INQUIRING MINDS

Tressa Olden

Library of Congress Control Number: 2011906119
ISBN: 979-8-89465-037-1 (sc)
ISBN: 979-8-89465-038-8 (e)

Printed in the United States of America.

Integrity Publishing
39343 Harbor Hills Blvd Lady Lake,
FL 32159

www.integrity-publishing.com

This book is dedicated to Bishop A.D. Reeves
My beloved uncle

CONTENTS

CHAPTER ONE

Surprise, Surprise, Surprise

Desmond Owens and his wife Mostalgia were sitting at home remembering a time when she was pregnant. They recalled fond memories of her lying in her hospital bed awaiting a nurse to bring in their bundle of joy. Neither had shared with their parents about what gender it would be. Since they already had a sweet little baby boy named Jordan, selected by his father who had taken the name from his favorite basketball player of all times was his claim. Both would only say they wanted a healthy baby and the gender didn't matter. "We will be happy with whatever gender God blesses us with". Desmond often shared that with his mom who was visiting them.

Desmond and his wife both lawyers were being visited by both sets of parents at this time. Des and Mossy were excited about the new baby she was having and chose to keep it to themselves and surprise their moms, who constantly bickered back and forth to them about what gender the baby should be. Martha Owens, Desmond's mother a former law clerk and retired schoolteacher had come earlier to help them through this difficult time. She had wanted her first grandchild to be a girl. Though she loved little Jordan and spoiled him rotten. She had birth two sons, Desmond and his older brother Sidney and had raised them to be fine young men. But she wanted the pleasure of a little girl and was sure that's what Mossy was carrying this time. "You're carrying very high Mostalgia I just know you're having a girl! Martha shared with her daughter-in law, coming into her bedroom with a large bowl of ice cream she had been craving. 'Well mama Martha you could be right" Mossy smiled, while lying in bed sitting up and reaching for the delicious treat. Mossy was following her doctor's orders to the letter with bed rest only in her last month of pregnancy.

Martha Owens her mother-in-law always spoke her mind and was adamant about having a little baby girl so she could spoil her with bows, ribbons and lace. She was sure it was time for the Owens family to bring in a girl and led the argument that statistics said it was time. She being a very astute but classy woman was unwavering about her wants about having a little girl to follow in her shoes. She stood her grounds against the rest of the family regarding a baby girl. Martha had come a month before Mostalgia was due to deliver. The later months proved to be very difficult for her. Her mother-in law came in from Palm Springs to help her through this rough time she was having with this pregnancy.

"Desmond, I talked a little with Mossy about names for our granddaughter" Martha would say "Have you and she selected a name as yet? She asked as she sat with him at breakfast sipping on her tea sweetened with honey. 'We have picked out some names but we're waiting for our baby to arrive, Desmond said choosing his words very carefully has he spoke with her. 'Well I like Margaret! For a girl, I've had that name picked out since I was carrying you". "That name belonged to my mother's sister she was one of my favorite aunt's who made the best banana pudding when I was growing up, Martha explained as she sipped from her teacup. "That's a big name for such a tiny little person mom don't you think?" Desmond questioned only to get a reaction from his mom. "Maggie is what we will call her Desmond, 'little Maggie" looking at her son sternly as she explained. "I'll share it with Moss. I know her mom wanted us to give the baby a Yugoslavian name" he teased, so we'll wait and see okay mom", kissing her on her forehead as he left for the hospital to meet his wife who had been waiting all night but still had not delivered. Desmond had quickly come home to shower and change clothes armed with advice he had received from the doctor that he had plenty of time. He would never live it down if he missed video taping the big event for his mother and mother- in- law to view later. He quickly got a bite of breakfast and out the door again. As he walked in the hospital room Mossy was still lying in the bed the doctor's advice was right nothing had come yet.

Dalmatia, Mossy sister was on her way to the airport to pick up her parents. They had just arrived from Yugoslavia and she didn't want to be late. Dal was there as well to help her sister with the baby. Little Jordan was only a year old so she had her hands full. But for now, she was left trying to get everyone settled in while Mostaglia was in the hospital having another baby. Speaking better English but still broken she tried her best to communicate what she was doing. Mrs. Owens, she said, "I'll be back soon". Dal had come back to America again a few weeks before her parents arrived to visit their daughter and see their new grandchild. Their first visit to America was three years ago during Christmas time and Dal loved it. She only went back home to Yugoslavia to help care for her aging parents and her dad's business affaires. Their dad owned a men's clothing store in Yugoslavia. He was a tailor by trade. Dal looked at her watch, "Mrs. O "I go to get ma'me and popee". I will be back", she said again to Martha. "That's fine dear. "That's just fine, drive carefully. Little Jordan and I will be right here when you get back" Martha replied.

The couples had not been together for this length of time before. They had met briefly after one Christmas and the New Years holiday gathering some years ago. Now they were coming together sharing another precious grandchild. Mossy and Desmond were hoping for the best from this visit. Both mother-in –laws were strong willed. Mostalgia's mom raised two sons and a daughter. And she wanted a grandson she'd said like Slovenia her youngest who did not return home after a visit to the United States but chose to stay in the states and had gotten a job working for the United States post office. Slovenia moved downtown near the law firm in a small high-rise apartment that he enjoyed. Lela wanted a boy and had picked out the name of Vlade for his name. And in her own way was very adamant about her daughter having another son.

Leron and Flaga, Martha and Lela's husbands were just trying to get through this visit enjoyable and save face. Leron Owens

Desmond's dad a lawyer from Palm Spring was teaching Flaga Filta, Mossy's dad how to play pool on the beautiful large pool table their children had in the game room. The huge walnut finished table sat the end of the couples' great room had become a ideal conversation place for the two dads. "Hold the cue like this and hit the ball" Leron advised to Flaga. He had been trying all day to learn this "American game of pool". Flaga leaned onto the table and hit the white ball. It in turn sent the other balls flying all over the table. He stood up smiling and looked at Leron again who acknowledged is accomplishment. "Way to go!" raising his hand and showing him how to high five.

Meanwhile Desmond stood by the bedside holding his wife's hand. Several times he would look at his watch checking how far her pains were apart. "They are still five minutes apart sweetheart!" Desmond shared with Mossy as she grimaced at him in pain. After much laboring pain the doctor came in. The nurse said after monitoring the pains "I think it's time". "Let's see Mrs. Owens," the doctor replied checking to see if she had dilated fully. "They are ready Mrs. Owens, are you? Doctor Henry asked smiling. Mossy said nothing she just looked very angry. Desmond was glad to hear the news it was time. Mossy had sworn at him, pushed him away when he tried to comfort her. She asked him to leave and then got mad when he wasn't holding her hand, and she was miserable sweating and just very irritated she was going through all this PAIN! Desmond and the doctor were standing by the bedside waiting for the new arrival into this world. "I love you Mossy, Desmond shared holding her hand again. "PUSH, Mrs. Owens, the doctor exclaimed. Push! PUSH. "I see the head, keep pushing! Desmond put a cool towel on her sweating forehead while another nurse stood by with the camcorder. He'd asked her to record the event. He explained he would watch later he couldn't bear to now. He just kept his eyes on Mossy. As time went on the birthing was complete. Desmond took a deep breath. "How are you feeling dear?' hugging her as she was crying and apologizing for what she said while in pain "I know you didn't mean what you said dear. "I understand you were in pain", he said smiling with her.

Dalmatia had brought both sets of parents to the hospital and they sat in the waiting room. Both mothers were sitting there. Mrs. Owens with her soft pink blanket for her little Maggie and Lela putting the finishing touches on a hand knitted blue blanket for her grandson Vlade. Little Jordan was playing happily at a little table filled with small toys without a care in the world.

Leron and Flaga were thinking of somewhere else to go for two weeks they had planned to be with the children. The doctor walked out first with this huge grin on his face to the waiting grandparents to announce that mother and baby or both doing fine. "Mr. Owens will be out shortly to speak with you". After a short wait Desmond emerged. "Thanks doc! Desmond said extending his hand as he came out to get the first set of grandparents with a large smile on his face.

The Owens nodded for the Filta's to go first. Lela and Flaga went in Mostalgia's room. Lela was carrying her beautiful knit blanket for her grandson. Flaga walked over and kissed his daughter and Lela caught her hand and spoke to her in their native tongue. "Where is little Vlade?" Lela asked. "Oh, mom he is so perfect so beautiful, Mossy told them. Mrs. Filta was smiling from ear to ear. She kissed her daughter again and after a few more minutes they walked out to allow the other grandparents to come in leaving her knit blanket on Mossy's bed. Lela walked out into the waiting room and hugged Martha and sat down on the hard-plastic couch playing with her grandson Jordan and speaking with her husband in their native language, with Flaga sounding very proud. Martha wasn't sure what the hug meant because no one had share whether it was a boy or girl? She looked back and caught Leron's hand and walked toward Mossy's hospital room. When she saw the big smile on Desmond's and Mossy's faces, she sensed she and not Lela had got what she wanted. "Where is that beautiful baby? Martha asked. "In the nursery Mom, Desmond confirmed. You will see her soon "Oh my!" Martha started to cry, holding on to Leron's hand tightly. "Did you hear that Leron, we have a granddaughter?" Martha said walking over to give Mostalgia and Desmond a big hug. "Congratulations to both of you", she said laughing loudly. "Now Mossy, you get some rest" "You'll need it when you get home." she explained. "I love you both she stated leaving the room but not without leaving the fluffy pink blanket with its wide ribbon trim on Mossy's bedside.

The day they all waited for had arrived. Poor Dalmatia was so happy that Desmond was bringing Mossy home from the hospital with the baby. She was left with the responsibility of entertaining the in-laws wants while her sister was resting a few days in the hospital. She had to take the two women shopping for the already over crowded nursery. Martha buying and loving anything pink and Lela favoring the color blue. Neither was going to say what their baby was. They chose to leave it up to their children to give the good or bad news to the other.

They sat anxiously waiting for Desmond to return with his wife from the hospital. The door opened. In walked Desmond with Mostalgia carrying her bundle in a blue knitted blanket secured tightly in her arms. Lela expressed cheerfully, Oh! Look its Vlade my sweet little grandson" she replied. Martha looked shocked. She stood staring at the door with her mouth opened. For the first time she was speechless. She still said nothing but turned and looked at her husband. "I thought they told us our granddaughter was in the nursery Leron? positioning her hands on her hips. Desmond didn't say anything he knew his mother so well. He carefully sat Mossy in a comfortable chair and went back out to get the luggage from the car he explained as he went back out the door.

Lela had walked over to see her grandchild and nodded for Mostalgia to put him in her hands. She gently held her precious grandson in her arms then went over and sat in the large rocker she had purchased for holding the baby. Mrs. Owens' rocker sat empty in the corner of the same room. "He is so beautiful and perfect," Lela said holding his little hands counting his fingers. Flaga stood looking and Leron who came over and rubbed his head. "He has a big head just like his dad! Leron teased to break the ice that was forming around his wife. Tears were forming in Martha's eyes. She walked over and kissed her grandson on his little hand as Lela held him in her arms. "He is beautiful Mossy! A beautiful healthy baby boy! Martha said turning to hide the tears streaming down her cheek. She turned around after wiping her face as though undetected and saw Desmond walking in with another bundle and it was pink. "Who is this? Martha exclaimed noticing her fluffy pink blanket. "Mom this is little Maggie!" "What?" she questioned looking at Mossy. "Two Mossy? You had two? "Yes, Mother Martha, "one for you and one for mom, Vlade and little Maggie" Mostaliga added. Leron and Flaga were happier that anyone in the room things had turned out this way. 'Thank God! Leron said, Thank God!

CHAPTER TWO

What a friend!

Billy sat by the pool at his parent's home. He had taken several weeks leave away from the office, thinking only of Jillian his fiancée whom he missed dearly. "Son would you like something to eat?" his mother asked as she looked out at him sitting on the deck out back. She was leaving for the Center where she worked. "No thanks mom I'm fine" he told her and sat looking out across the pool and extended backyard. Tetra was so concerned about her son. She felt his loss too. She had come to love Jillian as her daughter-in law. What an awful way to die. "DID SHE EVEN GET TO SAY GOODBYE? Tetra thought as she drove in to work.

Billy was torn to pieces. Even the news of his son Davie couldn't overshadow the pain he was feeling from losing Jillian his fiancée to 9-11. He was going to be good to her and take care of her and be true to her. WHY had God taken her? he questioned. "I have never felt pain like this! Even when Mr. Parsons, my dear friend died in that bus accident he thought to himself. How could God love me when he let this happen to Jillian? Billy sat there looking out beyond the sky very angry at the whole world. He didn't want to see anyone, and vowed he'd never love again. He had not taken any time to talk with Davie even when his mother told him the story regarding Dana his old girlfriend. As a matter of fact he was angry with Dorca who had now changed her name to Dana for the hurt she caused Jillian. And once again Davie his son found himself in the middle and didn't know what to do.

"Yello, Yez yello thez iz the Parker residence, Mrs.Laine said answering the Parker's telephone. "Uncle. Billy please?" "one moment plez, Mrs. Laine replied and walked out back where Billy had been all morning since she arrived. "Mr. Billy, you have a friend on the telephone" she announced. "Who is it Mrs. Laine? he asked not wanting to speak with anyone and she knew it. "I thin you should speak to your friend, handing him the receiver. He looked at her she knew of his pain and everyone wanted to help him through it but he wanted only to be left alone. "Thank you, Mrs. Laine, he finally conceded seeing that she was not going to go away. She gave a nod and walked away to stand in the glass door until I started speaking. "Hello, this is William Parker" making my formal announcement not knowing who was on the line. "Hi" could be heard very softly. "HELLO! HELLO! who is this? I asked. This person had disturbed me and now I couldn't hear what they were saying. "Hello Uncle Billy, this is Davie". The words were still not very loud but I could make out the person calling. "Hi Davie, how are you doing? I finally asked. I had not spoken with him since that awful day a month ago. I had forgotten about everything. I just wanted to be alone. "I asked grandma Tetra if I could call you" she thought it would be alright". She gave me the number. "I know how to call now. Before, when I was younger, I was forgetting to use the one first in front of the numbers" he explained to him. "Oh, I see." Then Billy thought about how this child probably dialed those numbers over and over in his head Jillian had taught him getting no results. "I'm glad you called is everything alright at home?" Billy asked not really knowing honestly what to say. "Yes, Justin took me to a movie last night he confided. "It was fun. But I called to tell you that I loved aunt Jilly too!" he said sounding sad. "Mom explained to me about what happened and said that if I be good someday, I will see her again in heaven" Davie shared. "I really don't know what all that means yet, except I really want to see aunt Jilly again" he confessed. I sat listening to this child whom mom had said was mine. I realized I had to live. Jillian had practical raised him too. She had scrapbooks and pictures of their life together that spanned over four or five years. She loved and knew him better than I did. He felt abandoning Davie was like burying Jillian all over again. And for me that still had not happened. "Uncle Billy are you there? Davie asked. Billy guessed he was so silent but he was just thinking about a lot of things. "Yes Davie, I'm here he told him. "Well, I'm on my way to school now and I just called to tell you that" he remarked. Billy really wasn't listening and something else was on his mind and he really didn't hear why he said he had called, so he asked again. "I'm sorry Davie why did you say you called?" I'm listening this time" he told him. "Oh yes, Davie repeated, "I just called to tell you I loved aunt Jilly too. Bye Uncle Billy".

Billy sat holding the phone receiver for about and hour. As if he was holding Davie or Jilly in his arms. He had to find strength through this he vowed. It's what Jillian would want. She would not want me to give up Davie! She loved Davie as much as I loved her. AND I LOVED JILLIAN SO MUCH.

Tetra sat behind her desk at the Center waiting for her friend Christine to come by for their morning break. She knew Christine for a long time and could talk with her about anything. She had shared with her the concerns about her son Billy. He had withdrawn from society and for the most part moped around her home GRIEVING. He didn't want to call or speak to any of his dear friends and she prayed continual for him. Tetra knew how much he loved Jillian. She and David both shared their son's pain for the entire Fleming family. Though there were many families involved in this tragedy. Jillian's family was close to their hearts.

"Good morning Tetra," Christine said walking in with her coffee mug filled with coffee. "Let's head to the lounge I think James brought in croissants and glazed pastries, she informed her. "Sounds wonderful, Tetra replied. However, I'm not indulging this morning I just needed someone to talk too" "Why what's wrong Tet? you have always enjoyed a good pastry!" Christine teased. "I know you're right, but I'm fasting, I need God to bring Billy out of this slump he's in" she confided. "I do understand how Jillian was taken away so suddenly, and I understand the pain and grief of the tragedy but it has been almost two months." And he's still grieving her lost." "I tried to get him to go back to work part-time anyway just to get his mind on something else. He told me everything reminded him of Jillian." "Oh, Tetra this can't be easy for him being so young" Christine" replied while they sat at the table in the Center's break room. "His leave is up at the end of this month and I'm just afraid if he doesn't do something soon, he will never go back to law, Tetra confessed. "Well Tetra, be careful don't push to hard it could be devastating for him and yourself." Christine reasoned. "I know that's what David keeps saying and I know it's probably true, but it hurts me that he's hurting so much" Tetra added. "You're right Tetra, something's only come by fasting and praying, so that's what we will do." Starting tomorrow and the rest of this day I will fast with you". And we will pray for God to do what only he can in Billy's life" Christine shared with her dear friend. "Thank you" thank you so much.

"David and I have prayed fervently, and now we're completely turning it over to Jesus. 'We've been keeping it to ourselves not letting anyone know just what this lost meant to him" They knew he would be hurt and rightfully so. She was his fiancée. "I called Pastor Hathaway last evening and asked him to pray and shared my concerns with him. He wanted to know if it would be alright if he shares it openly with the congregation." "At first I thought no." Billy may get upset with me and also I thought it was not my place to share" Tetra reasoned. "But I read where two or three gathered touching and agreeing on the same thing God is in the midst. "So, with everyone praying everywhere for this cause will surely make a difference" And I said please Pastor share it for there are a lot of hurting people and families that were affected by this terrorist's attack."

Tetra sat conversing while Christine finished her cup of coffee and her pastry. "Tetra let us pray right now for Billy". Now that you have given it over to Jesus, we can now just thank him for doing it," her dear friend suggested. And Tetra and Christine joined hands and thanked God for what he had already done.

CHAPTER THREE

Storm is passing over

Dana had finished seeing all of her clients for the day. She still had not spoken with her young son Davie about his past. She would sit down and explain some of his questions he was now posing about Billy his dad and grandparents. She had thought it over and over again how she was going to do it. What exactly should I say was a question that she went over and over in her mind? Davie was a bright young man and he was not going to be satisfied with just any answers and Dana knew that. But just how much to tell him at this time was the issue she was faced with. As she logged out of her computer for the day Justin his uncle walked in. "Hello Dana" how are you today? He asked coming in pulling up a chair. Justin was now in medical school and often stopped by to talk with Dana. He to had lots of questions after finding out that her son was his brother's little boy. Justin wanted to know everything about Davie and Dana but was reluctant with asking some things. She explained she wanted to wait until she spoke in detail with Billy his older brother. Which was taking longer than anyone had thought, giving him his time to grieve the loss of Jillian.

"How was your day?" Justin asked getting comfortable in the chair. "It was alright Dana responded knowing it was the first of many questions. 'Have you spoken with Davie yet? He asked. "He's always asking me questions about Billy" Some of the questions I can answer and some I don't think it's my place to answer" Justin stated. Then he looked up at her with a wide smile. "Dana I can't tell you how to raise your child, but I do think you should take the time and share with Davie about all the questions he has." Justin suggested. "I know, I have plans of doing that, she replied. I want to speak with Billy first about some things that may be difficult for Davie to understand." "Well that may be true, but I haven't heard from Billy in a while, he is still dealing with the loss of Jillian and I understand that" Justin shared. My mother Kat openly shared everything with me about my absent father David Parker and it helped me. Things about him did not surprise me when I finally met him. But if you keep things from Davie, he is lead to believe a lot of things that may not be true and some will come back to haunt him later in life," Justin said looking at Dana.

"Hey wait! Who works in psychiatry here! Dana asked smiling. "But you are right procrastinating and delaying until another time only gives temporary relief, I don't really know where to start to be honest Justin," Dana confessed. "I'm constantly giving my clients advice on these matter's and I realize it's not easy as it seems" she said now pacing the floor in her office. Justin put both hands on the arm of the chair and pushed himself up. "I will do my best not to tell him what I think you or Billy should tell him when he asks. Though I think some things should be addressed soon Dana", looking at his watch. "Hi honey, Ariel replied coming into Dana's office. Are you ready?" she asked Justin then looked over at Dana. "Hello Dana has Justin been talking your ear off?' "No not really, he had some sound advice this time, he may be going into the wrong field of medicine." Dana teased, brushing her hand over his wavy hair. "Justin reached over and gave Dana a hug and Ariel followed with a hug also for Dana. "We'll see you around Dana, Justin said holding Ariel's hand and leaving Dana's office. Dana knew what Justin said made sense. He had told her how Katherine never kept anything from him about his past and he turned out all right. Maybe that will work for Davie. She sure hoped it would. He and Justin did share the same bloodline. Davie was only eleven years old. And she didn't want to overwhelm him with past information. So, she thought, I'll answer only the questions that he asks right now. She put on her coat, briefcase in hand and turned off the light. Going home to talk with Davie about his dad William Parker.

When Tetra arrived home from the Center, she was greeted at the door by Billy her son and his luggage. "Hi mom! I'm so glad you made it home before I left" he said coming over and giving her a big hug. "Billy where are you going?" she asked surprised by his mood. "Mom I'm going home back to Maine" he replied. "I've been here long enough don't you think?" My desk is probably under a pile of briefs that need immediate attention and my office is expecting me by week's end he added. 'Billy that's wonderful but aren't your rushing things a bit? Tetra found herself saying. "Mom you're the one who told me I needed to go back to work for my minds sake!" Well, I heard you mom, I heard you! Billy explained. "Yes, son I know but." Tetra paused then her mind reflected on her conversation earlier with her dear friend Christine. God had already answered her prayer and the human part of her wasn't ready. It's supposed to take longer she thought to herself. But if God is in control, he can do it however he wants to and when he wants too.

"Well be sure and call me when you get home. "I'm planning a visit there soon to see my grandson and spend some time getting to know him, Tetra shared with Billy. "That's wonderful mom. "I have plans to see Davie too." I know there is a lot he wants to know and there are a lot of things I need to know" he explained to her. "Billy be careful, don't rush things" Tetra reasoned. "Mom, I'm not going to rush into anything but so much time as been wasted in our lives not knowing each other. I've learned from my relationship with Jillian that time moves quickly and we must cherish each second each moment everyday, he told her.

Tetra had moved to her great room still talking with her son. "I'm waiting for a cab mom, to take me to the airport. Sit for a minute and let me talk to you." "Tetra was nervous. She didn't know what Billy had to talk about. Her prayers had been answered and she didn't know what to do. She was just thanking Him. And before she could digest it God had moved. She went over and sat next to Billy on the sofa. Her little boy had a son of his own now. She looked at him with tears in her eyes holding his hand. Billy reached over and gave her a big hug. "My favorite girl! he said "I spoke with your grandson today" he started "he called to tell me he loved Jilly too." "Oh, Billy that could not have been easy for either of you" Tetra reasoned. "It made me realize what Jillian would have wanted." Tetra sat silently and listened. "Jillian loved Davie. She spent more time with him than I did." She knew him better than I did" pointing to himself as he said the words. She was a remarkable lady mom", he shared wiping the tears from his eyes then wiping Tetra's tears also. "And I will always love her though Davie needs me now and I must go on. Life is to short! Billy shared. "God bless you son" Tetra thought, then the doorbell rang. "It's probably the cab mom" he acknowledged reaching over again to give his mom another hug and getting up from the sofa heading to the door. "Son I can take you to the airport, Tetra replied running to get her purse and coat. Billy opened the door and yelled to the cabbie "I'll be right out! Handing him the luggage "No mom, you have done more than enough putting up with me all these months". "I promise I will call when I get there," he whispered in her ear hugging her and heading out the door. "Tetra stood in the foyer watching the cab pull away. Her heart was full and her eyes filled with tears and she was just letting them stream down her cheeks and on to the floor. Soon Tetra followed. She fell to the floor and gave thanks and prayed mightily for strength and understanding from God.

Billy's flight left on time headed for New York. He had to go there one more time he thought as the cab rounded the corner where the two tall towers once stood. He looked at the place where bulldozers had come through and cleared away all the debris. They were preparing to build a memorial for all the lives that were lost on September 11. He walked around on the surface of ground, wondering how Jillian must have felt. Her last breath, that instance when she made that attempt to call him. He put his head down and covered his face to hide the tears. Others were walking around also probably for the same reason a lost loved one. Though each said nothing they all had their own secret pain. He must have stayed there close to an hour. He thought of ever conversation Jilly and he had. He remembered when she tried hard to cook breakfasts to satisfy him. "Oh Jilly! he thought why did you leave me? His anger that he had come with was gone and all he felt was sad and so disappointed. He wanted to give her the world. "She deserved that from me". "Oh, my sweet Jillian, he cried out as he fell in the dirt on his knees.

He sat back on his bent knees with his head hanging down and wept. He felt someone touch him. He looked up to see this lady standing over him. She didn't say anything but she handed him a Kleenex to wipe his eyes and stood there praying softly with her hand on his shoulder. He sat up first and looked at her. His first thought was maybe she knows Jilly. He hurriedly got up from the ground and stared at her. "Why did you bother me? he asked. She had her back to him and he couldn't see her face. He caught her on her shoulder and turned her around. "Why did you bother me? You had no right! I wasn't bothering anyone! He stated loudly.

She looked at him and smiled. "I'm sorry" she replied. "I was in that state earlier this month you see. I lost my husband in one of the towers. I do identify with your hurt, your pain, and loneliness." Someone came by and tapped my shoulder and now I can stand". I come here everyday Monday through Friday just like Chad use to. And when I see the hurt, this attack caused. "I vowed to help each one by giving them something to wipe the tears even if only for a little while" she shared. Then she just stood looking at him. "I do apologize but I will probably do it again it's how I get through" she confided. "I feel many lives were saved by the brave firefighters that day. But because of it there are many more lives that need saving". "The lives of the families of those left behind" she confessed using one of her tissues to wipe her eyes.

This lady he'd say middle aged looked again and walked away toward someone else aimlessly moving around ground zero. She was still there when I left handing out Kleenex to those in need. Thank you! "I yelled to her but she couldn't hear me. She had now made her way to someone else sitting on the ground. But her act Billy thought toward him was selfless. "You are not alone". "Do whatever it takes to get through this and then help someone else is what he came away thinking.

His flight left New York heading to Maine his home. He wasn't quite up to seeing Frances and Roger Fleming yet. Jillian's parents, what they must be going through. He had spoken with them a bit after the memorial service. Frances and he had someone they shared and loved. He vowed to keep in touch with her. He then found the strength to call Glen Reed his lifetime friend. He had been avoiding his calls and not returning the ones he had promised to. Billy shared with him he was headed home to Maine and like old times they shared a laugh. "GLENN SOMEHOW SINCED HE KNEW HE SURE NEEDED ONE! But right now, his focus was on uniting with his son. He needed to talk with Dana now and hold Davie in his arms. He will call as soon as he gets in. And of course, I promise to return all of mom's calls immediately!

CHAPTER FOUR

Mr. Right meets Ms. Right???

Sidney was waiting for Jessica to finish packing her suitcase for the trip. She was on her way to a singing engagement in Lake Tahoe. She was the lead singer in a group of three women and a total opposite from the conservative Sidney Owens, Desmond Owens brother. Jessica Strassburg and Sidney met while he was covering a story regarding a new Sports arena being built by the Fisher Brothers in Greece. Her singing group was over there performing with some of the top artist in the business, Rhapsody and the Deuce Boys to name a few. Sidney just happened to be having a lunch meeting in the posh restaurant when the group came in to dine. She was awestruck by that cute sexy journalist and asked her manger to arrange a meeting. Jessica insisted it was love at first sight! He was her soul mate. Sidney on the other hand is intellectually appealing and handsome the women say. He's a bit shy which they find sexy. You know a Morris Chestnut kind of a guy! And I'm told he knows how to treat a lady. Whether are not he and Jessica's lifestyles will work I guess depends on them. He has changed a lot for her. Staying up late and partying till dawn is so unlike Sidney. But that's her lifestyle because of the business she's in. Desmond says according to Mrs. Martha Owens' their mom she hopes Sidney stays that way with this one," SINGLE." I just hope Sidney knows what he's doing Desmond shared. They seem to be very happy and it's been three months and counting he says. They are both constantly traveling all around the globe. So, their time together is precious to them, again according to Sidney when asked by Desmond his brother to come for a visit.

"I told you I would get around to it brother. I will be in Kansas City about five 'o' clock after I get Jessica on her way" he replied to Desmond. "Is mom and Dad still there?" "No man, they left last week dad had some important cases to get too," Desmond responded. "Jessica isn't coming this time she has and engagement but she sends her love and hopes to see you two soon" Sidney added. Well we looked forward to meeting her as well". We have heard so much about her from mom". "Hold your comments until you meet her for yourself you know mom is hard to please!" Sidney confided. "Mossy's sister is still here, but there is still plenty of room if you decide to stay here instead of a hotel Sid. You know you're welcome". "It's been a long time since we talked. I'm really looking forward to spending time with you, Desmond remarked. "Has your game improved any?" Sidney asked referring to golf. "My game, you're asking about my game! You know my game is sweet and I'm going to make a tee time as soon as I get off this phone to show you." Desmond stated. "Well you know I'm always up for a game of golf!" Sidney replied and I will see you soon. Hanging up and going out to close the trunk of his car filled with luggage heading to the airport with Jessica in the passenger seat.

"Jessica when do you think we will have time together to visit Kansas?" I know it's not the Ritz but I really want you to meet my baby brother" Sidney confessed as he drove into the long-term parking at the airport. "Kansas! I don't think I've been there before, what's in Kansas?' she chided with her British accent. Well my brother for one thing he explained to her, "we are very close, and I want him to meet you, what's wrong with that?" Nothing, but you make it seems like you need his approval!" Jessica replied getting out of the car grabbing her handbag and scarf from the seat. "I thought it would be a nice change from all the late nights and glitz and glamour of the lifestyle I have become accustomed too he argued. "I don't think there's anything wrong with glitz and glamour, what does he do in Kansas anyway? Who would go there?" she asked in a factious tone. Sidney hugged her as they talked and walked to their assigned gate. His flight left an hour after hers. He planned it that way so he could see her off. Well Jessica, you enjoy your singing engagement and I'll meet you in Vegas, right?" "We will fly back to Baltimore together". Sidney had chosen not to discuss Kansas anymore. Maybe Jessica was kidding but this was not the time to find out. Sidney had been to a few of her performances but wasn't wild about her fan base. Just something he'd rather not be a part of. She's all mine when the show is over, he'd say. They sat together with him holding her hand. A few of the passengers recognized her and asked for an autograph. She loved her FAME and didn't mind obliging them. Sidney was in loveeee. Soon they called for her to board. Jessica stood up and hugged and kissed Sidney. "Be sweet" she always said and turned and flirted with her eyes at the male stewardess. He recognized her and boarded the plane with his rolling carryon in tow quickly behind her.

Sidney was on cloud nine. Jessica had kissed him in the airport in front of all those people. Some he noticed were even her fans. He wasn't accustomed to that. Her usual departure was a tight squeeze of the hand. Things were looking up he thought. She's famous a lot of people know her! Sidney had a nightly show and could be seen locally on WFTZ television in Baltimore but as he says "I haven't hit the big time yet! I'm trying to be a "Rather or better yet Bradley." To look at him you would think he could have any girl he wanted. And that was probably true. But his shy personality always landed him with the strong-willed women that usually took him for a ride. And this one didn't seem any different according to Desmond's mom. But he would have to find out himself. Sidney had put Desmond in his place a few a times before when he tried to tell him about the other women. So, Desmond chose to just be there when he was needed.

Sidney sat in his first-class seat on the plane and thought about Jessica. Timing was off regarding meeting his family. Every time he brought it up, she cuddled and suggested doing something else. She's got her mind on her singing right now. He was in love so he covered every excuse for her. We'll talk about it later. He thought has he sat on his flight going to spend a few days with his brother in Kansas City.

Billy sat in the living room of his cottage and looked over some papers he had gotten from his dad regarding Dana. He was preparing to call her and wanted to be familiar with the facts. "Hello, Dana answered her home phone that evening. "Hello Dana, this is Billy" how are you?" Dana's, heart stopped, she didn't know what to think. She had not spoken with Billy since the day she took Davie from school. That was a long time ago. And so much had happened since then. Nervously she responded "Yes hello, this is Dana. "I think we need to talk," he stated. "Yes, I guess we do" Dana replied. "How about lunch or dinner this week" he suggested. "I think enough time has passed already" I'll call you later this week and we can make final plans. Is that okay? "Sure, Dana replied softly. "I'll be going back to the office this week let me look over my schedule and we can set the date" Billy suggested. Not really knowing exactly what was waiting in terms of caseloads. He continued making conversation aimlessly suggesting plans as he spoke. "My partners were gracious enough to keep me on board during by bereavement". "That's sounds great, Dana replied, I really wanted to talk with you before I spoke with my son Davie. He has so many questions?" Dana confessed. "Well then that's even more reason to speak as soon as possible" he stated. "How is he doing?" I mean what kind of questions is he asking?" "Just questions about you and Jillian mostly. Wanting to know how come?" Dana hinted. "Okay, give him my love. I will call you soon and arrange a meeting." he told Dana. "Call me at the office during the day." my number is 547-2999 x 42 Dana responded. "Thanks, I will and let me give you my number if things change alright," he shared with her. Allowing time for Dana to write down the number Billy replied "We will talk soon bye" hanging up the phone and moving on to the next item on his list of things to do this evening.

"Hi mom. Yes, I'm fine I got in about and hour ago" I love you and I will be in touch. "I'm going into the office tomorrow call me there if you need me" I love you too mom bye. Billy sat there thinking after he had hung up the phone. Now how do I get my son away from Dana without hurting him? I want him. But after what she did to Jilly, I don't want to spend one moment more than I have to with her! I don't know her anymore!" But I'll have to play along until I get what I want. He thought as he stood in his shower after a long day. Soon he was retiring for a restful evening.

Dana was excited, about the call. Surely, she was looking forward to seeing and talking to Billy. She had never stopped loving him. She had kept her distant because of her looks. For sure he would understand that. So many times, she wanted to tell him about Davie but he was so in love with Jillian so she kept her distant. Dana walked out of Davies' room after tucking him in for the night promising to answer all of his questions very soon.

Desmond was out in the back yard playing with the twins when Sidney came. "Whoa!" you guys are way out here," he said after getting a car and driving out to Langley Estates. "Hi bro, Desmond replied walking toward him after Mossy had greeted him and pointed him to where Desmond was playing with the children. "My they have grown so much since I saw them" Sidney said looking at the toddlers now climbing on the large activity set Desmond had put together in the yard. Little Jordan was trying his hand at riding a tricycle. "Yes, that shows how long it's been since you were here", embracing his brother. "Come to uncle Sidney", he said to little Maggie. Who was trying to follow Vlade who was the oldest by about two- minutes? "He reached over and picked her up in the air. Wheeee! He said moving her around like an airplane. She liked it and laughed loudly as he continued making sounds. "How was the flight?' Desmond questioned. "Not bad you know I'm so accustomed to flying." It's routine. "Well, are you staying here? Let me show you around, and added last time you were here, you came to the hospital and didn't make it by our home. I remember you had a big story to cover." Desmond understood. "I plan to spend these few days with you bro just to see how the other side lives". "Jessica and I are very much in love I don't know what might happen." Sidney confessed to his brother. "Well like I said on the phone I looked forward to meeting her". When do you think she'll be coming?" Desmond asked as they walked into the house with Sidney carrying Maggie and Desmond holding Vlade who was not ready to come in and was crying to voice his opinion. "Babe, are you finished with those letters?' Desmond asked his wife Mossy. She had been working from home transitioning back to the office. They had agreed that the twins would be two years old before Mossy leaves them with a sitter. And then finding the right one was proving to be a task for them. She had interviewed about three so far and still had not made a decision on any one. 'Vlade's not ready to come in and I want to show Sidney around the grounds" he shared. "Oh, Desmond, Vlade is so spoiled! Look at Maggie she's content no matter what!" he gets that from you!" she stated coming over taking the crying Vlade in her arms.

"Sidney come this way," Desmond said leading him to his favorite place the game room in the basement. "You're still living in that bachelor pad in Maryland?" Desmond asked. "Yes, but if things keep going like I think they are things may be different." Sidney confided again with his brother. "Oh, is it that serious with you and Jessica?" Well I don't want to jump to conclusions but things are pretty together with us" Sidney confessed. "Nice table, very nice room." he added. As they walked through the game room "Oh thanks, right this way the other guestroom is right off here. Heading down a short hall way opening the door to a very spacious bedroom with a fireplace and a king-sized bed.

"Here's your room, I'll help you bring in your luggage from the car." Desmond suggested. "Man, are you sure, where is your other house guest staying?' he asked thinking he had put her out. "Do you see the size of this house!"? Desmond asked heading to his guest room downstairs. Mossy and I planned for family. There is another guest room upstairs. As well as the pool house if you'd rather stay there." Desmond said going out to the car with Sidney to get the rest of his luggage. "No this is fine, but I'm only here for three or four days I have to meet Jessica in Vegas Friday night" he said. "That's fine, I'll let you get settled and I will see you in a little while. Desmond closed the door and went back up to find Mossy and their twins. Little Jordan had gone out with his aunt Dal.

Dana was restless all night. She was thinking about Billy. What was he thinking? What would he think about Davie?" She woke with questions still on her mind. What if he didn't want to be a Daddy?" she had so many questions running through her head as she drove into work. Her calendar was full she had client after client with problems she had to let them talk through. She had just closed her book on the last client for the day when her phone rang. "Dr. Williams, how may I help you?" Hi Dana this is Justin," Oh she sighed Justin I was expecting someone else. "Yes, Justin why are you calling?" "I promised Davie I would take him and a friend to see that new space movie in theaters". So, I'm calling to ask. I'm off this weekend and I wanted to have and answer for him WHEN HE CALLS?" "This weekend, Dana repeated. "I want to say yes" but you know Billy is back in town". "He is! I didn't know. "Yes, he called me last night to set up a meeting so that we can talk". Dana shared with Justin. "Whoa! I didn't know he was back" Justin said." I'll have to call and maybe go by and see him". "THANKS! But let me know about taking Davie to the movie. "Got to go" Justin said disconnecting the line. Dana finished writing in her charts and closed out her computer and sat staring into space. "Hello! Oh my, he startled her. It was Billy. She recognized him right away. "I thought you were going to call. Dana said touching her hair putting it in place. "Oh, I decided to stop in hope it's alright?" he said looking around her office. "Nice, very nice he was making reference to the office space and décor. But it blew his mind to be speaking with Dorca but her face said Dana, which by the way had "Halle" written all over it. So, I would have to get use to that. "Dana can I be honest with you, I said it's going to take me a while to get use to the new you" I guess the name change was necessary if you changed the face" he told her. "I thought that would be best. My face was so messed up believe me this one is a lot prettier" Dana smiled starting to feel comfortable with Billy again. "If you say so, "I made reservations for tonight at 6:30 is that all right with you?" I suggested without letting Dana say a word. Sorry for the short notice, but I don't believe in procrastinating any longer" he shared. 'I'm not dressed, where are we going?" Dana asked nervously. "You're fine' he told her. She was wearing a wool black shirt with matching form fitting jacket and a silk white cowl neck sleeveless blouse underneath. "I have to call and let Mrs. Bea know I'll be late. She doesn't mind sitting with Davie until I come home" she said hurriedly. "That's fine" I'll wait".

Billy moved to the waiting area until she made her call and he read an article in a magazine. "Okay, she said after going to the powder room to freshen her makeup. "Fine let's go. Where are you parked?" he asked. In the garage upper level Dana responded. Billy surprised her by walking her to the car and having her follow him to the restaurant. He doesn't know what she was thinking but he wanted to go over everything in his mind before he sat at the table with this woman whom he felt had caused his pain with Jillian.

As Billy drove leading the way to the restaurant his cell phone rang. "Hello! William Parker" he answered. "Bill this is Justin, what's up? Oh, Justin how's things going? he asked. "Not bad, not bad. Justin replied. Dana told me you were back in town are you staying long?" Justin questioned. Billy answered without thinking. "as long as it takes!" he replied. "As long as what takes are you staying in Maine?" "Sure, I mean as long as life treats me good, I'll be here" changing what he really meant. "Maybe once you get settled again, we can do something together bro!" "Count on it!" he said 'I gotta go but I will be in touch soon." "Oh yeah, I asked Dana if I could take Davie to the movie this weekend if it's ok". He didn't say anything. Justin was still spending time with Davie. Davie didn't need him anymore he was there now he thought. "Look Justin we will talk soon bye! Disconnecting the line as he pulled up to the valet with Dana following.

Dana didn't know what to think. Billy waited out front while the valet parked his car. Dana waited and another valet came up and she handed him her keys. She walked over to where Billy was standing. "Well I have never been to this place", Dana remarked but then I've only been to a few places since coming here to Maine". It's quite nice and the food is great Billy replied. "Jilly and oh I'm sorry it's just so hard to accept she's gone," he told Dana. They walked in and the waiter showed them to their table. "I hope you don't mind I chose a place off by the window where we could talk" he said. "No that's fine" Dana replied. He pulled out her chair and Dana sat down. Then he walked over and sat at the other side of the table. "Something to drink?" he asked her. "Whatever you're having Dana replied. "I'm only having water but you feel free to order whatever you like", he said to her. "I'm not much into drinking Billy!" I thought you knew that" Dana stated. "I'm sorry, just trying to accommodate you," he replied sarcastically. The waiter standing at the table threw his cloth over his arm and walked off huffed until further instructions.

"Billy can we start over?" Dana asked. Obviously, this place is where you and Jillian came frequently maybe we should try another place at another time" Dana got up and started to walk out. "Wait, wait, I'm sorry this was my idea!" I do miss Jillian a lot but that's not why we are here." he said holding her hand pulling her back. She was not about to spoil his plans by leaving. "Please come and sit down". Dana looked at him and came back over to the table. Billy motioned to the waiter and ordered a bottle of his best wine and two glasses. The waiter smiled and walked away to get the expensive bottle of wine.

Dana sat with tears in her eyes. "I said I'm sorry" Billy stated again. "Please excuse me she said, "I need to go to the powder room!" She got up and walked over to the lady at the front podium and headed in the direction of the lady's room. After a while she returned. The waiter had brought their wine and poured a glass for each of them. Billy lifted his glass to her and said. "New Beginnings" Reluctantly Dana lifted her glass and echoed "new beginnings". Both drank their expensive wine from the crystal goblets. Now that wasn't so bad was it? he asked seeing Dana seem to be feeling better. "Billy, she said "I thought we were here to talk about our son David? "Well we are! But I now know it was you who sent that package to Jillian at her office, why? Dana swallowed another gulp of wine and motioned for Billy to fill her glass again. "Billy, I had every intention to come to Cambridge to be with you! But when my face got messed up, I knew you wouldn't want me any more". Every girl you dated was so pretty and then you met Jillian and fell in love." I couldn't let her have Davie." And I tried to stop her from having you". I gave you so many hints and you still chose Jillian" Dana confessed.

"I waited for you for years Dana." I looked everywhere including under a rock! he said sounding very frustrated at this point. You had no right to involve Jillian and hurt her feelings that way! "What you did was wrong! he expressed in a tone very harsh at this time. Dana sat quietly across the table looking at his expressions. She knew he was not happy and Davie was the last thing on his mind right now. The waiter came over and asked if they were ready to order? They had several times got a bit loud with their discussion regarding the past.

No! Billy responded, "in a few minutes" And picked up the menu as if reading it. The waiter was miffed and walked off. "Dana, I waited for you! I put Jillian on hold for you! Billy was calm on the outside but he confessed that he was fuming on the inside. And Dana sensed it. "Billy, I'm so sorry this happened to Jillian but I'm not responsible for what happened to her and neither are you!" I'm sure if you knew that was going to happen you wouldn't have let her on that plane" Dana voiced. "How dare you say what I would have done after the choices you've made in your life? Billy tried to be pleasant but he was mad! and as furious at this moment as one man could be and still be civil.

Dana got up from her seat. "Billy this is not working! She admonished "Call me again when you're ready to talk about Davie" and she walked out. He thought that was best too. As pretty as she was on the outside to him, all he saw was all the ugly things she had done to Jillian and he hated her for it!

Desmond and Sidney were just returning from a day of golf and met Dalmatia coming in with an armload of books. "Hi Dal, how was your day? Desmond asked. "Okay" she said. She had driven to the university across town a few miles into Kansas City to enroll in the University of Missouri in Kansas City. Dalmatia was only nineteen and had graduated high school in Yugoslavia prior to coming here two years ago. Since things seem to be settling down with Mossy and the babies, she had enrolled to pursue her degree. "Oh, Dal this is my brother Sidney Owens, I'm not sure if you two have met'. "No, I don't think we have" Sidney replied extending his hand to her. "Hello" she said blushing from shyness. Desmond opened the door and they all walked in. Mossy was coming from the nursery, everyone was down for a nap and she was breathing a sigh of relief. "Well what are you majoring in Dalmatia?" Sidney asked seeing Dal move toward her room upstairs. "I haven't decided" she said as best she could so he would understand and hurried off before the next question.

She's still learning the English language Desmond said to Sidney. "Oh, I see he said heading to his room to freshen up after a day of golf. "Honey, Henry needs you to call the office," Mossy said walking toward the kitchen to prepare dinner. Dal had put away her books and came down in the family room to watch television. "Mind if I join you? Sidney asked coming in after a relaxing shower. "No, what would you like to watch? she asked. "What you're watching is fine" I don't watch much television as a rule" he shared. "Dal didn't say anything she was a girl of a few words. Desmond tells me you are learning the English language?" Yes, she smiled She felt better knowing he knew that. She didn't want him to think she didn't want to talk to him. She found him cute! Sidney was older than Dal by about ten or eleven years. Anyway, that was the last thing on his mind he was in love with Jessica Strassberg!

"What do you do?" she asked bravely. "Me, Sidney said modestly I'm a journalist. "Interesting work" she said. "Yes, it keeps me quite busy but I do enjoy it." "What things do you like to do? Sidney asked 'Umm I like to sew. My family is in that business she shared. But mostly I love to dance" she said beaming from ear to ear. "Dance?" Sidney thought for a moment. "What kind of dance?" "How you say, "ballet". "Oh, I see, that's great" he smiled realizing the type of dance she was speaking of. "I would love to be on center stage spinning around and around" she voiced excitedly. Desmond came in from the study. "Oh, I'm glad to see you two communicating." I had some business to attend to with Henry at the office" he shared. Dal got up and went into the kitchen to help Mossy with dinner. Desmond your sister-in-law seems to be coming right along with her English", Sidney said. "Yes, she is, Desmond said "it took us a long time to get her to talk in front of any one. I hope she didn't make you feel uneasy she really doesn't mean to" he shared.

"Not at all" Desmond I'll be right back; I'd like to call Jessica before dinner. Sidney got up and walked to his room. Dal was humming a tune as she helps Mossy put the meal in serving dishes for the table. "Well you seem happy?" Mossy said to her. "Oh, I only met this very cute guy today?" "Oh! where?' Mossy asked. "At the university" Dal replied still smiling and humming. Mossy thought that's all right she had been around this house since coming here after the twins were born. I guess it's time she found someone her age to talk to.

CHAPTER FIVE

New beginnings

"Dana Williams" she replied answering her phone. Dana! Roger Dodger he said laughing. His name was Roger Haskell and he sold hospital supplies to the hospital. He was in sales. She had met him one day coming out of Dr. Baisden's office. "Oh, hi Roger, how are you doing? He and Dana had shared lunches a few times when he was in town. He traveled quite extensively. His covered area was from Maine to Florida and all along the Atlantic coast. "I'm great! in town for a few days thought we might have dinner?" "Dinner? Dana thought. She had only saw Roger for an occasional lunch and now he's asking her for dinner. "To what do I owe this pleasure?' she asked. We have a seminar here this weekend and my days will be very long and boring, did I mention boring" he said again laughing. So, I would like something beautiful to take my mind off of business "Dinner, maybe a movie, if you're up to it this weekend?" Beautiful! there's that word. No one except Roger had said that to her in a very long time. She was hoping the call was from Billy, but two weeks had past and except from having Davie over his home and taking him out for an outing he had not spoken to her. "He did talk with Davie and explained to him he was his father. "Until you feel comfortable enough, just call me Billy okay" he said to him holding his hand for confirmation. Davie had told Dana all about it when he returned home after a visit. Roger that sounds good." "Let's plan on you picking me up from my office Friday about 7pm." I'll be there! Roger said. "Goodbye.

Justin and Ariel had come back from shopping. She had asked him to come along with her. She was shopping for her brother's and sister who were growing like weeds she thought. "Babe I'm glad you're finally allowing me to help you with your family," he shared lovingly. "Justin you know I can't let you spend your money on my family that's for your education! Ariel replied. "Ariel, I have more than I need for that" thanks for letting me help anyway". Ariel was glad Justin was in agreement with her decision to help her family. It made things much easier on her. But she didn't want to take advantage of his kindness because her mother could do a lot better than she was doing. And Ariel wouldn't abandon them all together either. She wasn't aware Justin's medical school had already been paid for. He was saving that to share with her after they get married, she figured. But he had a good salary from his job at the hospital and didn't mind carrying the load.

Justin had changed a lot since high school. He was the head nerd. Ash blonde curly hair and bucked teeth. Katherine put him in braces his last year of high school before entering college. A trip to the local barber and the removal of his braces and walla! Handsome hunk! I think getting past adolescent had a lot to do with it too. So, he didn't have a lot of girls after him yet. He and Ariel were set now to attend his high school reunion. They had been out now for five years and calls had started coming in from his former classmates regarding the event. 'Hello, may I speak with a Justin Parker?" 'Justin isn't in right now; may I take a message?' Ariel asked. "This is Menae Sanchez "I'm one of Justin's high school classmates, I'm calling about the reunion in June, I am on the committee." Do you know if he plans to attend? "I think he does plan on attending, Ariel replied. "Is this his mom?" she asked. No, I'm his fiancée Ariel Hodges" she replied. 'Will you be attending with him" she asked. I'm on the committee to gather as many former classmates as I can find. So please express to him if he knows any fellow classmates, to please let them know about this event". Okay, so you both plan to attend, right? "Yes, that is correct" Ariel responded. "What is the address that I can have some information sent to? It is information we'd like to have prior to your attendance. "Oh, I see "Ariel replied giving Menae the address information. "Thanks" allowing time to write the information down. "Will you be buying your tickets at this time? Tickets are available now for one hundred and fifty dollars". Most people who are going have already purchased their tickets" Menae shared. "Can we count on you? not stopping between questions. "Yes, that's fine I will purchase them now" Ariel said. How will you be purchasing your tickets? She asked again. Ariel knew she had tapped out on her card so she asked Menae' Sanchez to hold for a moment. Walking into the bedroom she looked at another card but knew it wouldn't do any good either. It had caught the big shoe sale at the Vintage mall. Then, laying aside what she vowed to never do she looked in a small box where Justin kept his cards and other important items. She took the key from its secured place in the drawer. She knew where it was but never had yield to the temptation of using it. This Menae made it seem like she and Justin couldn't afford to attend the reunion. Opening it she saw a gold master card and a silver visa in Justin's name. She didn't even think twice about removing the card for this purchase. He never flaunted what he had. Just this time he will never know she thought. I always get the mail. She walked back in and picked up the receiver. Sorry to keep you waiting I was trying to decide which card to use. Put it on my silver visa" she said. The number is 128957648302. Ariel got off the phone put everything back just like she found it and ordered pizza for the night's dinner.

Billy had reasoned it was not yet time to speak with Dana. But he wasted no time getting reacquainted with his son Davie. "Justin, how are you? he said calling him one evening. "Hi Billy just got in how's things going? Well I can't complain, he said: but I've purchased tickets for the baseball game this weekend and thought you might want to come along with Davie and I, he asked. "Oh, bro that sounds great! I'd love to!" Good! I'll pick you up say Saturday morning 8:30a.m we can do breakfast before the game." That sounds wonderful Billy I'll see you then" Justin replied. Billy hung up and went back to what he was doing. He was looking over some briefs that had been there for a while with resolutions pending. He knew he had to find a way to speak with Dana and be civil about the whole matter. Davie had questions about his mother and Billy couldn't stand even the mention of that name "Dana!

I'll call her he said; and let her know Davie is spending the weekend with me. Small steps, very small steps then maybe I can be civil with this woman for my son's sake anyway.

Dalmatia was swimming in the pool with Little Jordan and Mossy was sitting out with the twins in their wading pool. "Kick your feet Jordie! Kick your feet. Dal was teaching him how to swim and Mossy sat watching from the yard chaise near the twins. Little Jordan had on his floaters around his arms and he was braving the pool water. "Dal. I'm going to take the twins in for a nap they have been out here long enough". I'll let Jordan stay a little longer until I get them settled in, Mossy informed her sister. I have a potential sitter coming by at 2:30 she added. "Oh, that's wonderful! Dal said then I can spend more time at the library practicing the language" "I'm getting pretty good don't you think Moss?" Mossy had noticed there were a lot of things Dalmatia was asserting herself to do these days. She was cheery and lighthearted. And she was asking constantly about how to pronounce words correctly. This to Mossy was comforting to know she was communicating more effectively and breaking out of the shyness that shelled her for years because of it. "Dalmatia that's wonderful you're getting use to the United States but remember when the school year ends you have to spend the time off with momee' and popee" she shared with her. "I know Moss, I know. Mossy walked in carrying both twins who were falling asleep in her arms as she walked. "Need help? Sidney asked coming out of the door. He put Valde in his arms and followed her into the house carrying Valde to the nursery lying him down for Moss. "Thanks! She said. "Not a problem.

Sidney went back down stairs to his room and sat on the bed to call Jessica. He rang Jessica's phone. Ring! Ring! ring! He had been trying to reach her all morning. "Hello came a groggy voice. "Jessie, Jessica is that you? "Hold a minute chap" came the voice. Sidney sat listening for minutes but to him it seemed like and hour. "Hello, very quietly came a voice. "Jessica? "Oh hi" then silence "Jessica? Is that you? "Yes. "This is Sidney, what are you doing?" "I'm in bed Sidney it's the middle of the night here," she said. "Who answered your phone?" "That's Marty one of the band members". There was a big mix up with rooms we're all over the place" she told him. "Babe let me call you in the morning. I promise I'll explain everything," Jessica said rushing him from the phone. Sidney didn't really know what to think and he didn't want to think the obvious. He loved her and she said she loved him. "I'll await your call, he said disconnecting the line.

David had just returned to his desk after an extensive staff meeting. "Ring! Ring! 'Hello David Parker". "Hello David this is Katherine, Katherine Heller". David took a deep breath "Yes Katherine, why in heavens are you calling me?" "Well I was just calling to say hi!" Justin shared with me a while ago he had met you, Katherine expressed. "Yes, I've seen and spoken with him briefly. David was being cordial even when he felt betrayed by the call. "Have you acknowledged to him that you are his father?" she asked and step over the line. "Katherine listen to this, and listen good! Justin is a grown man now. What happened with us has long been over. It is definitely the past! He knows my son Billy and they seem to have a good relationship! I don't feel you need to get involved". And yes, I do still love Tetra dearly. "Have a wonderful day Katherine! And David disconnected the line. Katherine sat back in her comfy chair in her den sipping a martini. For the most part she steered away from directly asking Justin questions about what was going on in that family. She knew he probably wouldn't tell her anyway. But she often tricked Ariel into getting information for her. Like David Parker's office number and the state, he lived in.

Dalmatia headed out to the university bright and early Thursday morning. "Can I get a ride into town with you? Sidney asked running out to Dal's car. "I missed my brother he left so early this morning. I need to get down to KLFG broadcasting station. They have opted to let me used their facilities to broadcast a program to be aired later" he shared. He was feeling good again Jessica had called back and somehow explained away the phone call he had placed yesterday. "That's fine hop in!" She said and pulled away. The two got along well. They drove along having conversations about school, careers and other interest they had in common. Soon Dal pulled up to the broadcast station where Sidney said he was spending his day. "Thanks, he said I'll ride back with Desmond". I have to leave tomorrow thanks for keeping me company these last few days. I really enjoyed it. Have a good day" smiling as he got out of the car. Dalmatia walked onto the campus full of glee. She saw a friend who she had met a month now she thought to herself. "Let's do lunch to celebrate she suggested. They had enrolled in the same class. And both were walking aimlessly around campus looking for the classroom that was taught by professor Vogel.

Dana had logged off her computer and was set to leave for the evening. The last patient had left from her office an hour ago. The hospital offices were clearing rapidly. "Ring! Ring! 'Hello Dana answered cheerfully. 'Hello Dana this is Billy. Dana took a deep breath remembering there last meeting. "Yes, she responded hesitantly. I'm wondering if you would mind if Davie stays the weekend. I plan on taking him to a baseball game on Saturday. he asked cordially. "He never mentioned it" Dana replied but that's all right with me. When will you bring him back home Billy? Dana asked. "Sunday evening okay? I also plan to take him to see my grandparents here in Maine. "Oh, Billy I think that's wonderful". I spoke with Davie this week and tried to answer most of his question about us". But I'm leaving all the questions about Jillian up to you" Dana explained. "Are you picking David up from the house? No actually he tells me he has learned how to ride the bus, Billy stated is that true? I'm sure he'll do just fine" Dana said remembering when he and his friend Tommy had ridden the bus across town to the batting cages but stayed to long and had to call her to pick them up. "You two have a wonderful time and I'll see you Sunday" Dana added. Then she turned to see Roger Haskell standing in her door with an arm filled with flowers. "Dana! Billy replied "I'll have David home early, good bye". Dana hung up her phone and walked over to Roger. She had never seen him in anything other than his unformed jacket and slacks with the medical logo over its' pocket. Now he sported stylist blazer and wide leg slacks. "Well you clean up nicely" Dana commented. 'And may I say you look as beautiful as ever" Roger returned walking in handing her the beautiful bouquet. "Aren't you sweet, thank you, "I'll put them in water". Dana went into the back and came out with a crystal vase filled with water. She carefully put each flower in and arranged them and set them on the corner of her desk. The flowers are lovely Roger! She smiled and walked over and kissed him on the cheek as he sat waiting for them to leave. 'Ready? Dana asked. The two walked out. Dana locked the office. Both walked down the hall to the main door and left for the evening.

Davie walked in as soon as Billy hung up the phone from talking with Dana. Hi, I'm here to see William Parker" he said walking into the building. Annie Clark the legal secretary at the firm was walking to the receptionist desk with some files for mailing. "Hello there she said looking at the young man and walking up to lay the letters on the desk. "I was just going to show him to Mr. Parker's office the receptionist replied. "I'm going that way I'll show him extending her hand. "Hi! My name is Annie" she said walking David down the hall. "My name is David ma'am David Parker." "David Parker" ummm she repeated. Soon they were standing in Billy's office. "William you have a visitor" looking at him smiling. She and Billy had dated when he and Jillian was on the fritz though nothing really came out of it. She knew he loved Jillian so she moved on.

"Oh Annie! this is my son David" "your son! she said surprised! "It's a long story and I'll share it with you someday. "Well it's a real pleasure meeting you" Annie said, we'll talk later and walked away. "Good you made it here son" Billy said coming over rubbing David's curly locks of his head. "I did and it only took me two buses to get here," he acknowledged very proud of himself. "That's good Billy replied but call your mom and let her know you have arrived safely." Billy sensed he had not done a lot of this before. I'll be ready to go in a little while." David sat in Billy's big chair. It wasn't as big as he remembered. His feet now touched the floor. Reluctantly though quickly he dialed Dana's number, she answered. "Dana, she said. Hi Dana, "Yes Davie? "I'm here at uncle Billy's I mean Billy's office, he said. David had been practicing saying daddy in his mirror at home. His friend Tommy had asked him why he called his mom and dad by their first names. He still wasn't comfortable with it yet. "Dana! He said "Billy said I should call and let you know I am here. "Oh, that was thoughtful" she responded. Have a wonderful time tomorrow sweetheart okay? 'Okay Dana bye! quickly getting off the phone.

"Well are you ready for a fabulous evening Dana?" Roger asked tapping her on her knee as she sat on the passenger side of his car. "I am, I really am she thought. Roger was very handsome. Dana and he had been having an occasional lunch for about four months now. And she enjoyed his conversations. Not only was he intelligent and knew the business of his job. But with his dark auburn hair and big smile accented by his tanned skin he was very appealing. Not to mention he was a gentleman in every since of the word. Even with her striking new look Dana hasn't had anyone to open a car door for her in a long time.

Billy went toward Annie's office down the hall. He turned to the right and stopped in the middle near the file cabinet. "Annie, he said walking over. I saw the look on your face when I introduced my son" I thought I might explain he said. "No, the look was for "I didn't know you had a son William". You never mentioned him one time when we were dating "she said. "I know that's because until recently I didn't even know he existed" he replied. "What? Annie stood there with her mouth opened. "David is from a relationship I had in high school. And until recently I never knew she had a son for me". I knew it was a possibility but I didn't know what had happened to her after high school" he explained. "Whoa! So, you have to become instant dad. How's that going?" Well I'm learning. Jillian would want it that way." "Jillian? What does Jillian have to do with this?" did she know him? "Yes, Jillian practically helped to raise him "How?" Oh Annie, I really don't have time right now to explain it all but I'm sure over time I will. "You know we have a date next week right, you didn't forget you promised to be my partner for the bowling tournament" Annie explained reminding him of his promise. "Oh, I remember Annie! he responded; walking over and gently hugging her." I'll see you Monday".

Dalmatia woke up to talking she thought was loud. Sidney was saying goodbye to Mostalgia and the children in the nursery. She slowly peeked out her head and saw the lights go off in the nursery. Mossy and Sidney along with Desmond were heading toward the stairs. She walked out quietly down the hall. Desmond was taking him to the airport. "Brother, please don't make your next visit so long in between" Desmond suggested hugging Sidney as he got out at the airport. "I promise" he said, "I really enjoyed you and your family. And little brother your game looks great! Sidney responded returning his affection. Dalmatia had watched from her room upstairs as the car drove away. She would miss the talks in the evening with Sidney.

CHAPTER SIX

Deuces are wild

Billy and David his son left the office going home. "Billy did you play baseball when you were little? David asked riding along in the car. I did! very excited to tell his story. "My best friend Glen Reed and I put together a team every year and we always won the championship that summer. "Whoa! so you guys were good?" I'd say, but most of all we had lots of fun. "What position did you play Billy?" David asked. I played first base, I loved to be in the game" he again replied finding himself reminiscing his younger days. 'Then you were good! I'm a pitcher and I have pitched a no hitter inning before" Davie bragged to him. They went on along the highway talking and getting better acquainted all over again. He shared with him about school and Billy shared with him about what he does at the office. He shared with Davie they would be going over to see his grandparents Sunday and Saturday they were spending a day at the baseball game. Before long they were pulling into his driveway. "Do you live by yourself uncle, I mean Billy?" "I do now but things could change." he said getting out of the car opening the back door to secure his briefcase from the seat. They walked up to the door and he soon realized he had not prepared for Davie to stay there. His place only had one bedroom and the sofa was not a comfortable place to sleep. "Your house is nice! David said coming in with his over stuffed tote of clothes for the weekend. "Put your bag in the bedroom" and after dinner we will have to go and get something for you to sleep on" Billy said "one of those air mattresses or something. "That's going to be fun Tommy and I always sleep on one of those when I stay at his house." "Well, I said it's just temporary until I get a bigger place" Are you getting a bigger house and moving away Billy?" Oh no! "Now that I have you, I can't live in this small place. A young man needs room to grow" he replied.

Sidney landed in the Las Vegas airport and began looking around for Jessica. She was meeting him there. He was joining her for her last performance night in Vegas. He had checked all the flights on the flight board and all the scheduled flights were on time. After sitting for about thirty minutes he went over to baggage claim to retrieve his luggage.

There he saw Jessica standing with a friend who looked a bit like her blonde hair and hazel eyes. She shared they were waiting for him. Walking toward him she introduced herself. "Hello my name is Bridget we have been waiting for you!" standing in front of Sidney extending her hand for a shake. Sidney turned to Jessica "I'm sorry darling but I was up in the other area awaiting you." he replied. "I got an earlier flight out dear. "I just want to get out of here! Jessica stated, "Let's go! Seeing Sidney had gotten his luggage she walked away very quickly. Bridget followed. Sidney didn't know yet where she fit in so he walked along trying to keep up with the fast walking Jessica. "Our flight leaves here in an hour. 'Let's get something to eat and maybe I'll feel better," Jessica stated looking for the nearest eatery at the airport. They found a small café that served sandwiches hot or cold. Walking up with rolling luggage Jessica asked. "May I have a cold beer and hot pastrami on rye please?" Bridget and Sidney both ordered and soon they were all sitting down eating. Bridget had a beer also. He still didn't know what part this lady named Bridget played so Sidney decided to ask. "So, Bridget, are you an entertainer also? No, she said very British sounding. "Jessica and I are going to London for a few weeks" "She needs to get away. "Her performance was sub par this last time out and I think she needs rest", she informed him. "Jessie! You're not performing tonight Jessie? You're not going back home to Baltimore with me either? Sidney questioned. "I will be there in a few weeks Sidney. I really need to get away for a while. "I will see that you get rest honey" Sidney insisted. Jessica motioned her head for Bridget to leave the table. She got up and walked away. "Sidney darling look, I need to get away. I need to get myself together so that I can once again enjoy what I'm doing". I am not happy right now with my performance it needs updating". She was holding his hand and crying quietly. "What happened? You were so happy when we left each other last week" he stated. "I just want to do well every time I step on that stage and lately it's not happening". I've been so preoccupied with being with you and pleasing you my performances are suffering!" Sweetheart you know you don't have to do this" Sidney said. "But this is what I love, a few weeks away honing my craft I will be fine you'll see! Please understand! She stated. Sidney wasn't finish talking but apparently there was nothing else to say. Bridget walked over and stood by the table. Jessica got up and started to walk toward the gate to check her luggage. Sidney knew that no matter what he said things were not going to change. He walked along side Jessica asking questions trying to understand. Bridget was very quiet and didn't interrupt one time. Soon after the luggage had been checked and they had walked to their boarding gate Sidney conceded. Sadden by the news that Jessica was going in another direction without him. After a while he found himself sitting in his first-class seat alone. Her kiss this time had less meaning.

Dana had practiced and practiced before her mirror at home after her renewed look. She worked on refining her taught social skills and manners. She had no use for them for years. But of course, now she would have lots of dates. So dancing was on the list as well. Wouldn't you know the luck of the draw her first date was to a very nice dance club, and she fit right in moving around on the floor. She remembered she hadn't dance like that since those high school dances. "This is so much fun!" she said swerving her hips to the beat. "You certainly know how to move" Roger expressed smiling. Dana was feeling pretty good on her first time to the floor in an actual dance environment in a very long time. "Thanks, she said smiling. Soon they made their way from the dance floor and sat having drinks and conversation until another song they liked drew them once again to the dance floor.

After about two hours of conversation and dancing they left to get something to eat. Roger had made reservations at this very elegant restaurant in Maine called the Wedding cake house, named according to legend. The two sat dinning on Steak and lobster and getting to know each better outside of work. As the dining got close to the end Dana expressed "Roger this has been a spectacular evening. I didn't know these parts of Maine were here thanks for sharing". "My pleasure" he said but we're still on for a movie, tomorrow right?" We are" Dana smiled. 'You know Dana this would have been another boring weekend if you hadn't said yes" Roger confessed. A flirty gesture of thank you from Dana and the two were back in his car and headed to her car they had left in the hospital's parking garage. Saying goodnight with a kiss on the cheek Dana was safely in her car and headed home. Putting the key in the door she walked quietly in realizing what a wonderful time she had.

"Hello Dad, Billy said calling his parents in Spokane. What time does your flight come in tomorrow? He asked. They were not only coming to see Davie but granddad was ill also. "Son we are heading out now so we will be there bright and early." "How is everything with you and Davie going?" "Davie and I are fine. We're bonding. We had a wonderful time together at a baseball game last weekend. Justin even came along with us" he shared. "Well that's wonderful son. "May I speak to Davie please? Tetra asked coming over to get the receiver from David's hand. Tetra talked a short time with Davie before he gave Billy back the receiver. "Will you bring Davie by while we're there Billy?" Tetra asked excited. "Yes, mom Davie and I will come by," he confirmed to her. "I can't wait to see him again." she said. "He is looking forward to seeing you as well mom". "Have you spoken with Dana?" Tetra asked? "One step at a time mom", right now I just want to get to know my son". "I understand dear, love you, she said and handed the receiver back to David. "Son, speaking of Justin there's something I want to talk with you about." "Oh, Something about Justin! Billy exclaimed. "Not directly about Justin. But I got a call from Katherine the other week and I was not happy about it" David replied. Katherine? he asked. "Yes Katherine Heller, Justin's mother.

Why? he asked thinking it could be important. "Come on David we're going to miss our flight! I heard mom saying in the background. She had walked into another room to get something she had purchased for Davie and had returned to the study. "Are you two still on the phone?" Son we will talk when I see you". Safe flight dad" "thanks son.

Sidney returned to Baltimore alone. Walking into his bachelor pad he could hear his telephone ringing. Running hurriedly over to answer it, "Sidney' "Man I'm so glad I caught you". It was his brother Desmond. "Man, I know I didn't mean to interrupt what you have going; I just call to say you left your electronic scheduling pad on the bedside table. And if you're like me your whole life is tied up in it". "You're right, thanks Des I would have turned this place upside down looking for it." Sidney replied. Well Sid not to worry I'll send it first thing in the morning on my way in." And Sid, I'll send it to the station that way you'll be guarantee to get it" Desmond added. Thanks bro Sidney responded sounding a bit down. "Sidney you sound down is every thing alright?" Do you need to talk? Desmond questioned. "No! You caught me coming in the door I just got off the plane" Sidney shared. "That's right I'm sorry we will talk soon" love to Jessica he said hanging up. Sidney put his luggage in the bedroom and flopped down on his sofa. He really missed Jessica. Ring! Ring! Hello Sid, "Sid this is J.T. J.T. what's up man? Sidney was trying to sound upbeat this was a co-anchor from the station. "I saw the piece you shot in K.C. old man Finster would like to speak with you about it in the morning, Great job by the way!" Thanks man, thanks for the call. Sidney got up went into his bedroom unpacked his luggage to get ready for his meeting tomorrow morning.

Dana hummed through breakfast. Mrs. Bea was out at a social with her church group and her son David was with his father Billy. She had the house all to herself. She hoped Davie was having a wonderful time with his dad as she moved around humming a tune, she heard last evening. "Ring ring! Hello" Hi Dana" "Hi Roger sounding giddy answering the call and threw herself on the large sofa in the family room. "To what do I owe a call this time of day?' she asked very cheery. 'They do occasionally give us breaks you know" he said teasingly. "I see, Dana commented. So, what types of movies do you like? I'm trying to decide what we're going to see tonight", Roger asked confirming their date for the evening. "I'll let it be your choice this time Dana said." I'd like to see what you think I'd like, deal?" "Deal! this was Dana and Rogers second weekend date together though they had sat down to quite a few lunches at the hospital. He laughed. "I'll pick you up at 6:30 or 7:00. 7:00 Dana agreed. "Just call when you get near. See you then." Dana had already explained to Roger her living arrangements. Roger was all right with calling which somehow impressed Dana greatly. Dana liked the fact that even if Roger was thinking what she would consider at this point the wrong ideas he never showed it. And he never made advances inappropriate toward her on their first full date. He always complimented her on her attire and was very attentive to her through the whole night. She moved around the house thinking about tonight and what would come out of it.

Ring ring! Hello, Dana answered "Hi Dana! "David how are you doing? She asked. I'm having so much fun! He exclaimed. "You already know I went to the baseball game last weekend with Billy and Justin." Davie was so excited. "You did, you told me, Dana responded. Justin went with you?" Yes! He is my uncle and Billy's brother. "You're right Davie. "That's cool. I can't wait to tell Tommy! He replied still excited about his discovery of family. "I ate so many hot dogs and I got lots of autographs too". Billy says next time I can ask Tommy to come with us." Well that's good Davie, mommy's glad you're having fun! Dana was starting to tear up. Dana I'm going to see grandma and grandpa this Sunday" he shared with her. "No Davie you mean you're going to see great grandpa and great grandma again this Sunday. "Well Davie sighed, "They are coming from Washington! Billy said. "Oh, then you're right son". Why is everyone coming here is everything alright?" Billy says great- grandpa is sick. "Oh, I see well tell them all I said hello". Dana had never met Billy's grandparents and was glad David was getting a chance to. "Also tell Billy thanks for keeping me informed," she added. "He's not in right now, but I'll tell him Davie implied. 'WHAT DO YOU MEAN? ARE YOU ALONE DAVIE? ARE YOU FRIGHTENED? Dana questioned loudly getting very excited. "No Dana he's outside on the deck with Annie" Annie! She repeated quietly but Davie heard it. "She works at his office. "Okay, Davie you have fun" she told him. "I will, Bye Dana." Bye sweetheart."

Ariel had gotten comfortable with using the credit card she had discovered in Justin secret hiding place and paying it off. She could now shop at the stores Kat had taken her to for special occasions only. Now she shopped on her own without questions. She would use it one month and pay it off. She wasn't noticing her purchase amounts were getting larger and larger. And one month she barely paid it off before Justin used it to buy his schoolbooks and supplies. But she felt so empowered just handing over the card for all of her purchases. She felt success. They were practically married anyway she thought walking out of the department store with lots of shopping bags almost everyday after work. A new outfit for the reunion was definitely in order and certainly a new fragrance of cologne for Justin. Cash advance for her mother one month. At months end all was well. "Honey did you get a raise at work? No why? I've been noticing some things around here". Ariel needed something to tell Justin so she lied. I have just been saving she replied. "That's great! I'm very proud of you Ariel. She smiled and walked in the kitchen coming back with their dinner plates putting them on the tray tables in front of the television Justin had set up. "Justin remember we are attending your high school reunion this month she said taking a bite from her meal. "Yes, I almost forgot about that. I saw Franklin last week and he asked if I planned to attend. I think it will be fun you wanna go? he teased her again. "Yes, Justin we are going I've already purchased our tickets Ariel said smiling, looking at him and pushing slightly on his shoulder. I'm surprised you have been spending time with Kat and it's rubbing off he said. "Is that good or bad babe?' "Taking care of business is good sweetie and leaned over and kiss her.

David, Tetra and his mom sat in service early Sunday morning in Maine. Mr. Parker David's dad was home with his nurse who was caring for him in their absence. Tetra's eyes were flowing with tears as she sat thanking God mightily for her family. They thanked Him for returning Davie their grandson back to the family and restoring their son Billy's heart and mind. The atmosphere around them was less charismatic and moved a lot slower than their church service back home in Washington. But the Lords presence was all around Tetra felt it as she stood basking in His glory. David's mother Mrs. Ruth Parker requested a special prayer for her husband as the Bishop Slage gathered everyone around the alter to pray. Most in the congregation knew him and was aware of his recent illness they stood in agreement also. Setting aside the fact that he was seventy- six years young he'd say. His health was failing. Mr. Alfred Parker was a very active businessman in his day. Ran successfully several companies which his son David now over sees. Until recently he was very active on the board of two of them. His son lovingly asked him to resign from his duty because it was obvious to all he was forgetting things and calling boards meeting where the previous agendas were already discussed. They retired him with a big celebration shared by hundreds of his business associates, employee's family and friends.

Alfred Parker was known as a screwed businessman and as fierce a competitor as you want to meet. His daughter Sarah Parker runs the companies on the east coast with David Parker his son handling the ones on the west coast from his corporate office in Spokane Washington where he lives.

Truthfully Bishop Slage brought a heartfelt message and God reigned supreme throughout the service. After being introduced around by Mother Parker, David and Tetra left going back to his parent's home to enjoy their visit with them.

"Ring, ring, Hello, Ruth answered her phone it was Sarah her daughter inquiring about her dad's health. She was on a cruise and couldn't come now but would be there as soon as the ship docks she told her. "That's fine dear he understands, Ruth replied. Their dad didn't want them to fuss over him. Didn't want them worrying over him he was fine he'd tell them. Ruth excused herself and took the receiver to his bedside so Sarah their daughter could speak with her father. Maybe she sensed a week would be to long for him to wait for her though doctors never said.

The hired staff had prepared mid-day dinner brunch and Tetra, David and Ruth sat down to eat. Ruth had come from the bedroom after making Alfred comfortable and he seemed to be resting.

Well Tetra how are things going with the Center? "she asked passing the serving dish to David. "Things are going well we have expanded so much since I was here last" she replied to her mother in-law. "That's good the Lord is for ever working dear" she said in her sweet soft voice. "David tells me you two are grandparents now?' she smiled and laughed softly patting Tetra on top of her hand. "That's wonderful. "Sarah is not thinking of marriage or babies she's so much like her dad I should have named her Al" Ruth chuckled softly. "We need someone to carry on" she added. Ruth was very sweet and very soft-spoken but she stood up for her son when he said he wanted to marry Tetra. Saying the heart has not color it loves whomever it wants. "Yes, Mother Ruth, Billy is supposed to be bringing him here to see you and pops," Tetra confirmed to her. I'm sure he'll be here that child sure has grown" she giggled. And now he has a son." He comes by every week since he moved back here to sit and talk with me and Alfred." I remember when he was younger and use to run around this house and Alfred would be just yelling running after him. He spoiled him rotten when he thought I wasn't looking" she said shaking her head with a soft grin.

'I'm very proud of him he's a good son." Tetra replied. "I was so hurt when we heard about his fiancée" Ruth shared. We had gotten our invitation in the mail and had made plans to be there." "Yes, mom that was a tragic situation all those people's lives!" David said putting another helping on his dessert plate. "You know, Ruth said "I have all the letters Billy sent me over the years when he was in school and college stored in a beautiful handmade box. The beautiful cards he never forgot about us." I was going to put his engagement announcement in it last week and I sat there looking and reading through them" she explained.

Soon there was a ding! dong! at the door. The maid came from the back to answer it. In walked Billy and Davie with big smiles on their faces. "Hi grandma! and grandpa! Davie said very loudly. He was so excited to see them. It had been months and he thought he might not see them again. Tetra quickly moved from the table and ran and hugged him. "My you have grown! I can't even pick you up, she remarked. "But I can! David said standing up and lifting him in the air. "How's my grandson? He asked hugging him tightly. And son, how are you doing?'

he asked placing Davie back on the floor. 'We're fine" he responded. "So, what are you two up to? Tetra asked standing aside of her son Billy holding him around the waist. "Well first we're hoping we're not to late for a good meal." He replied. Hello Nana, how is granddad, he asked leaning over kissing her gently on her forehead. "He's resting, but you two sit down there is plenty" she said acknowledging her grandson with a hug. Another maid came in and refilled some of the serving dishes and quickly heated others. "Now! Ruth said as the two sat eating "Who is this young man?"

"I'm David Parker, Billy's son" Davie said and I'm eleven years old" he added putting another bite into his mouth. He noticed grand nana looked a lot like the older lady he called Grandma Bea "Nana, Billy said "this is David remember the one I wrote you about in a letter" "I told you we were babysitting Jillian's friends' little child. Well it turned out to be my son" I'll explain it later. It gets to be a bit complicated" he said. "Well! Welcome to the Parker family" Ruth said smiling. "I'm your great grandmother. "Whoa! I'm so lucky! Davie expressed "I have lots of family!" I can't wait to tell Tommy". He's my best friend! Davie remarked smiling at his great grandmother Ruth. They all sat around the large dining table getting better acquainted with Davie.

Davie asked all the question that were important to him and Nana brought out picture albums I hadn't seen in years. It was wonderful. After a while we moved to the great room with Nana leading the way holding Davie's hand. The nurse rolled granddad in from his rest. "What's all that laughter I hear going on? He asked now taking control of the chair's wheels. "Granddad this is your great grandson David". Billy announced very proudly.

He locked the wheels on the chair. 'Let me out of this thing" he said trying to stand without assistance. David his son and Billy his grandson got beside him and sat him securely on the sofa. "Now come over here" he smiled patting the sofa's pillow beside him looking at his great grandson David.

CHAPTER SEVEN

Memories of:

Desmond and Henry were out looking at a new location for the law office. This winter proved to be plagued with troubles. A leaky roof that the building owner kept promising to fix and a heater that was thought to be used by Thomas Jefferson they'd joke. No matter the cliental and business had grown so much they really needed a larger space to spread out and to modernize. Mostalgia refused to come in some mornings opting to work from her home office if needed. The weather in Kansas gets very cold. She had finally found a reliable babysitter to care for her three children and was back working full time at the law firm. 'Desmond how is the search going for a new building? she asked. "Were making progress the realtor has a building he wants us to look at today. He thinks it's a great location" That's great! Mossy replied as long as I don't have to spend another winter in this one" getting her briefs out to start the day. "You're right our folders are so compacted in those files it takes me longer to find what I'm looking for than building a whole case" he teased. And poor Emily tries her best to keep things in order. Emily Pickens had now joined the staff and had proven to be a very good secretary for the growing law firm.

Dalmatia had embraced her newfound freedom and Mossy tried to keep a close eye on her. This was her first year of college in a new country. But she had somehow come out of her shell and was venturing into new places and becoming very comfortable with the language and had become successful with it. "Dalmatia, what are you doing coming by this time of day? Slovenia asked when his sister stopped by for an unexpected visit to his apartment. Slovenia worked the night shift at the post office and was home during the day. "I only had to be there for an exam today so I came by just to say hi" she told him. He was just getting up for the day it was around noon. "Slovenia this is Marsha Turner she goes to the college with me" Dal said introducing Slovenia to her friend she had brought by with her. They had become very good friends since meeting earlier in the year. Both went everywhere together. "Marsha this is my brother Slovenia" Dal said going into his small kitchen to get her a soda or some juice from his refrigerator. Slovenia said hello and went into his bedroom to make himself presentable for company. He had bed head and stripped bottom pajamas. Though his hairy chest wasn't bad Marsha thought as she sat on the sofa looking around at the stark walls of the apartment. She was from California and her parents had sent her off to college in Kansas saying she could focus better on her studies. She came because it gave her independence away from their watchful eye; she explained. So, she and Dalmatia were helping each other learn the ropes of college life. She lived in the dorms and was glad she had Dalmatia living off campus. She could escape and better see the world was the story she tells. She confessed she didn't feel so confined and limited in her new environment. They spent time at Desmond's and Mossys' home as well as the local malls. She helped Dal update her wardrobe and to fashion her look. She was a true valley girl in every since. 'Marsha would you like something to drink?' Dal asked standing at the refrigerator. "What ever you're having is fine" she replied. Dalmatia came from the kitchen with two sodas and put them on the bare cocktail table in Slovenia's apartment. 'He's cute' she whispered to Dalmatia. "If you say so" Dal replied. Slovenia was two years older than Dalmatia and the two were very close. He always dreamed of coming to America, finding a beautiful girl and getting married. Dal wanted to see the world through the eyes of a ballerina. She had come by to use her brother's telephone at the apartment most of the time she confided. Calling a friend, she was still keeping secret from even her friend Marsha she would lay on Slovenia's bed when he wasn't there and talk to her friend before going back to Langley Estates. "Mossy know you're off today? He asked coming from his bedroom. "Only if you tell her! Dal replied sipping from her soda can. Slovenia walked in his kitchen looking for something and had his back to them. Marsha got up and quickly peeked into his bedroom. She saw that it needed a woman's touch she thought sitting back on the sofa before he turned around. "Slovenia may I use your phone? Dal asked has he came back and sat in the smaller chair in his living room. "Surely but why do you ask? He knew she came there when he wasn't home, he gave her the key. His apartment was downtown and closer to the college campus than Langley so she came by often and he was all right with that. "Just felt like being nice" she said hitting him as she passed by. "Keep Marsha entertained, I won't be long." She remarked going into the bedroom and closing the door. "How do you pronounce your name again? the bright-eyed Marsha asked. "SLO-VEN-IA" he said very slowly. Marsha repeated it smiling "SLO-VEN-IA She had long silky dark hair that hung to her back. Very fashion conscious and today had her mid drift showing. Slovenia went into his kitchen to prepare him something to eat. 'Would you like something? he asked as he took the bread from the cabinet. Marsha was far from shy. She got up and walked into the kitchen. Two people in his kitchen were the maximum it would hold comfortably. "Let me help you" she remarked. "I make the best sandwiches ever" she affirmed.

Roger was on time. Dana came out shortly after he arrived in front of her home to pick her up for their third weekend date. 'Hello she said getting into his car. "How was the seminar?" 'Well I made it through another one" he joked saying it was fine. Now let's see if I know something about you" Roger stated. "The premier starts at eight o clock. Mind if we stop by Maui, Maui for a cocktail? he asked. "That's sound wonderful and what are we seeing tonight since you think you know me so well Dana questioned smiling. I thought we'd go and see the "Titanic". I'd like to get your take on that movie. "Okay. It was one of Dana's favorite movies and DeCapprio played his role. They sat and had appetizers and some fruity cute drinks with umbrellas before heading to the theater. Hi Roger!" a voice said as they went out of the door at the Maui restaurant. He turned to see one of the salespersons he had just been with in the seminar. "Oh hi! He said "I see you survived as well" he told her waving and continuing out the door. Giggly but very relaxed Dana shared her day with Roger. And he informed her on the seminar that was not as boring because he knew he would see her tonight. At the theater they stopped at the concession counter and got a large box of popcorn and two bottles of water and went in to enjoy their movie.

Ariel had gotten dress and was waiting for Justin to come home. His medical class should surely be over by now she thought. She was moving around very carefully as not to get anything on her designer dress she had purchased. She had everything ready for Justin including having his new slacks from his suit professionally hemmed and pressed. Where was he?" she thought. It was getting very close to the time they should be going to the big event is what it turned out to be. Where? Ariel thought was Justin? Suddenly a very angry Justin emerged through the door. He looked like he had been drinking beer she suspected. "Justin did you forget about your reunion? You look terrible where have you been? Ariel questioned puzzled by his lateness and appearance. "Oh, he mumbled I stopped by to buy you a corsage earlier today and maybe a sprig of perfume since you have been keeping on top of things." Ariel's heart began to pound where was he going with this. He continued "that was before I went to the Norfield's Department store earlier to by you a piece of jewelry" he said. Ariel's legs began to shake under her new gown. They told me my card was declined. And I knew that couldn't be I only use it occasionally for special purchases" he confessed. So, I called the company and you! Ariel Hodges! he screamed You! have been using it all over the placed. Why Ariel? Why! I put my trust in you!

Granddad Alfred began telling Davie stories of when I was younger. "Now your dad and I built a tree house one summer" he said. "A treehouse a real one you can sit in? Davie asked. "Yes, he said it's still out there" he confirmed. "It took us the whole summer to build it but we were able to climb into it and we had lots of fun" he laughed. "Your Great Nana Ruth always saw that the boys had plenty of snacks in it." I sat remembering Harry and Ernie aka Munchie" "Munchie! Davie chuckled. Munchie wasn't his real name but he was always eating so we nicknamed him Munchie and it stuck. Can we see it please great grandpapa Alfred? Davie pleaded sitting next to his great grandpa who had by telling his stories gotten younger. "No Davie another time granddad's not up to it right now" I explained. "I'm sorry I understand" Davie replied sadly holding his head down. "Well now, who told you all to speak for me?" Alfred said clearing his throat. "Get me in this contraption and let's head out to find it". Granddad had a muscle disorder that was causing all kinds of strange things to go on in his body including recent memory loss. But speaking to him this day we knew his past had been tucked away safely and every bit intact.

Dad and I headed out back with my son David pushing Granddad's wheelchair. Mom and Nana followed. We walked out toward this big oak tree that had grown in size but still looked the same size now to me since I had grown also. The gardener had the lawn freshly cut and manicured way out there. As we got closer Davie became so excited. "Whoa! Great Grand you built this all by yourself?" My nana stood back smiling she remembered how hard Granddad had worked on that tree house for me. And he was so proud the day he could say it was finished. The wood was now worn from the rain and the years that had long passed. No one had played in it since I had grown up and went off to high school and or college. Nana remembered how Alfred her husband had asked her to make character pillows to sit on. One for each boy to have has his own in the clubhouse. She knew he enjoyed seeing our smiles as much as she did. We all stood looking up at it. "Can I climb in it? David asked. Before anyone could answer he was headed up the tall but rigidity ladder leaning on the tree. The boards that had been used for steps were very worn and as Davie made the second step the board broke and down, he fell laughing.

"Be careful! Granddad Alfred exclaimed. Yes, David be very careful mom and nana both said with nana holding her hands on her head. Dad and I helped David get back to his feet. Another try and he was at the top with dad and I close behind. "Whoa this is great, wait until I see Tommy! he said excitedly. There were spider webs, and dust so thick covering everything. The rickety floorboards were to be walked on very carefully. But David loved the tree house his dad played in has a young boy. Granddad Alfred sat looking at his work that years had worn away. He was very proud it had withstood time.

Dana and Roger walked out of the theater after about two and a half hours. "Well what did you think of that movie?" he asked. "I liked it. A very good choice she said. "Well I want to thank you for making this another enjoyable weekend for me." "We will have to do it again the next time you come this way" Dana replied. She knew Roger usually came to this area every three or four months. His sales route extended the coast and being very successful at what he was doing was not looking for a career change. Which didn't matter right now she just enjoyed his company. Well thanks again he said pulling up outside of her home. She knew Mrs. Bea was home so she was not going to ask him in. "Turn the car off for a minute" she suggested. Dana had waited for Roger all day. She had been all to herself since coming to Maine. And having someone else to talk to besides Mrs. Bea or Justin was a welcome change. Besides he was male and interested in her. She really wasn't ready for the date to end. Roger seemed to genuinely enjoy being with her to but was not going to rush things though he sensed Dana wanted more as they sat in the car talking. He turned the car's ignition switch off. "Come here" he said pulling her shoulders over to him. The compartment divider in the middle of the seats kept them separated. She laid her head on his shoulder. "This was nice Dana!" Roger said turning her head to look in her face. She lifted her head and kissed him. And he kissed her. She hadn't felt liked in so long. They talked some more very little regarding the movie. It spoke for itself. It was obvious to the both of them that this was not the ending either wanted. Soon the car started up again before returning the next morning early to bring Dana back home.

Sidney walked into his office bright and early the next day. J.T. greeted him. He was headed out after having broadcast the early morning segment. He and Sidney anchored the weekends together. "Good morning man" he said extending his hand out to Sidney. "Good seeing you "How was your vacation with your brother?" 'It was cool, I needed that in my life" Sidney confessed. Did Jessica go with you?" he questioned. They all knew down at the station he was dating Jessica Strassberg a big music diva and most couldn't wait for a bit of news about her to come across the airwaves. "Briefly but I'm cool he told him. 'She's very busy and has a lot on her plate right now so I'm trying hard to stay low key" Sidney added. 'Well I'm out, good luck with your meeting, J.T. said heading back to the dressing room in the news station. Sidney looked at his watch and headed to his meeting with Finster the station's director. "Come in, come in Mr. Finster said seeing Sidney approaching his office door. "Have a seat". "How was Kansas?" He asked allowing Sidney to position himself comfortably in his chair and set his briefcase on the floor beside him. "Not bad, not bad" "Well, this won't take a lot of time I'll get right to the point". The piece you shot in Kansas for us was very good! What we have discussed is, the committee and I of course" he smiled. "Is that we would like for you to expand on it" My executives were really impressed about this human-interest story and so was I," Mr. Finster said raising his bushy eyebrows. 'Thank you, sir," Sidney replied. "Now when you say expand exactly what or you making reference to? He questioned. "We would like you to go more in depth. Stay around the people, do some interviews and lifestyles stories" he recommended. And we're sending you with a crew to assist you" Mr. Finster added. He and Mr. Finster continued discussing the planned project for about an hour. Sidney knew he was making headway with the big guys in the business. "Mr. Bradley here I come, he thought sitting in his director's office suite. "Thank you, sir," getting up shaking Mr. Finster's hand and leaving very pleased. Most journalist strived for the inside television spot. But not Sidney He loved being outside on the street. That's where the real stories were, he explained.

Justin went into his bedroom without saying another word. Ariel could hear the shower water running. But still she had no clue what he was doing or planned to do. She sat in their living room on the sofa crying not knowing what to say. After about an hour he came out dressed in his suit "ARE YOU GOING WITH ME? He asked pointedly. They would clearly be more than an hour late. Ariel at this point was so shaken and nervous of what she had done and not knowing what Justin was doing behind the close door in their bedroom. She really had never experienced his temper even though Kat had told her it existed. He never said anything else about the credit card since coming through the door but clearly, he was upset. "Ariel didn't feel beautiful anymore she didn't at this point feel anything but fear.

Ariel? he asked coming out of the bedroom dressed in his designer suit walking over to the door and turning the knob "are you going? He asked again very harshly. What kind of an evening would it be with Justin in this mood? She thought to herself sitting alone in their living room. Her beautiful designer gown was for not. Justin looked great in his G.Q. styled suit standing there near the door. I'll make this up to him. I will she reasoned. I'll let him enjoy his friends and this reunion night alone and explain everything tomorrow! Justin did ask another time before heading out the door to his car. Ariel still sat trying to decide what would be best for this situation. After a moment or two in time it seemed had gone by, she decided staying home was not the solution. And besides he had never asked her to! But when Ariel hurriedly ran to the door looking out all she saw were the taillights of the Beamer pull out and turn the corner.

CHAPTER EIGHT

Let's do it again

Dalmatia and Marsha were laughing loudly in Dal's bedroom at home. They had recently come back from shopping and were taking out their purchases laying them on the bed. "What are you girls up to? Mossy asked coming in the opened door. "Look, Dal said bravely tossing a pair of skimpy underwear to her. "Who are these for?" she asked looking at Dal for and answer. "They are the latest fashion in lingerie" Dal replied. "FOR WHO? Mostalgia exclaimed. Mossy was very conservative; this purchase the girls had made clearly caught her off guard and she blushed. She allowed Dal to wear what she wanted, she wasn't her mother and she was of age and she was in college. But she was her guardian here in the states. She didn't want her growing up so fast. She shopped for her own clothes that were mostly influenced by Marsha like the short skirts and very tight jeans. Most of the time with exception of color they dressed exactly alike. "Oh Dal! She gasped, "I know you're not wearing these!" "No! Those are for Marsha," she alleged. 'They are very comfortable Mossy you should try them" Marsha suggested smiling at her. Desmond will love them! She added falling over on the bed laughing even harder at the look on Mossy's face. "You two!" Mossy stated walking out of the bedroom.

The realtor had found a prime location downtown for the law firm is how he described it. And after viewing it Desmond and Henry agreed. Moving day was approaching fast and the movers were busy with the deliveries of office furniture, computers and other office supplies needed that was not being brought over from their old office building. There new office was smack in the heart of downtown in a brand-new high rise building with and adjoining covered parking garage. The fresh smell of paint and new plush pile carpeting that Mostalgia had chosen filled the huge spacious office elegantly. She had spent long hours with the designers on their plans for the layout of the new space the law firm would soon occupy.

Some furnishing was arriving while Desmond was there checking on progress of things going on. Most of the furniture was due in by next week to give them enough time for the big opening they had planned. Desmond, Mossy, and Henry stopped for a moment to look as the very large floor to ceiling drapes were being installed. Contractors, installers, technicians were moving all over the place. Installers were putting in phone systems while technicians were connecting computers. "Let's get out of here Mossy, Henry" things seem to be progressing along fine" Desmond said leading her to the front entrance of the law firm. "Tomorrow I'm sure it will be more settled and then we can make a final opening day assessment" he added. The front entrance of the law firm after entering the building itself had very tall wide wooden doors with detailed cravings engraved deep into the wood. Each door had an ornate rod iron handle attached with a beautiful crystal chandelier in the entrance foyer.

They had made their clients aware of the move and the new location and planned a tentative opening in a few weeks. Desmond and Mossy walked out to see Mr. John Owens, Desmond's grandfather walking up. Henry greeted Mr. Owens and waved goodbye. "So, this is the new office yeah? He said looking at his grandson. "Hello, grandfather, Desmond returned giving him a big hug. Mossy came over and hugged him also. "It's good to see you" Desmond said. "You are going to speak for us on opening day, right?' he asked the seventy-two-year-old retired lawyer. 'Well, how are things going around here?' his grandfather asked. 'Very busy today, tomorrow would probably be a better time to walk around. We can come together tomorrow if you like Desmond replied to him. Well that sounds good grandson." He voiced with his baritone sounding replied. John Owens had worked what he would say all of his life. "Grew up right here in Kansas City" he'd say, was fortunate to go away to Philanders Smith College in Arkansas to better myself. Met and married after graduating my lovely wife Amelia" who then worked in a diner called "Alice's" near campus. Then he returned back here to start my own business. "Grandfather will you have lunch with Des and I. I have some new pictures of the children to give you" Mossy explained. "If it's not a bother, I'd love to he replied. He had loss his wife Amelia ten years ago to cancer and lived alone. His son Desmond's father who lives in Palm Springs California visited him at least once a year. He has been out to California several times to but not has much since Amelia passed away. He was so glad his grandson had moved here and enjoyed it when they brought the little ones, his great-grand's over to see him or he visited with them.

Justin drove into the parking lot of the Marina Inn. The reunion was in its elaborate ballroom. Going in everything was in full swing by the time he arrived. Walking in Menae Sanchez noticed him right away. Mainly because she was looking for the nerdy guy she knew in High school. She was standing near the welcome table where everyone came to get their name badges. Hello Julia Cook said, your name please?" Justin Parker, he replied suave as can be. He was not going to let anyone know how he was feeling.

"You are who? Julia exclaimed looking over her very thick glasses. They had several classes together back then. She began turning the pages of the yearbook stopping on the "P's" Justin quickly pointed to the bucktooth young man now staring at him from the pages of the yearbook. "Justin Parker! Well the years have certainly been good to you! Julia said using a voice like Mae West. "Are you alone? Menae asked coming closer to the table now interrupting the conversation. "Yes, I am! he replied not feeling very cordial right now. He had just arrived. Justin loved to socialize and most times the life of the party. But now all he wanted was his name badge and to move on. "I'm here alone too maybe we can share a dance later", Menae suggested quickly seeing how handsome Justin had become. "Maybe, he smiled taking the badge pinning it to the lapel of his jacket. "Thanks, he nodded at Julia and walked in. Most people were on the dance floor getting their groove on. Justin looked around for a moment and after getting a drink of punch he looked for somewhere to sit that was not occupied. But by now every table seemed to have someone sitting there. "Hi, a voice said noticing him passing through the crowd. "Hello, he stopped apparently she knew him. "Justin, right? She asked. "Yes, he replied. "I'm Pamela Ostrowski I met you the other week. I'm Franklin's wife she responded back. "Oh yes! Franklin, I remember. Do you mind? he said taking a sit next to this very pregnant lady. Can I get you something to drink? "No thank you she said softly. Taking a drink from his glass he knew someone had spiked it. 'It's a pleasure meeting you again" he shared making small talk trying to get comfortable. 'Where is Franklin? he asked looking around. It was obvious he was not at the table. "He'll be glad to see you". He just went to the car to lock up my purse" she said rubbing her large stomach for comfort he guessed.

They sat for what seemed ten or fifteen minutes looking at one another and making very little conversation waiting for Franklin who could have gone to the store and back by now Justin figured. Then the deejay played and old tune that Pamela liked. 'Will you dance with me? I love this song! she explained. Are you sure? Justin asked. He already felt awkward sitting alone at this table with her and now she wanted him to dance. When she stood up it was plain to see she was due any day now he thought. Justin moved carefully to the beat as she enjoyed his company and moved actively to the music.

After a few grimacing minutes for Justin it was over. He sat down finished is drink and politely excused himself to move on. Franklin still had not returned to the table. Justin walked around trying to see through the crowd. Eventually they would turn up the lights but right now everyone was enjoying the romantic atmosphere of the amber lights keeping beat with the music.

All of a sudden everyone was crowding around this pair that was moving to the beat on the dance floor. "Go! Go! Go! Go! When Justin got closer, he could see the red head Franklin freckles and all spinning around on the floor, then coming back up to join his partner and resume dancing. Justin stayed close by him until the music stopped.

"Frank, Franklin man, it's good to see you" he said. "Justin my man you made it! Embracing one another. Justin walked from the crowd leading Franklin back to his table. "Oh, honey this is Justin Parker my biology partner from our high school days" he laughed. Franklin and I ruled biology we were nerds and since there were no girls in our lives to distract us, we put our energies into our studies. "Hi! Justin smiled looking at Pam without an explanation. "Yes, we met" she replied. He sat and talked with Franklin for a few more minutes. It's good seeing you I'm sure we'll run into each other again" Justin said leaving the table. He doesn't know how long Franklin sat there but at least his wife knew he was back from the car.

Mr. John Owens walked up to the very tall brand-new office building that housed the law office space with his grandson. Desmond pushed the button to open the elevator's door. They waited for a moment sharing a laugh anticipating the upward ride together. The doors slowly opened. After getting in he pushed the button for the sixth floor. Soon the elevator opened again after a quick ride up. He and his grandfather got out of the elevator and walked up the long wide hall to the law office. He stopped before he entered and took out his handkerchief from his inner suit-coat pocket. "Grandfather is everything alright? Desmond asked. "Everything is fine" he smiled. They had put the names on the door and "MacFinney was there too. "Desmond smiled realizing the need for his grandfather's handkerchief. "Well, John said stopping short after entering through the foyer. "I'm proud of you grandson" he added fighting back tears. Desmond went on to show him how they had arranged the office. How this works, where they kept all the documents that were handled by the court. He raised his eyebrows pleased at the much-needed wall of file drawers for the now grown firm. He walked around in the office knowing that this sprung up from his foundation. "You have fulfilled my vision attorney Owens" he said smiling and hugging his grandson, as they looked out over the city from the window view in Desmond's office where his old desk was sitting in this new space. "You have put this law office on the top! He laughed looking down at the city below. "I'm very proud grandson, very proud of you."

Justin moved around the floor meeting Grace Riley and Brenda Edwards two of the young ladies who once made up the cheerleading squad. "Hi Justin, could be heard once everyone figured out who this cutie was in their midst. Desiree Singer had married a minister and he stopped and spoke with them before moving on. They were sitting in the corner conversing and watching everyone enjoying the reunion he surmised. Leonard Smith and Mary Applegate were still together they dated all through high school. Everyone all thought they were married the whole time anyway. Justin walked back up toward the front entrance. "Would you like to dance? A very soft voice asked as he past her table. It was Menae Sanchez she had been watching him walking around getting reacquainted with his old classmates. "We're going to slow the pace down a bit!" could be heard by the deejay playing and announcing the music. "Sure, Justin said. He had walked around meeting and greeting a lot of his old friends so he thought it was time to enjoy himself. He was starting to feel a lot more sociable after two more trips to the punch bowl. Extending his hand, he slowly pulled Menae to the floor and they embraced. Moving slowly around the floor with other couples sharing intimate moments Justin asked Menae about her life. She being quite the lady whispered quietly in is ear her successes and her journey getting there. Menae had spoken with Ariel who stated she was his fiancée' so why was he here alone? she thought has she drew closer embracing Justin's touch. "if he's here alone he can be got! She reasoned rubbing close to him on the dance floor. He was impressed that she had gotten her degree from the University of Maine in business and had a career in local government. He not only found her interesting to talk with she was also very classy and soft spoken. Feeling pretty good about things he took time and shared about himself as they sat now talking having another drink he had purchased from the open bar.

Justin and Menae sat enjoying one another's company getting better acquainted with each other. She reminded him she had come late in the school year from Philadelphia. "That's right he said now I remember". Soon they had another intimate dance and exchanged telephone numbers before parting. "Thank you she said softly "I enjoyed that". "Are you trying to get rid of me?" Justin asked moving back over to the table. His plans were to go and be with some of his buddies he saw gathered across the room and probably come back before the night was over anyway. 'He felt totally comfortable with her. 'Oh no! she said so sweetly, I just didn't want to cause trouble you know?" smiling naively holding his hand. Justin was going to enjoy himself. He did not tell Ariel not to come. And had asked her several times if she was coming! "May I say since I'm alone and you're alone. Let's do this thing together?" He suggested. gently lifting her up by the hand from her seat and hugging her around the waist very innocently. Menae smiled that's fine with me! Come this way let's go through this line and show them how it's done!" pulling her gently through the crowd to the line Franklin had formed in the center of the room. Bruce Mason and Joe Winston were two high school All-star football players who was still showing of their agility moving down the line that was getting longer and longer by the minute. The loss of Bruce's physic was not slowing him down one bit. He still had moves. Willie and George Perkins were buddies they both shared their dad's dream and were dressed in military uniforms. They stood clapping their hands to the beat after going through the line. Both seemed very proud with their gorgeous girlfriends by their side Justin had found out from conversation with them earlier. "Yeah guy! Walking over he saw his good friend Sam Spencer. He was voted most likely to succeed. He headed up a lot of the fundraisers for the school. He owned a very successful textile company in Bangor Maine. Justin and Menae talked a bit with Sam before moving on. "Hi Justin! Shirley Story said as he past her on the dance floor. Where is Ariel?" Shirley was a clerk in the pharmacy at Bayside Medical. "She's at home" he answered quickly and kept moving. He and Menae stopped again short of their table and danced to and upbeat tune before sitting down. "Justin?" she said softly, I don't want to cause you any problems? She was holding his hand then. "Justin thought about all he had went through before getting here and reasoned she was not his problem. "I'm having fun, are you?' he asked. "Sure" she said softly.

Then the lights went up. Everyone took his or her seats as Ranae Pritchard and Johnny Joyce announced and read the names of those who had sent in a bio of their selves. This was the time when everyone got a chance to meet you as you cross the stage while the audience viewed you on the big screen in the background. It was a very large photograph of you in high school. There were lots of laughs and pointing at hairstyles clothes and mostly over all look changes. But everyone had a good time. After and fun time of laughter the lights were dimmed again. The music struck its first cord and Franklin was on the floor. His wife had apparently left. The table where she sat was noticeably empty. All the single young ladies now knowing who Justin Parker was were vying for a dance. They were impressed with his bio and wanted to know more about this geek turned hunk. MEDICAL STUDENT. He really hadn't thought about himself that way. Hanging out with his older brother Billy had brought some stares but that was for Billy certainly not for him he reasoned. Ariel had met him right after he came through the informative years. Braces bucked teeth and dish watered brown colored hair. He really hadn't thought of himself as a lady's man. Menae sit back very politely like a lady and Justin danced with several of the single young ladies. As Justin danced, she walked over and whispered to the deejay a requested song she wanted to hear. For tonight she thought he belongs to me! "Justin what are you doing after this is over?" someone asked from the crowd. "Don't know yet he responded back to the female voice as they moved around to the music. It was close to 1:00 p.m. in the morning. Menae had come back and sat down when the deejay announced the last dance of the evening. Another young lady came over to dance with Justin but he turned and walked over to Menae who was sitting and hoping it would work out that way. "May I have this dance?" he asked She put her hand in his and they embraced for another intimate memorable dance to end the night. Justin's cell phone clipped to his waist went unanswered all night.

David and Tetra stayed the entire week with his parents in their home. David spent some quality time alone with his Dad and enjoyed his mom as well. He knew they were getting along in age and he always tried to visit them as often a possible. Many times, for a day or two. But this time he had set aside a week and just enjoyed and relaxed with them. His dad would have some very good days when you couldn't stop him from conducting some kind of business affair to days when he could hardly sit up in bed. "I'm so glad you're here son" his mother

Ruth said one night before going to bed. "Your dad is proud of you you know? she added patting the top of his hand. David embraced her he prayed to God daily for her strength. He knew losing her companion was not going to be easy for her. "I know mom. I love you too, he responded. He always made sure their affairs were kept in order. His dad always stayed on top of those things anyway. But since his recent illness David would meet with their financial consultant/lawyers to assure everything was in order. His mom didn't like to fuss with those matter's she'd said. David was glad he had Sarah his sister close to them to keep him informed. Ruth was glad to have him and his wife around the house this week it brought so much joy she reasoned. Her great-grandson David and his friend Tommy came over and helped her son David repair the tree house. And boy did they have loads of fun! Nana and mom made homemade cookies and they had a choice of Nana's iced cold lemonade or milk. Granddad even sat out on the deck in the backyard a few times and watched them with his binoculars from afar.

As the week ended David had to take his mother downtown to sign some legal papers while he was there. "Tetra honey Mom and I are going downtown are you coming" David asked. She had been helping Ruth in the garden earlier and decided she would stay and finished reading her book. It was at its' climax and she would have to wait until she was on the plane to find out what happens to the main character if she didn't read it now. "You two have a good time" she said I'll stay with Pops". Are you sure his nurse is here and the staff, he has plenty of help Tetra", Ruth explained "I'm sure go ahead," walking with them to the door? Tetra sat in the family room reading when she heard over the intercom a bell ringing. 'That's Alfred" she thought I'd better see what's going on.

They had moved into another master suite downstairs and Tetra took the long walk down the hall meeting his nurse at the door. "I'll see what he needs" Tetra shared with her. "Are you sure madam? the nurse asked holding the doors' knob. "Yes, I'm sure Tetra replied nodding her head going into the large bedroom. Alfred seeing Tetra come in said "Oh sweetie I just needed a cool drink of water seems the pitcher is so far away." 'No bother". She poured a glass of cold water from the iced filled pitcher on his bedside table. Then she lifted his head as he took a drink from the glass. Carefully she helped him hold it in his shaking hands. She placed the glass back on his side table and lifted his head again and fluffed his pillow and turned it over making him comfortable. 'Thank you dear but I do have a nurse for that" he said. "You're suppose to be visiting not working" he smiled at her. His eyes were weak and his wrinkled skin caused him to look much older than he really was Tetra thought smiling back at him. Tetra suspected he was putting on a good front for her but she knew he was really sick. "Well sit for a minute, he said nodding his head for her to sit on the bedside chair" as suggested. He closed his eyes for a moment it was obvious that whatever this disease was it was moving fast through his body she thought as she watched him squirm trying to get comfortable. He had lost so much weight but his appetite Ruth says was fine. He opened his eyes and caught her hand. "I'm so glad you're here dear" You make my son happy" Alfred said. "I was an old fool to try and stop him from marrying you. And look what I would have missed out on my great grandson and my grandson" he said, letting out a cough that put fear in Tetra's face. 'Pop's just rest okay" she said and began praying silently to herself. "I have had so much fun seeing everyone here this week it was good, very good" he acknowledged. Tetra wiped his forehead to settle him down again. "Tetra dear please forgive and old racist man like me," he said with a tear slowly running down his cheek. "Oh, pop Parker, I've forgiven you a long time ago" and I have always loved you pops". She stood and leaned over the bed hugging him and holding his feeble body tightly in her arms. "Please read to me from my book?" he asked. He pointed to a table near the window. Tetra walked over and saw his bible with pages that had lots of worn edges. She could tell he enjoyed the Psalms. She walked back over to the bed and pulled the chair closer to the bed's edge and began reading to him. Tetra could tell for a while he was listening then had fallen fast asleep. "Just like a baby needing to rest but fought all the way" she smiled quietly. With the sound of silence all around she took a moment and prayed silently in his room ending with "God thank you for allowing me the opportunity to forgive". With Alfred once again fast asleep she stopped praying and went back to the family room. Billy had called to check on his granddad and to say hello to his parents and find out when their flight leaves heading back home to Washington State.

Sitting back down Tetra hears the doorbell ring. The butler answered it. It was Sarah Parker, David's sister. She was back from her cruise. "Hey Tet, I'm glad you guys haven't left yet! She said walking over giving her a shared hug. She was glad to see her sister-in-law. They spoke often over the phone but it had been a while since they all sat together. Sarah was the girl of the family though labeled a tomboy most of her growing up and still today not much had changed. She and Tetra were still enjoying conversation when David and Ruth their mother returned. Sarah stayed talking with her mom a while in the living room while her brother David and sister-in-law strolled around the grounds of the beautiful estate until their dad woke again. Billy and Davie had come by also with Davies young friend Tommy. Everyone stayed for dinner and it made nana smile a lot. Tetra had a feeling she told her son Billy; your nana would need a lot of these days. Granddad Alfred even felt good enough to take his sit at the head of the table. We were not certain how long it would last but once again I saw the whole family was united again.

CHAPTER NINE

Red flags

Sidney was anxiously waiting for his assignment to start in Kansas City. He had family there but his real reason was he loved his chosen career job and that drove him. But for now, he sat in Jessica's private plane waiting to spend a beautiful week in the Bahamas with her. First, they were making a stop in Chicago for a big celebration. He had forgiven her for dumping him he says at the airport in Vegas and she seemed to have her focus back he thought upon her return, so maybe it was a good get away. She looked well rested. And thank God there were no signs of Bridget! Jessica's long champagne blonde hair was cut off. She wore it very short in a funky mussed up style. It fit her. Truth is she looked good in anything! Sidney reasoned. After Marty one of the last band members boarded the pilot announced over the plane's intercom, "Buckle your seatbelts! Jessica had put a pillow under her head and after take off confirmed she would recline to sleep. Marty secured himself in his seatbelt with his guitar in hand strumming the cords. And secured also in his seat was Sidney. He had taken out his research materials of the work he was to do in Kansas City and read quietly to himself.

Dana was so lighthearted around the office these days. It had been nearly three or four weeks since Roger was there but he called once a week and sent fresh flowers for her desk often. Seeing that the relationship was getting serious Dana had started looking for a place of her own. She wanted a bigger place for her growing very active son and his friends who by the way were constantly playing in and around Ms. Bea's home. Ms. Bea said it didn't bother her she liked it. It kept her young she'd say smiling. Dana's young son's friends visited mostly everyday after school and during weekends when the boys club was closed. Davie and Tommy stayed around the home in the evening every day. "Dana can Tommy and I go to nana's? she said we could come as much as we wanted," he shared with her one day after school. Dana knew how far his dad Billy's grandmother lived from them and opted to say no! Tommy wanted to play in the tree house he and Davie had bragged about over and over again before returning to school the next day.

"I don't think this would be a good time Davie, remember your great-grand is very ill your dad tells me." "I know Dana, but Billy goes by almost everyday, I wish I could go" he said sadly. "Call your dad and ask him, Dana replied going back to what she was doing.

Ms. Bea never said the boys were brothering her. Dana felt as involved as she was with her church group, she would be fine with someone coming in every now and then to check on her. Besides Dana wanted some privacy for herself. Deacon Willis had stopped by a few times lately for ice cream. Dana smiled watching Ms Bea and Deacon Willis sating out under the large maple tree in the front yard eating their strawberry ice cream cones.

"William Parker', Billy replied answering his phone. Hi' Billy" "David how are you doing today son?" "I'm fine he replied quietly. "David what's wrong?" Oh, nothing I just called to say hi" he responded. "You just called to say hello". Well I'm glad you were thinking about me" Billy said knowing there was more to this story. Dana and he now shared weekends and this one was hers but Davie had other plans he reasoned. "Where's your mom?" She's in the kitchen". Let me speak with her please" I asked because I wasn't getting anywhere with him. He was just breathing on the phone saying nothing until asked and not hanging up. "Hello, Hello, Dana this is Billy how are you" I asked "I'm good Billy, Dana replied surprised I wanted to speak to her. I had been trying to forgive her for past things and move on so when I got an opportunity I tried. "Our son called to say hi!" he laughed. Dana held her head down and looked to see David and Tommy hiding around the corner peeking into the kitchen as she spoke. "Is that what" he said?' Dana was trying to get him to be more comfortable with Billy. Her life seemed to be heading in another direction and it may not include Billy other than for his son David. "Well, she paused, I asked him to call. He says he wants to go to your nana's house this weekend". "I suspect it's the tree house" she laughed as she said it. "It is contagious that way." "I'm really busy this evening but have Davie call me tomorrow and he, Tommy and I will spend the day there if you don't mind me taking one of yours" he responded. "I'll do that" Dana replied shouldn't be a problem." understanding fully getting off the phone. David's little face grew sadder. He knew from her response he wasn't going today to see the tree house.

The plane landed in Chicago at O' Hare international. Jessica had been up exercising her vocal cords getting ready for the big show. She had sat in the back of the plane with her headset on practicing an opening tune for tonight's concert in the park. Jackson Park had been transformed with a huge stage attraction with lights all around. Security walls had been put up around its perimeter. And security patrols were all over the place Sidney noticed walking in with Jessica to her trailer. They had designated a large trailer for her along side the other entertainers that had come to perform in this event. After settling in they sat kissing and hugging enjoying each other. Jessica was giving him all of her attention these next two weeks she had shared with him "Did you see that?' Sidney asked. Someone was looking through that window he said pointing in the back of the trailer. "No not really Jessica replied. But did you see all the people when we came in!" Everyone is moving about" Jessica responded. "You're right" but Sidney felt uncomfortable. He got up and closed the shutters on each window. He and Jessica had been and exclusive lately showing up on the red carpet and the Music awards in Los Angeles. He picked up a newspaper from the trailer's magazine rack that Jessica was featured in. "That's mine, he said to himself looking at the sexy outfit she was wearing. Then in the picture's background he saw a face. "Jess I didn't know Bridget was at the awards" he said. "Oh Bridget, I didn't see her but she may show up anywhere" she replied continuing now to start her shower and dress for the show. "You told me she had gone back to Paris?" Jessica said nothing but ignored the statement and continued to the shower for tonight's big show. Sidney and Jessica had engaged in more than one heated argument regarding Bridget and their departure in Vegas. But things seemed to have smoothed out and he had not seen her around of late and that's how he wanted to keep it! Bridget gave him the creeps.

The entertainers were all there to perform after the big parade given for their basketball team 'The Chicago Bulls" The team had put together a winning season and won their championship for the second time in a row. The crowds already had started to gather. People brought blankets and lawn chairs and umbrellas. Some even had strollers. Cars were bumper to bumper. They were coming by the bus loads into the huge park. Sidney left the trailer to walk around in the crowds with Jess still in the shower. Who knows when there's an assignment he thought moving around watching the crowds grow larger and larger by the minute? After about an hour he decided to head back for higher ground. With his pass visible for all to see he headed back only to see someone he thought leaving Jessica's trailer. It was dust and the commotion from the team entering the park was a constant roar for what seemed to be about twenty minutes or so taking his mind off the trailer. After a while he turned back and headed again toward her trailer and walked in "Jessie! I thought you were almost dressed? he questioned surprising her. She was standing bare bottom with just a sequined top on. "It didn't look right she said throwing the bottom of her outfit she was holding in her hand on the bed and getting another pair of pants to wear from the spacious closet of her trailer. Sidney looked around the trailer. Something just did not feel right to him. Did you have a visitor? he asked. "No, a couple of the band members came by to see where to set up but that was an hour or so ago" she replied moving around hurriedly. Not wanting another airport episode, he concluded "Oh well you'd better hurry and head toward the stage the opening act just ended and according to the schedule you're up in half and hour, Sidney informed her still standing at the trailers door looking around. I'll watch you from behind the stage on the monitors" he told her walking out after her.

Dana was in her office behind closed doors with a client. As she walked out, she saw Roger sitting in her waiting room. "Roger! What a surprise! I didn't know you were in Portland Maine now. "I'm not working here I came by to see you! he replied to her delight. I'm working in Lewiston right up the way but I had you on my mind" he told her. "Oh, that was sweet" Dana responded trying to hold her cool. But what she wanted was to run over and throw her arms around him and make love right there in her office. Composing herself she walked over and kissed at his cheek but he turned and their lips met. Dana smiled and stood back. "Well I have a full day. I wish you would have called" she said. "I'm here until tomorrow morning call me when your day is over and we will talk, Roger suggested throwing that long curly piece of hair that sometimes covered his sexy brown eyes. Someone walked in Roger reasoned it was another client and back toward the door. Very professionally Dana showed the person into her private office and shut the door leaving them on the inside. She came back and gave Roger a kiss with more meaning and said she'd call later and went back into her closed office smiling.

The weeks were very tense around Ariel and Justin's apartment. He would leave without announcing where he was going or for that matter coming back. But he always came back and for the most part things were back to normal so it seemed. Ariel had taken care of the credit card bill and wouldn't even look at the box that Justin kept it in again. He probably wouldn't have objected to her using it if only she would have asked and saved her the hurt and him some embarrassment. Two months had passed though he remembers having to go back home that day and get the other card to take care of his book purchase. He later explained to Ariel he was saving for something special. Ariel figured their wedding. But she still walked around on eggshells regarding that thought right now. 'Ariel I'm going out he informed one evening. "Billy invited me over he wants to talk to me about something private" he shared with her. "I'll get my coat" Ariel replied. She had gone with him to Billy's several times before. "No! he says this is important man talk "I'll see you later kissing her cheek and walking out of the door.

An hour later he pulled up in front of Billy's home. "Hey guy" he said walking into his brother's home. It is so nice around here! so quiet so peaceful" he added. Ariel and he had lately been having lots of heated arguments about any and everything since the reunion he enjoyed the peace over there. 'Have you eaten?" Billy asked chewing on something that had his attention. Justin walked over getting a plate from the cabinet and as usual made himself at home. "Hey bro" Justin said "I had a fun time at my five-year high school reunion a few months ago." "Those are fun I try to go to mine every five years just to see old friends." Billy shared with him. What about the girls?" did you recognize them?' Billy asked laughing. "And I'm sure the guys changed he laugh. Hairstyles alone made the difference! They agreed slapping the high five with their hands. "This geek made his rounds with the ladies" Justin shared sitting down to the table with his plate. Billy had saw Justin's high school picture and there was quite a change. "How did Ariel like the girls cooing over you?" he asked. She decided not to go! That brought on another high five between the brothers. Those kinds of things are better I find if I go alone, Billy affirmed smiling to agree. With brotherly conversations, and laughter both finished eating their carry out meal Billy had brought home on his way from the office. "Justin, I called you over to ask you about a phone call Katherine made to dad" Billy started "A phone call? How did she get his number?" Justin questioned. "I don't know, but that really doesn't matter she did! And I was hoping you knew about it." he added. "This is the first time I've heard about this Billy honestly" he said feeling bad about what happened. "What did she say? Justin asked curious now about the call. "She was questioning dad about acknowledging you as his son! "What! I knew it! I told her it was none of her business! I'm sorry man if she caused problems." "I'm sure dad handled it but please know you have as much right to our family as I do. But what happened with dad and your mom is the past". Please ask her to not call again please bro! he asked to the very angry Justin about the information Billy had just given him. "Its' taken care of believe me! he said in a matter of fact tone. "Now don't do anything silly it was a phone call and I'm sure a slap on the wrist will make it go away" Billy again shared.

Ring, ring, "Hello" Billy said answering his phone looking over at Justin "Hi Billy" oh hello Ariel" how are you? he asked. Without a response she quickly asked. Is Justin there?" He is, we were just doing the brother thing, hold on." "I handed him the receiver. "Yes Ariel" still a little miffed about Kat. "What's wrong Justin?" Nothing, why did you call?" knowing she was checking up on him and his whereabouts but composing himself to be civil. "Tell me what's wrong and I'll tell you why I called" she responded. 'Ariel it has nothing to do with you! It's about Kat?" Kat? What about Kat? she kept questioning. Justin looked at me. I shrugged my shoulders indicating it was his call to say. She called David Parker that's all and I was just wondering how she got the number? Thinking she would make points because of the story Katherine had told her why she needed it. "I gave her his number she said she needed it! 'What! You did what? Justin hung up the receiver. "Billy do you mind if I just crash here tonight? "I promise I'll be out before you get up. I have an early class schedule" Justin explained a bit miffed from the call. 'Sure, the air mattress is in the bedroom closet" I replied. Reasoning things will look better tomorrow. I got up to get the mattress from the closet and Justin was now talking quietly on his cell phone to someone. "Billy thanks bro but I want be needing that bed" "I'll talk with you later" and with "goodnight" he left.

Davie went to bed very excited about tomorrow. He was going to visit his great grandparent's home again with his dad. Tommy had begged his mom to let him spend the night so that he could go also. She said he couldn't spend the night but Davie could come by and get him on his way over tomorrow.

Dana had call and said she would be home a little later and asked Mrs. Bea to keep and eye on Davie until she returns home. After a round of cartoons Mrs. Bea came into the family room. "Time for you to turn in" she said. "Is Dana due home yet?" Davie asked. "I' don't think so Davie, now run along to bed. She hugged him and kissed his cheek as he passed. "Goodnight grandma Bea he said walking into his room turning out the light. He had already taken his bath but since it wasn't a school night Mrs. Bea let him stay up a bit longer. He went to bed thinking only of the fun he would have tomorrow with Tommy in the tree house.

Dana had met Roger after work and they stopped by the Maui for cocktails. "Well would you like to go dancing he asked spinning her around in the parking lot after leaving the Maui. 'Let's do that! she replied. They went to the elegant dance place where he had taken her on their very first date. Dana moved her hips to the beat and laughed and smiled all night long. On the slow beats Roger embraced Dana so close and they seemed to genuinely care for one another. They even shared several kisses on the dance floor. When they left for the evening Dana was not headed home.

Davie woke up in the middle of night in a cold sweat. He was frightened and went into Dana's room but her bed was empty. She had not come home yet, he thought. He went in the kitchen to get a drink of cold water and went back to his room. He didn't want to disturb Grandma Bea. But a warm glass of milk might be what he needed. Most of all he sure needed someone to talk too. He lay back in his bed trying to go to sleep and tossed and turned again before being startled once again and he sat up straight in the bed and YELLED! He was shaking when Mrs. Bea heard him and came running in to see what was wrong. She had already looked to see Dana's bed was not touched and it was very late. "Dear what's wrong?' she asked coming slowly to his room. Looking at him she could see he was visible shaken. "Mrs. Bea sat on the side of his bed" "I want to see my great-grand," he said. "Oh, dear it's the middle of the night" she tried to explain. "Your dad will take you there in the morning". After sitting near him on his bed with her arms tightly holding him, it calmed him down. After a bit Ms. Bea left the room again. All seemed quiet again for a while. Suddenly something appeared at the head of Mrs. Bea's bed. "David dear what's wrong? she asked rubbing her eyes trying to focus. "I have to see my Nana" he said again. Mrs. Bea looked at the clock it was clearly too late to call anyone's house and she couldn't drive this late at night. Dana's cell phone was going to voicemail. "Call Billy, Davie suggested. "Good idea" Ms Bea reasoned. I'll call Billy he will understand" she said trying hard to focus dialing the number again and again. Davie at this point was hysterical according to Mrs. Bea. Mrs. Bea saw know other way she explained later to his dad. RING! RING! RING! RING! "Hello my very sleepily groggy voice came across the line. "David handed the receiver to Mrs. Bea. "Hello Mr. Parker, this is Mrs. Bea. Hearing her voice knowing something must be wrong for a call to come in at this hour. I sat up in bed. "Yes Mrs. Bea is everything alright? I asked. I was startled from the wake up. And looking at the clock that read three p.m. "We're fine but Davie seems to be having some sort of nightmare and can't go back to sleep" she explained. 'Did he eat too much junk food today? That will do it! "I don't think so" she said. 'What does Dana think?" I asked. Trying to find a solution and get back to sleep. "Well, she paused, Dana's not here right now. "Oh, I see' "I could have gone into a rage but Annie was lying aside of me in the bed so I could not point fingers. I sure wanted to. "Have him get dressed I'll be over to get him as soon as I can". It's going to take a bit Mrs. Bea I'm about forty-five minutes from you. Please make sure he gets dressed. I repeated" and Mrs. Bea thanks for calling" I acknowledged hanging up the receiver.

I got dressed quickly explained to Annie kissed her and headed out to get my son and bring him home. I was speeding across the highway breaking all kinds of limits I knew. In my hurry to leave I had left my cell phone by my bedside table. After about 30 minutes I pulled up into Mrs. Bea's driveway. They were standing in the door. I shared with her I understood and I quickly let her go back to bed. I promised to call and check on her later. She kissed David on his forehead and we left. We got into the car and I headed in the direction of my home. "No! No! He said I have to see Nana! "I told Grandma Bea to tell you! He said loudly, he was crying. "David we will see them in the morning it's late! I stated a little inpatient at his insisting.

They are asleep," I yelled still trying to reason with him. "Dad please, please dad he pleaded. Please! he was crying harder. Conceding I said if it's that important we'll go by and I'll show you they're asleep okay? Okay dad, he said wiping his eyes with his fists. I handed him a Kleenex from my glove compartment. I was now driving down the highway again at an alarming speed. Within 4 minutes I got off at the next exit and headed out to my Nana's at around 4p.m in the morning. I was moving quickly down the highway looking at my wide-eyed son in the passenger seat still wiping his tears. I didn't have my cell phone to call Annie who was probably sleeping anyway. Thirty minutes later we pulled into my Grandparents driveway. Just minutes later aunt Sarah screeched in behind me almost hitting the large fountain sitting in the yard. She then jumped, out of the car. "What's wrong?" I asked seeing her go pass my car, she was crying. She ran and struggled with the key trying to open the front door before ringing the doorbell. I quickly ran to her thinking only of granddad. I helped her. She was shaking so badly. The butler ran to the door to open it as we entered. He had called aunt Sarah, I found out later. Aunt Sarah didn't stop she went into the bedroom passing granddads bed where I had stopped from following right behind her. She had stood by nana lying over in her bed. She gently touched her cold lifeless body. "NO! She screamed NO! NO! I fell hard to the floor in tears looking back at my son Davie standing in the bedroom door.

Sidney watched the entire celebration from backstage. The groups that performed rock the house. Jessica and her sexy sultry way of dancing and moving was a show- stopper according to Sidney and the tabloids. The bands were out of this world. The crowds screamed and yelled and danced to a non- stop celebration that lasted for about four or five hours. Chicago knows how to party! After a long day of celebrating they were headed for a good time in the Bahamas. Away from all the cameras and fanfare!

Dad and mom had made the unfortunate trip back to Portland Maine. Mom had sat up with him most of that night after their son Billy's call. He had called to give them the news. Seems Nana Ruth had called David Parker her son earlier that morning while she waited for his dad at his routine doctor's appointment. "She sounded fine" David shared crying in Tetra's shoulder. He was prepared for his dad but not his mother" "Oh my God, he cried out sitting in his bedroom. Tetra felt his hurt and their pain. They both knew the Lord intimately and were searching their being to thank him through this unforeseen time. The nurse said Mrs. Ruth Parker felt tired when she returned home that morning and decided to lie down for a nap. She was resting most of the day her nurse reported sadly. When Thomas the butler went in to give her some warm milk, she had request he found her and called Sarah her daughter. Granddad had to be taken to the hospital the next day where he stayed and passed away within a month. We concluded from a broken heart. My son David Michael now lives with me.

CHAPTER TEN

I need to know

Jessica was in her lavish penthouse preparing to go for another singing engagement tour. And Sidney was once again headed to Kansas City. It had been months in coming but the assignment he had been preparing for was awaiting him Monday morning and he was very excited. He was given a crew of three eager young energetic journalists of his choosing and three camera persons. He had packed and was awaiting Jessica to complete her conversation on the telephone to an overseas friend. She was flying out on her private jet and they were riding out in the limousine to the airport together.

He had called Desmond to let him know he'd be coming, but he was in court so he'd try him later. Sidney wanted to share with him about the assignment and looked forward to maybe a game or two or golf while he was there. As he sat waiting for Jessica, he called again from his cell phone. This time Dal his sister-in –law answered. "Hello Owens residence" "Dalmatia this is Sidney, how are you?" "Oh, hello Sidney, when are you coming back for a visit? She asked cheerfully. It had only been about six months and that was a good time frame for Sidney's visits. He usually tried to visit at least once a year. Most of the time it ended up being a year to a year and a half between visits. "Well that's why I'm calling is Desmond in?' "He is, he's working behind closed doors and asked not to be disturbed but I don't think he meant you" she said knowing he was family. Dalmatia walked over to the study and knocked on the door slowing peeking inside before walking in.

"Des it's Sidney" she explained. Desmond picked up the receiver of his telephone and Dal backed out of the door. "Sidney! Brother, how are you?" sounding glad to hear from him. "I've been viewing you on the screen man. Jessica has you large and in charge" he joked. "Well what can I say the girl is hot right now" I can't keep up" Sidney responded "but I'm enjoying the ride", he said sharing a laugh. Though the reason I called is I have an assignment out your way little brother" Really? Desmond asked? "I have and human-interest story to shot in Kansas City" he explained. "That's great should I get the room ready for you?" Desmond asked hoping his brother was through for another visit. Thanks, but no thanks" the station is putting us up at the Sheraton there "us is Jessica coming?" No! They have given me a crew for this one" Sidney said. "Oh, things are looking up. I'm happy for you and look forward to seeing you while you're here. How long will you be here? About a few months maybe longer" Sidney replied. "I can see a few golf games in my future" Desmond loving mocked. "Oh, and Sid, plan on seeing grandfather while you're here, he's getting up there you know"

"Yeah, man I'll do that! I'll certainly do that" Sidney replied smiling disconnecting the line.

Justin had hopefully gotten through to his mother Katherine regarding the phone call. He had spoken with Ariel who had given her the number from his phone book letting her know he was not happy about it. He was miffed because he had explained to her that Kat was not to have it under any circumstances. Ariel, he thought had given him more reasons to wonder off. He couldn't trust her with anything! Ariel was hoping to make points with Justin through Kat but it had backfired. He was spending more time now at the hospital opting to stay and sleep in the designated assigned quarters for interns. His style of clothing had changed a lot. Overall, his whole outlook on life had changed. He had talked with his brother Billy about updating his wardrobe to fit a young successful "BACHELOR". Honestly, a love bug had bitten Justin, and his interest had seemingly changed overnight. He had shared with Billy about how he walked straight out of Katherine's house into a committed relationship with Ariel. Justin concluded he really had not lived. Besides meeting Menae, he saw all his friends living what he viewed as a productive full life and he felt stuck now sitting around them thinking over his. He wanted to experience life and see what else it had to offer he shared one night in conversation with Ariel. He loved Ariel but she had disappointed him, caused him to mis-trust her with the finances, his dad and of course there was Menae! Although it really wasn't impacting him now, he was looking further ahead. But all of that aside, a lot of his thinking came after meeting Menae Sanchez at the reunion. She seemed to have everything together her career and her own apartment. She said she enjoyed the single life. Justin had begun changing some things too. And "shhh" was even seen recently in the company of an unknown young lady at a very elegant outing given by the State department. It was mentioned to Katherine by one of her co-workers who went with her husband who works there. Katherine always wanted that life for Justin and felt like he deserved it so she was not going to tell Ariel even though she was Justin's fiancée. She knew very well about their evolving problems. Ariel befriended her in that also. But Kat was glad because she always knew Ariel was not from good stock, no class! were her exact words? "Justin, are you coming home tonight? Ariel asked one day as she visited him for lunch at work. "Why are you asking?" Don't I come home?" and if I don't, I'm here at this hospital" he explained unequivocally. He didn't always stay at the hospital and he didn't always come home lately. But she didn't know when he did or didn't stay at the hospital not with certainty anyway! She only knew he wasn't in her bed! But to him Ariel kept giving him reasons to move further from her. His interest in her was fading. He knew it and didn't really want to hurt her but he had got a taste of another life and he liked it.

"Justin, I like the new you! A young nurse said walking by while he and Ariel were eating lunch out on the patio of the hospital's bistro. He smiled back at them. Ariel threw her cup of soda down on the ground. The young ladies moved quickly out of the way as not to get any of it on their uniform. "Sorry about that" Justin said jumping up handing one of them a napkin if she needed it. Ariel stormed off. "It's alright, you're still cute". she giggled. "Thanks, he said, watching Ariel walk away quickly. He had styled his hair to reflect the G.Q. image he had begun to embrace. Emulating Billy when he wasn't in his intern greens his look was torn right from the cover of style magazine.

Ariel was having a very hard time keeping up. Not the clothes she had clothes. But his newfound self-confidence since the reunion was unmatchable.

When Dana arrived home the next day, she was taken by what she had heard. She was very sad for Davie and Billy finding out what had happened with his grandmother. Dana decided to stop fighting him for custody and reasoned it was best that he lives with his dad. Davie had chosen to stay with Billy his dad anyway until after his nana's funeral. So as long as she could see him and she still wanted her weekends that would be an acceptable arrangement. Billy happily agreed and had her sign the legal papers to reflect it. He did not want her changing her mind in midstream. On the other hand, Dana said she felt so bad that she wasn't there for her son that night. She had figuratively beaten herself up over and over again in her mind about it. She thought at this time in her life he was better off with Billy. Something was happening to her. She was falling in love with Roger. She loved her son dearly and thought hard about letting him go. But she didn't want another episode like that again and she had no plans of giving Roger up either. Since she didn't have Davie full time, she purchased a VERY LARGE TOWNHOUSE near the hospital. Spacious enough for when Davie came for his visits and close to the hospital so that when Roger was in town he could come in and stay the night without the hassles of and expensive hotel room EVERYTIME! She wanted Davie to meet him but things hadn't turned out that way yet. Their visits seemed to be on opposite weekends not purposely planned that way. With her still at Mrs. Bea's home she and Roger would stay in town on the one or two nights he was there which to Dana had become an inconvenience. They spoke everyday over the phone. He called her but for the most part she would call him between every client visit it seemed. Dana had fallen for Roger!

It had been several months and she was looking forward to seeing him when his route brought him to this area again. On his next visit she'd be all moved in and planned to surprise him. He pursued her sending candy and flowers to her office. Depending on how close he was to Maine he would always try and see her every two months without fail. He had been gone longer this time between visits and that caused Dana questions each time she spoke with him. He simply explained sales were going well!

Dana? Mollie asked meeting her in the cafeteria on break. "So, are you still dating that salesman Haskell?" Most in the hospital knew him. He had been doing business with the hospital for a while. Dana wasn't a kiss and tell girl so she questioned. "Why are you asking?' Oh, someone saw you two out at the Maui a few times. Just thought I'd ask?" "We're good friends" she said nothing wrong with that is it?" Nothing as long as you know what you're doing." "What does that mean? Dana questioned getting up from the table. "Well girlfriend you're sweating between the sheets every few months, are you sure that's what you want?" Mollie stated. "I'm fine with what we have besides we talk often" Dana responded. "And we have known each other for a while we're just getting to know each other better before we began to talk commitment. I'm having fun!" Well that's cool but the heart is a funny thing it doesn't always wait" Mollie reasoned. Dana knew exactly what she was saying. She felt her feelings for Roger were stronger than his for her though she did feel he loved her even if it was said during their intimate moments. "Well you sound like a woman who's got it all together" Mollie acknowledged. "I commend you" I had this guy who told me he loved me but when it came to showing me outside of the bed he failed miserably" she confessed. "Mollie I'm headed back to my office lets walk and talk". She went back to her office and put in a call to Roger who was unable to respond to the call according to his voicemail. And she and Mollie sat talking until her next client came in.

Billy had decided he needed a break from all the sadness the family had went through. He was helping his aunt Sarah get all the affairs in order for the family's estate. She was taking their deaths really hard but in her known business style toughed her way through it. We all were grieved one death right behind the other. So, most of what had been done rested on my shoulders Billy concluded. He worked with his grandparent's attorneys under the direction of his aunt Sarah when she felt up to it and his dad. Everything went well. Mr. Alfred Parker kept very accurate accounts on all business affairs. There were some minor hitches pertaining to some assets that were soon resolved. After his granddad's huge funeral consisting of his partners, co-workers and the many company executives he was looking for a peaceful get away. Nana's funeral had been somber and quiet just like she was. "It' s what she had requested in her will. And the family granted it.

Now with that behind him he was headed out to see his old friend Desmond in Kansas and taking his son too. "Dana, Billy said calling her at her office. "I'm going to take Davie on vacation. I need to get away for a while" Oh do you need me to keep Davie?" No! I'm taking him with me I was just calling to let you know we will be gone for about two weeks right now" he explained. If something changes, I'll let you know" he added. "That's fair" Dana replied. "Oh, is Annie going with you?" she bravely asked. Dana noticed she had accompanied him to both funerals hanging close on his arm. "Now I really don't feel like I have to answer this, but no it's just going to be me and David." Billy replied. "Since we're asking questions, how is Roger these days?" Billy smiled because he looked so much like Justin hair and all. Billy had met him when he waited to confront her about leaving David home that night alone. "We're fine". Dana laughed softly. "Does David need anything for the trip from me?" she asked. "Your love and blessings" Billy said. "I'll have David call you soon." Take care Billy" she said. "I will Dana I will". Surprisingly enough they had learned to get alone and speak cordial with one another. He was starting to understand her better he surmised.

Justin was looking for a place of his own. He and Ariel had talked about their relationship and tried to work things out between them. But the bachelor bug bit Justin and the relationship was growing further and further apart. Ariel was his girl. He had met her at the hospital during his first months working there. And they moved in together. He didn't want to stay at home with his mom and at the time couldn't afford a place in a descent neighborhood on his own. He didn't want to just stay with her and not be committed and he was. He had given her an engagement ring for her birthday their first year together. Katherine his mother liked Ariel but thought being engaged at his age was too soon. And now he knows she may have been right. As much as he knew he loved Ariel Hodges and she was the only girl for him. But now someone else had stolen away his affection for her. They had grown apart. Poor Ariel sat in their apartment crying. She was angry with herself she says for believing in him. He was her prince charming. If only she would have gone to the reunion, she thought then we would still be together. But then she reasoned if she took him away in one night did, I really have him at all! She stated as she paced the floor of their apartment. Justin had left for an evening shift at the hospital so Ariel decided to find out who had stolen her man's heart. She began going through his drawers and coat pockets and his bedside table. She was so angry she pulled his new clothes from the racks in frustration. She could not bear what was coming. Justin was leaving her. He was moving out as soon as he found a place, he had shared with her. And affordability has nothing to do with it now. He had taken over his trust fund from Katherine and his status had moved way up. Justin explained to Ariel he just needed time to think and still wanted her for a FRIEND. Ariel was not taking this news well. "Why! She yelled out loud. Why? She was hurting laying across the bed she and Justin still shared right now.

Jessica finally got in the limousine and they headed to the airport. The limo driver moved quickly as possible through the heavy traffic. They were behind schedule. Knowing it would be a few months before they saw each other again Sidney and Jessica try to make up for lost time. The limo driver turned and tossed them around in the back seat. He shrived around sharp corners quickly, quickly as to get Sidney to his flight on time. Pulling up to the airport Sidney button his shirt and buckled his belt, making a quick exit from the limo, kissing Jessica who was pulling her blouse over head and saying be sweet at the same time. The driver hurried Sidney's luggage to a bellhop as the two continued making themselves presentable. "Your plane is here" he said looking out past the landing strip of the airport. They both stood out by the limo and kissed again before parting. Sidney knew he was meeting his crew there but first a quick stop by the men's room to freshen up and then began the search for them. He didn't get to walk Jessica to her plane this time as he usually does. His flight was leaving soon and would not wait for him so she had to be on her on. After her plane was cleared by her security she boarded. The band was on an earlier flight and she stayed behind with her man Sidney. Jessica had the plane all to herself. She walked in and "Oh my! She said surprised. "Sidney would kill you if he knew you were here" she laughed walking toward the person standing in her plane. "But I'm so glad to see you. Meeting with and embrace and an intimate kiss.

Ariel followed Justin from the parking lot. She had borrowed a friend's car as not to be detected in her own and was determine to find out where he was spending his time. Days had pass and he still hadn't found a place. But his getting into bed and turning his back while not forgetting to kiss her cheek or forehead was the last straw. Justin was a very active person in bed and now nothing. Though his body still laid beside her in bed someone had stolen his affection and his heart. Even when she wore his favorite lingerie, it DID NOT faze him anymore and she wanted answers. He turned the corner heading for the entrance to the freeway. Ariel was close behind him. He sped up keeping up with traffic and she moved over watching the Beamer's taillight's move swiftly down the highway lane. She had never driven or been this way with Justin before. She couldn't imagine where he was going. Maybe he's going to see a realtor about a new place she though staying close as not to lose him in traffic. After several miles his blinker went on and he moved slower toward and exit ramp. She waited for a minute and pulled behind him as to not be detected for following him. After a while he pulled into this luxurious neighborhood. Large beautiful trees lined the street. Turning the corner Ariel followed. Slowing down he pulled up to the gate of a gated community. He dialed some numbers in at the gates intercom and the gate opened letting him inside. She looked from her car as the gate closed quickly behind him. She took out her pen and wrote the address and street of her location. As she was putting away her pen a car was slowly exiting the gate. Ariel hurried and pulled into it as the other car pulled out. 'Yewh! That was close. She rode around and around through the parking lot until she saw

Justin's Beamer. But his car was parked outside in a stall. He could be anywhere she thought sitting outside looking at all those condo's. She sat there for about and hour. And her anger was building up inside of her. Who is he with?

"Surely a realtor would have come out by now?" QUESTIONS WERE FORMING IN HER HEAD AND SHE HAD GOTTEN DESPERATE! She knew how sensitive the alarm system was on his car. She took a tool from the trunk of the car she was driving and tried prying the door open. "One. Two. BEEP!@#%%%%&^**&!! The beeper rang out over and over again. Soon Justin came running out with no shirt on from an apartment across the way. He scrambled to turn the alarm off as the residence of the complex looked on. He walked around inspecting what had set the alarm off and saw his door had been tampered with. "Darn! He said kicking it. 'I'd better call my insurance company." Ariel was crying now but sat and waited until he returned back to the apartment. She sat and counted again to ten before getting out of the car walking up to the door knocking. Justin came to the door probably thinking it was in regards to his automobile he opened the door to see "Ariel! What are you doing here?" She pushed her way in mad and trembling from this hold experience. "What am I doing here? She looked around the apartment. She saw a picture of Justin and someone sitting in an elegant frame on a shelf. "When were you going to tell me Justin?' she said pushing him in his chest. Whoever else was there still hadn't surfaced. "Go home Ariel, how did you know I was here anyway? Did Kat tell you?" Kat knows! Ariel sat on the sofa very hurt. "I thought she liked me" she said sadly. Justin why! What did I do to you?" Ariel please go home we'll talk tomorrow" he said trying to keep things quiet. "Then Ariel went postal! "Where is she? Where is she? She kept asking walking around through the spacious condominium. "She's probably upstairs! Ariel screamed. "No Ariel, Justin said standing in front at the stairs landing. "Move Justin! she pushed him in his face and scratched his nose. "Now see what you have done! Justin said pushing her back from the scratches sting. Move Justin! Move! she was furious! She headed back toward the stairs. Soon the lights upstairs could be seen. That seemed to make her even madder. Ariel kicked Justin so hard between his legs he doubled over in pain. He was down on the floor and moaning in pain and she was headed up the stairs. She tiptoed into one room, nothing. She turned on the lights in the bathroom at the top of the stairs pulling back the shower curtain, nothing. There were still two bedrooms and picking the wrong one could be fatal. One of them was closer to the stairs and she could get away and go downstairs to Justin, Ariel thought as she moved slowly around. And that would eventually happen but not before she speaks with her Ariel was thinking. She could hear Justin getting his composer and coming quickly up the stairs. She peeped into the bedroom closest to the stairs. The rooms were rather large so a quick glance wouldn't tell the story. She checked the walk-in closets. Steam was building. "I just want to talk to you!" she yelled moving a chair over to inspect a space in the corner. Suddenly she heard Justin talking with someone in the other room. Darn! She said heading in that direction. Justin had closed and locked the door. Ariel kicked and kicked the sturdy door until it opened. The shattered wood of the keyhole fell to the floor. By the time Ariel got up to enter Justin and whomever he was with had gone out the window. She hurried downstairs and watched as the Beamer left headed out. Ariel sat on the sofa in a stranger's home crying and hurt from Justin's deceit but she knew now for certain she had lost her man.

CHAPTER ELEVEN

Is it soup yet?

Sidney and his crew had got settled in and their plans were to spend the evening looking around the sights in Kansas City. Sending them off Sidney gave them his blessings again and asked them to just be ready bright and early tomorrow morning. He sat in his room and called Jessica. "Hi honey the flight in was great! "U7 and the band are ready to rock and roll! She said very excited. "That's great hon sounds like you're up for this one" Sidney replied. She had been amazing the crowds all over the world. The new choreographer had put together a new dance routine that was out of sight. Fans and viewers had raving reviews regarding her performances now. It was about an hour before she had to head to the stage so they engaged in conversation. He shared about the things he expected to accomplish here in Kansas City and she shared about the crowds that filled the stadium and domes in which she was performing. Sidney was in love and though he knew she really didn't understand his love for journalism she often pretended she did. She would ask a question about his work and then go off on a tangent of her own liking. But the publicity he was getting by being with Jessica wasn't bad. And he loved her. He was noticed several times even there in Kansas City when he was out as Jessica Strasberg's boy toy according to the magazines and tabloids. But he knew he was more to her than that. After giving his love again over the phone to Jessica he headed out to Langley estates to his brother Desmond's home.

Desmond and Mostalgia were out at a fundraiser dinner for the Mayor elect of the city and Dal greeted him at the door. "Hi Sidney" running over hugging him around the neck. "Well it's good to see you too. A lot surprised at her reaction to seeing him though. "Where's the other part of this family?" he asked removing her arms from his neck noticing no one else came to greet him. "They're out doing the society thing" she responded. Hi uncle Sid! He looked to see Jordan coming from the family room in his character pajamas. "We're in here Dal said heading back to the family room holding Jordan's little hand. She was letting him finish watching his movie before going to bed. Dal was just glad to have some one to talk to. It was spring break at school and Marsha had flown home to California to visit her parents. Little Jordan played with his uncle for a while and then went back to sit and watch his fiftieth episode of 101 Dalmatian's on the television screen video. Dal was talking excitedly to Sidney about his journalism work. She seemed really interested asking some questions that Sidney had to really search his knowledge to answer. He admired that! She wanted to know what he was doing in Kansas and he shared his assignment with her. Much to his amazement she had a pretty good grasp on it. He loved his work and enjoyed talking with anyone about it. She shared about her studies at the university too. "Have you noticed how well I am pronouncing my words?" she asked with Sidney smiling at her bravery. "Yes, I had and I'm very proud of your accomplishment" he told her giving her a touch on her hand. Despite his planned visit with Desmond he really enjoyed sharing an evening with his little nephew. Dal enjoyed his visit as well. Probably more than Sidney, he was looking to spend and evening with his brother. Dal was infatuated! Sidney could have gone out with his crew but didn't want to get involved in anything heavy. He knew tomorrow he needed to be at the top of his game. He had chosen some promising young journalist and had to be an example for them. So, his plan was to spend a relaxing evening with his brother and his family. Jordan went to sleep and Sidney carried him to his room with Dal following. She tucked him in and went back downstairs were Sidney had gone after lying him into his bed. Sidney thanked her for the hamburgers she had prepared and of the course the milkshakes. That was the extent of her cooking she told him. Little Jordan really enjoyed his milkshake. Dal had to change his pajamas after he finished it. "Goodnight Sidney said heading out of the door. Tell Desmond and Mossy I'll call tomorrow. "Goodnight, the giggling Dal said. She closed the door turned off the lights and stood watching from the window as Sidney pulled out of the driveway. Dal hurried upstairs and went into her bedroom to call her friend Marsha.

Desmond's schedule was really busy now so Billy decided to change his plans and visit his parents. He left the message on Dana's answering machine. Because their flight was leaving and she wasn't available anywhere by phone he knew she'd get it there. "Dad, are we really going to Grandma's and Grandpa's?" David Michael asked excited boarding the plane. "Yes, son we are, we will stop and see your Uncle Desmond on our way back home he informed David Michael.

Tetra was so happy and excited coming home finding her son and grandson waiting for her. "Oh, what a surprise she said finding them out by the pool. "Billy what a surprise she said going over and touching his hand. They were emerged in the pool and touching their hands was all she could do until they get out of the water. She smiled looking at them playing in the beautiful blue water of their backyard pool. Did you two get something to eat yet?' she immediately asked. "Yes mom Mrs. Laine was here when we arrived and was not going until we had eaten something" I told her. "Well how long are you staying son. "Oh, mom I have two weeks from the office so we'll see at least a week for sure" I said getting out of the pool grabbing a large towel from the nearby chaise to dry off with. I've been so busy with granddad's and nana affairs I needed time off" I shared with mom who I knew really understood. She said dad had taken some time off too. "When is dad due home mom? I asked now sitting with her on the deck watching Davie practiced his dives for us. "He should be in here anytime now" she said looking at her watch. "He is going to be so glad to see you two." Billy talked a bit with his mom before going back to show Davie some of the dives he was having questions with. She sat watching them interacting with one another. Billy was showing him how to dive without splashing the water when you entered. "Grandma watch!" he said heading to the high diving board. Tetra was so thrilled to have her son and grandson there she almost forgot about dinner. "Oh no fuss, we will just go out, she concluded thinking to herself. "Honey HONEY? David voiced coming through his home looking for his wife. He had seen the rental car in his driveway but he still had no clue about who was there. Soon he made his way to the back deck. Tetra heard him and was heading in the house to meet him. "Hello sweetheart you won't believe who is here! she said leading him to the back yard. She walked out with David her husband following waiting to see what had her so excited. "Hello dad" I said seeing him walk from the door. "Oh my! His face said it all! He was surprised. He came over and hugged me dripping wet standing in my trunks. He was so happy to see us. "Come here David" he asked looking at him frolicking around the pool. I'm wet granddad" but watch this! He said to impress his granddad. David stood watching and to Billy's surprise he had a pretty impressive dive. "Hold on I'll be right back" Dad yelled and headed into the house. Mom and I couldn't imagine why he hurried back into the house so quickly. Twenty minutes later he returned swimming trunks and all running and leaping into the pool. He was excited to play in the water with his grandson and son who joined the water games. Tetra smiled and watched from poolside with pride.

Dana was enjoying having a decorator in to help her decorate her new condominium. It was quite spacious and she had her very own Jacuzzi hot tub that was very elaborate. She loved it and was hoping to have everything ready for Roger's next visit when he returned. He had called and as far as she knew things were still going well with their long distant relationship. Mollie had come by to share with Dana about the new man in her life too. She couldn't wait to share the news about her trip with her either. Now Mollie was a full-figured girl. She felt that in order to keep her man she would have to lose some weight. Dana went with her to the athletic club to help her try and lose the unwanted pounds around her body. Encouraging her Dana did help her with her weight issues. Dana did not put her down like some others who claimed to be her friend. Mollie states they would pretend they wanted to help but often she had caught them talking about her when she walked into the lady's room. So, she took to Dana as a confidant. "Mollie I'll be by at six. You do remember today is our day to workout" Dana reminded calling her at work. "I'll be ready. I have a date with

Fredrick this weekend and I'm going to fit into my new outfit" she replied. "See you then".

Dana had logged off her computer for the day and was headed out of the door when her phone rang. It was Mrs. Bea. 'Hello Mrs. Bea is everything all right? Dana asked because she sound troubled "Dana will you please come by on your way home today? she asked. 'Sure Mrs. Bea, are you, all right? "I'm fine dear" she said hanging up the phone. Dana hurried out the door. Mrs. Bea didn't realize that Dana moved closer to the hospital. She had to drive about a half hour to get to her home but she didn't mind. Getting in her car traveling swiftly across the highway Dana arrived at Mrs. Bea's home. She saw Mrs. Bea standing outside with clothes in her hand. "Mrs. Bea, whose clothes are those? Dana asked puzzled as she got out of the car headed toward her. Getting closer Dana could see they were men clothing! "Will you tell this old coot he can't just move in here! She stated in her sweet but stern little voice. "I knew eating those strawberry cones with him was leading him on and that was not my intention!" she said so innocently. Dana turned her head to keep Mrs. Bea from seeing her laughing. Mrs. Beatrice Flowers was serious about her beliefs and wasn't backing down. Dana looked and saw Deacon Willis nervously sitting on her porch with other clothes now stuffed hanging from a suitcase. "Now Deacon Willis there has got to be a dating period before you move into a lady's house, Dana explained fighting back laughter. "That's true but Beatrice knows we are not spring chickens we've lived more life than we have left" he replied. "Well yes that may be true but you can't force yourself on a lady, Mr. Willis" Dana advised. "I'm not! I love Bea and I enjoy her conversations". She said she enjoyed me". "Well just because I said that it doesn't give you a right to move in my house without my permission" you haven't even given me a ring! She stated standing with both hands on her hips. "You didn't give me enough time" As soon as I opened my suitcase and put it down you started screaming at me and throwing out my clothes." Dana was doing all she could to compose her laughing at these two beautiful old people. Both obviously enjoyed one another's company. "I have the ring right here" he grumbled pulling the ring from his jacket pocket handing it to Dana "It's nice and gold with lots of handset diamonds" Dana said holding it in her hand. "Well that's what I asked for" Bea explained calming down somewhat. "But you still haven't asked! she replied scolding. Deacon Willis and older thin gentlemen in his late sixties or seventies got up from his seat and slowly kneeled down on one knee. 'Beatrice Flowers will you marry me?" he said holding up the ring to her. Dana stood back and allowed them to make up. "Well, Bea paused. "This just starts the dating and you can stay sometimes but not everyday until we get married" do you understand Harman Willis? She said looking at him kneeling down in front of her. "Yeah! YEAH! He responded. "Okay then I will!" she giggled taking the ring and putting it on her finger. "I thought you would never let me up from this porch" he said to Mrs. Bea with Dana helping him to stand securely. "Thanks Dana" Mrs. Bea replied "I hope it wasn't an inconvenience for you coming by here". "No not a problem, Dana explained as long as you're alright with your decision." "I fine now" Ms. Bea smiled. Dana kissed her and shook Mr. Willis's hand and headed to her car hearing "Come on Harman let's get us a cone" leading him into her home.

Sidney had everyone in the station's conference room for a briefing early before hitting the streets. Each was looking for coffee and sodas or something to wake them up. They had enjoyed the nightlife in Kansas City and were angry when their alarm clocks went off early that morning. "Good morning! the bright energetic Sidney said sitting at the head of the beautiful maple wood table in the large boardroom. Everyone there managed a hello from his or her sleepy faces. "Well I see you all have had a taste of K. C's night life. Now it's time to get to work". He began designating assignments and Sharon had her head lying on the table. "Sharon" he said the party's over you've got to bring your brains to the table now. She raised her head and said she was dizzy before throwing up all over the beautifully polished boardroom table. Sidney was not happy at all. He reprimanded all of his journalist crew and sent them back to their rooms with instructions other than dinner they where not to be out. As they were leaving maintenance was called in to clean up the mess.

Sidney and his cameramen hit the streets. They were just walking around trying to get a feel for a story. He knew from the demo he had presented that his story lies in the hoods of Kansas City. So, he and his camera crew went searching the streets for their story.

Billy took David his son around again in his old neighborhood where he grew up. David didn't really remember when he had come years ago with him and his aunt Jillian. He had so many questions about now and the visit that seemed a lifetime ago. They went by the old athletic club near where Tetra his mom once worked. He played basketball with a group of guys who were regulars there they told them. Billy didn't recognize anyone he knew. Many years had passed. Billy took him to the high school that Dana and he had attended and where he had graduated. The memories of those years came flooding from his inner thoughts. "Dad, were you and Dana good friends then?" David asked walking down the quiet halls of the high school. "Yes David, your mom and I were very good friends". "Did you love her?" he asked with his hands in his pockets walking up tall. Billy stopped for a moment and looked at him asking all those questions. But then he realized he was a product of this environment and of Dana and himself. "Yes, son I did". "Dorca, and I were friends before anything else" true friends! I said thinking about how long I had known her. "Why did she change her name dad?" "Son you'll have to ask her that okay", Billy replied. "Okay dad". "Let's get something to eat David Michael" racing with him back to the car.

David decided to take his grandson David Michael to meet a dear friend he had met years ago when he and Masony were looking for his mother. He asked Tetra and Billy to come along. He shared with both that this was the woman who had delivered David Michael into this world thirteen years ago now. "Besides it's a beautiful ride down the highway" he replied. Mom took him up on his offer but I decided to stay around the house. They were only going to be there a few hours so I chose to use it to just relax maybe talk to old friends, nothing to strenuous. "Hello, Billy, man, how are you? his buddy Glen asked smiling across the air waves. "Great! David Michael and I are down visiting mom and dad and he loves it". "Well you know how fun life can be at that age" I remember Billy replied laughing thinking over the years. "So, are you and the misses still enjoying the honeymoon? He then asked his dear friend. "Billy you know with all that has happening to me Cheryl has been remarkable" he confessed. "I'm happy for you man! "Take care we'll talk again soon". You know it! Glen replied hanging up his phone and rolling in his wheelchair down the hall of his office at JFK Space Center.

Dad had called to Oregon and the family was looking forward to meeting this bright young man, my son. After mom and dad left, I called Pastor Hathaway's home to just say hello. I heard he was in town and I hadn't spoken with him since granddad's funeral. He had rearranged his schedule to be with us. And we were so thankful. "Hi pastor Hathaway I said glad but surprised he answered the phone. Dad's always the last to answer the phone if someone else is in the house. "Hello he said, not really catching the voice yet. "Pastor its Billy Parker. "Oh, little Billy Parker how are you doing? "Is everything all right?" Pastor has started sounding older. He traveled so much. Mom said he shared one Sunday that he was going to slow down a bit but he had to be about his Father's business". So, stopping wasn't in the plan. "No, I'm fine pastor Hathaway. I was just down visiting my parents and thought I'd call and say hello". "Well I appreciate that son" he said. Let me find a sit, Mrs. Hathaway and Winnie are out shopping for something downtown, he shared as we talked. She's down visiting for our younger daughter's graduation from high school". "But things are good with you?" he asked. "Yes, they are pastor" I replied. I think pastor Hathaway wanted to talk. We talked about our little church and our growing church. He shared with me about the conferences. I had attended a lot of them. Not lately though but I told him I would try to start participating more. I told him about David my son. And tried to explain it as best as I knew how but there are still parts of it I'm trying to figure out. "I thought about telling him at the funeral. But it was not a subject that needed to be brought up because he was there to help us through a trying time and much grief and he did. He even came by and had dinner with my family at granddads and nana house before heading out again. "Well I do wish you well with your son" he said. "Now I would be amiss if I didn't tell you this son". "I know your mother trained up right" he said. And God also blessed you to have your father return back to the home. And they are two powerhouses for God". "Now you have a son and it is your responsibility to raise him right and train him to fear God too". He shared very fatherly. "I understand pastor. He had been slacking in a lot of things concerning the church. He would go every now and then and hadn't even included David. Some of his fun filled days were growing up in the church, he would admit. Billy shared with him he'd do better. He thanked him for his fatherly advice they prayed and said goodbye. I felt good talking to my pastor. He was always an encouragement for me. About an hour or so later Winfred his daughter called back. Her dad had told her I was in town visiting the folks. We made a date for dinner tonight.

Kat, Dan her boyfriend and some of her co-workers were sitting out back having a barbeque one Saturday at her home. Ariel stopped by uninvited to ask it she had seen Justin. Kat welcomed her in and introduced her to the five are six people sitting around the patio near her small in ground pool of her back yard. Ariel acknowledged each one looking around at the bottles of liquor sitting on a bar close to the wall of the back door. "Would you like something to drink she asked?" Ariel was hoping by chance Justin was there. He had moved out a few weeks ago now and she hadn't seen him except at the hospital. He had not given her his new address and was always too busy to talk. "No thank you she said. "I was hoping Justin was here" Everyone got quiet. Ariel sensed they all knew what was going on because of Kat's gossiping anyway. "No! Kat said with no explanation and kept dancing around with one of the guys in the yard. Everyone refreshed their drinks and Ariel sit looking at them smiling. Ariel was smiling because they were really starting to enjoy themselves at the expense of liquor. "Are you sure Ariel? One drink to take your mind off your troubles" Katherine said dancing now with her boyfriend Dan. Then she laughed and whispered to Ellen looking at one of her co-workers dancing beside her.

"Are you laughing at me? Ariel asked Katherine. Katherine snickered at Ellen and kept dancing. "I think I will have a drink" Ariel got up and went to the full bar and mixed a Vodka and coke and sat back in the lawn chair. Everyone continued enjoying themselves dancing to the beat of the music. Dan was dancing and attending to the meat on the grill pit they would later enjoy. "Excuse me? Ariel said "Kat may I use your restroom?" Since she and Justin were no longer engaged, she really didn't have a right to just go through the house except as a friend, and she wasn't even that, Kat had deceived her. Sure! Katherine said mocking her behind her back to her friends. Everyone was dancing with each other and one guy had gone over and dunked his head in the pool. He had apparently had too much to drink and was trying to clear his head Ariel guessed. Katherine was whispering to her co-workers from the office when Ariel came back out in her bikini. The men started whispering to each other. "Mind if I swim a few laps in the pool? Ariel asked. She was trying to get Kat roused. She felt Kat had pretended to be her friend and had aided in Justin leaving her. "Swim? Katherine asked do you see anyone else swimming Ariel?" No class that's what I always said, no class! Katherine stated again turning her back walking to take the meat from the grill. Ariel stood on the diving board preparing to dive with Dan and his male buddies checking her out. She dove in wetting her shapely figure in the very tiny bikini. Katherine led the small group of women who was telling her it was time to go! "Dan may I have another drink please?" she asked flirting with Katherine's man from poolside. One of the other women there grabbed her man and sat on his lap admonishing him. Dan despite Katherine's stern stares at him hurried over to the bar and mixed her a drink and ran it over to her. Ariel thanked him by rubbing her wet hand aside of his face saying, "thank you Dan" as everyone looked on. Knowing Dan's personality, he was hoping for more. Ariel turned the glass up quickly and sat it at poolside and swam a few more laps before getting out of the pool-dripping wet. Katherine was miffed. "I want you to leave and leave now! She shouted to Ariel who had put her on permanent ignore. "Her target now was to humiliate Katherine by using Dan her no good man! She walked over and mixed another drink. Katherine took the remaining Vodka and tossed it breaking it on the brick border around her flowers along the back fence. "I'm sorry, what did you say your name was? Ariel asked turning from Katherine and speaking to another gentlemen standing by his lady's chair. She wasn't happy either he quietly answered "Russ". Kat was fuming now. "My son would never be caught with you@#$%$#%$#$. GET OUT! GET OUT! she screamed. "Music! come on music, Dan said let's just all calm down! moving Katherine to the patio area to dance. Ariel had drunk too much now and was being very mischievous flirting with all the men there. Two of the couples gathered their things and left. Katherine's best friend and her husband stayed with Katherine, after all this was her house. Ariel was sitting there quietly drinking her vodka and Dan grabbed her "Let's dance" he said seeing Katherine over chatting with her friend Ellen about her unwelcome visitor. "I don't know how my son stayed with you that long! Katherine voiced. Ariel put both arms around Dan's neck and he pulled her up close. Ariel was having her way with him. Rubbing him on his head and swaying to the music in her wet tiny bikini. Katherine had had enough. She walked over and forced the two apart pushing Dan to the ground. It didn't take much he was sauced. Then she turned and slapped Ariel with her opened hand across the face "GET OUT! she screamed. But to her surprise Ariel slapped her back. Katherine flew into Ariel pulling her hair and screaming obscenities. Ariel tossed her to the ground and punched her in the face. Katherine kicked and knocked Ariel to the ground and they both were rolling around scratching and punching each other on the green lawn. Ellen ran over to help Katherine and Ariel caught her leg pulling her down. Her dress she was wearing went over her head. She was swinging her arms furiously trying to see what was going on and Ariel and probably Katherine at this point was punching her. The men came over breaking them apart. Katherine was fuming mad. Ellen was mad and had turned a beet red from embarrassment. Pulling her dress down knowing everyone saw everything. They all were covered in scratches. Dan held Katherine until Ariel got her bag and left. Kat slapped him and sat down taking a deep breath.

CHAPTER TWELVE

No place like home

David and Tetra with their grandson pulled up to Beulah Reeves home. She was expecting them and anxiously greeted them at the door. David had shared everything with Tetra about their meeting Beulah and she was glad to make her acquaintance also. "Please, please come in" she said directing them into her beautiful home. 'Can I get something for you to eat or drink?" she asked before taking her sit. "Oh no that want be necessary have a sit we're so glad to be able to come back with good news", David replied. He could see the years had taking a toll on Beulah, though she was still a very attractive lady for her age he thought to himself. "I'm glad too! she said laughing, "I had almost given up" Beulah replied "until you called two years ago. I still didn't expect to see you so soon". But I'm glad" she added sitting next to David Michael their grandson.

Her husband had come out of his study and extended his hand to the Parkers. Everyone sat in the living room laughing and talking. "Yes, my son and grandson paid me a surprise visit yesterday" David shared proudly. "Well I'm glad you thought of us" Beulah said "we've been praying for Dorca since the day you came many years ago". She nodded to her husband. "I am just glad we didn't give up' Tetra shared sitting hugging David Michael who at this point said nothing. "Oh my, we're just jabbering" Beulah reminding them "This must be David Michael" looking at his hands and how well proportioned and developed he was. She wiped her eyes. Her husband handed her a Kleenex from the decorative small box sitting on the end table next to the sofa. "Little David, I loved you from the first time I held you in my arms" she told him so glad he had not been harmed in any way. "I was the nurse who helped delivery you dear." Your mom did the rest" she smiled. "Thank you" he said shyly not really knowing what to say. "How's your mother? Beulah asked. "Dana's fine" he said. "Dana?" Beulah said jerking her head in surprise. "Yes, Dana is my mother. "She changed her name" David interjected. "Oh I see and he calls her Dana". Well she's doing alright then." I am certainly glad you're all right too" Mrs. Reeves replied giving David Michael a big hug embarrassing him even more.

Jonathan Reeves, Beulah's husband excused himself and left for a moment. He was seeing how uncomfortable David Michael was so he went and asked the young man across the street to share his basketball court with him so the adults could talk. David Michael was glad! "Thanks Mr. Reeves he said leaving to go outside. He was very happy to see and know Mrs. Reeves but he really didn't know what to say to her. He whispered to Tetra his grandmother that he would ask Dana about her when he returned home. Saying bye to the adults he walked out the doors to play with the Reeves neighbor's son.

The Parkers sitting now enjoyed a cup of coffee and homemade coffee cake right from Beulah's oven and talking with the Reeves. Sharing those lost years together brought back many wonderful memories for Beulah Reeves. They in turned thanked the Parkers for bringing closure to a prayerful situation. Beulah told David she was grateful they allowed her to see the young man she had help bring into this world. "And please give our love to Dor, I mean Dana as well" she acknowledged. David Michael enjoyed playing ball with Nathaniel the Reeves neighbor's son and gave Beulah and her husband a big hug from the bottom of his heart. The Reeves stood in their door waving as the Parkers got into their car and drove away.

Sidney had gotten everyone one the same page. His young journalists focused now and committed were getting precise details on the subject matter for this project. They were very interested asking thought provoking questions for clarification. With everything packed in the van they headed to the streets. After a while of riding around they stopped, parked their van and decided to walk. Walking around Kansas City's slums southeast of the freeway loop they had come upon this little jazz bar. It was a hole in the wall. They were tired from walking and went in to get something cool to drink. Most places sold soda even if it was priced too high. Sidney walked in and sat at a table with his crew following. The cameramen sat at the bar having a beer and Sidney ordered a soda for each of the journalist. They laughed they were of legal age though he said he was teaching them a lesson after the other day. After sharing a good laugh together refreshed from walking, they sat listening to this horn player. A young man who seem worn by the years of life? His appearance looked un-kept, shabby and his pants with tattered hems drug the floor. His graying kinky hair covering his head appeared in need of a cut. But closing your eyes you were swept away by the way he played that trumpet. Sidney sat there in amazement. He had not heard so great a player since "Louis Armstrong" the first internationally famous soloist in jazz. He turned and asked the bartender "who is that?

"The cat packed the place on Friday night." "Told us he's out of Saint Louis" the bartender replied and moved down to the other end to fill and order. Sidney sat and enjoyed his music. The melody was so soothing to his ear. He thought why was he playing in a place like this?" His clothes were worn and the soles of his shoes showed that they were probably the only pair he owned. He played the horn with such conviction you would think he had on a million-dollar suit. A few patrons that had stopped to listen were on the dance floor embracing one another moving to the beat on some of his tunes. He looked up with his somber eyes after the piece was finished. The bartender nodded at him and he put the trumpet back to his lips this time speeding up the beat. "Hey now that's it! Someone said from the crowd starting to gather. "That cat knows his jazz! could be heard in the crowd. "What's his name?' Sidney asked someone standing near him making rhythm with his feet. He pulled his head to the side motioning for him to ask the bartender. Sidney made his way to the bar. The small place had started filling up. It wasn't very big. "Hey what's the gent's name?" Sidney asked with pen in hand. The bartender was moving to the beat of the music with his towel over his shoulder taking it all in. "Tye he's says Tye P. is how I see it. Does he live around here? The bartender squinted. Sidney was bothering him asking questions and he was grooving to this jazzman that had everyone mesmerized. "We're renting him a small place round back" moving quickly away to enjoy the music down at the other end of the bar. Sidney gathered up his crew and said, "We have our story.

David Michael stayed with his grandparents and I went out on my date for the evening. I was picking Winifred up at 7.00 o'clock and didn't want to be late. I knew I'd go in and speak with pastor and Mrs. Hathaway and our reservations were for 8:00 pm. Wearing my very thin pinned stripped black double-breasted suit I pulled up to her parents' door.

They had moved into a much larger upscale home since our high school days. Having a Congress woman for a daughter came with its perks. Their home wasn't easy to find and security was visible. Since I was familiar with procedure the very secure homes property gate didn't slow plans down a bit. I passed through all the security points. We got through hello's fairly quickly and were on our way to the restaurant.

I made reservation at Freigo's. It was one of mom and dad's favorite places so I knew it had to be good. Winifred was lovely as always. She wore a white forming fitting dress that extended to her calves. She had chosen to accent it with a silver chain link belt that hung slightly around her hip line. Very sophisticated very Winnie! "You look lovely" I said opening the car door for her after we shared a laugh about me picking her up.

Winifred and I were long time friends. But life had not brought us together intimately. She and I dated when we were teenagers and going to the same school and the same church, we saw a lot of each other. I on the other hand was in love with a little girl name Dorca. "Well Winnie, may I call you Winnie? Congresswoman Hathaway", I teased. "Winnie is fine she said. Winnie was so reserved and so much the lady. I cleared my throat and started again. "Well Winnie what battles have you been fighting lately? I asked. 'Honestly she said my life was less complicated when I was a senator" she replied. I'm always at a meeting or having to go to a meeting" she laughed. My mornings are usually busy during office work" she replied. Yes, "I know how that can be" I shared. I just completed doing some work for my grandfather's estate and I needed a break" Not to mention my clients and the law firm". You're right, I meet so many visitors at the office from all over the world. Coming here, back home" she said is such a treat". "When I'm in the office" Winnie acknowledged "I'm waiting to hear that bell ring for a debate" she smiled. We rode along sharing about one another's careers and the day- to-day people we interface with. Soon we were pulling up in front of Freigo's door a very posh restaurant. Getting out the valet came up and opened my door. After I had gotten out, I walked around and opened Winnie's door. We walked in and were immediately shown to our table. I had asked for a semi private space out of the way of traffic so that we could enjoy conversation without so much fuss. They were very accommodating sitting us near a large window with a view of beautiful Mt. Rainier under a moonlit sky.

At night its breath taking. The sparkling lights of the city seemed magical. After we sat and were feeling comfortable our waiter came over and introduced himself and asked if we'd like an appetizer or something to drink. I looked over at Winnie whose smile lit up the room. Her personality was one of sheer elegance and I tried seeing the talkative headstrong girl I use to know but she was gone. Very posed and very in control was the beautiful lady that now sat across the table from me. Her sparkling handset diamond earrings were adding brilliance to the moment as she sat smiling at me. What was she thinking about me I thought? I turned to the waiter and ordered a bottle of Dom Perignon with our meal. He was very accommodating suggesting we have something called a Citrus Flip cocktail to compliment the large portabella mushroom we had requested for our appetizer. Winnie gave me a let's go for it nod. Soon we were laughing and sharing one another's lives and enjoying each other's company. We reminisced a bit. But we found our lives had grown so much and we had accomplished so many things that we could almost talk and share about anything. I felt comfortable in sharing about Dorca (who had changed her name to Dana) with Winnie who knew her as well. She was very surprised though we had conceived a son. She said I seemed timid even regarding a kiss. On that we share a laugh! I confessed to her it was a bit of a surprise to me too. And it was only the one night of the prom. We sat well over and hour in conversation before ordering our meals. Winnie and I shared good and bad times as we enjoyed our great meal. "Refill" I asked her holding the bottle of wine in my hand. "Why not? I don't get to be myself much these days! she confessed. She spoke of the prejudice situations she had to face in reaching her goals and how her marriage to Senator Aaron Reaching had almost sent her over the edge. She had come to Jillian's memorial service so she knew of the pain I had gone through. "Thank you Winnie I said after we were leaving the restaurant. "For?" She questioned looking over at me. "For just being you" I smiled walking her out of the restaurant to our waiting car.

Justin had found a luxurious upscale bachelor pad doorman included, in downtown Maine to purchase. He wasn't taking any more chances until he knew Ariel had gotten over him. He had heard Kat's story over the phone and stirred clear of her also and anything pertaining to Ariel. "Good morning "Mr. Parker the doorman greeted him coming in after a long night at the hospital. "Good morning Mort" returning the greeting as he walked by. Justin pressed the elevator's button and went up to the tenth floor to the spacious condominium suite. Walking in he smelled the scent of romantic candles. "He smiled knowing Menae was there. They had stopped seeing each other after the dramatic episode at her place a few months ago and he missed her but understood "that was crazy!

He slowly walked into his bedroom. His silk sheets were turned back on the king-sized bed. His Jacuzzi tub was being filled with steaming water. He could hear it running from the living room as he entered. He looked slowly around the room and saw a beautiful red satin lingerie gown draped over his clothing rack next to the dresser. "Yes! He exclaimed making a pulling motion with his fist. His heart was pounding, he felt so bad about what had happened, he just wanted to make it up to her. He wasn't aware Ariel would do something like that. But he certainly didn't want Menae involved. She was so sweet, and so soft, and so inviting. The way she would whisper Latin sayings in his ear was what he longed for. He put his keys and coffee mug down on the table. The scented candles had filled the room with sweet fragrances. He spotted her tiny little slippers sitting aside of the bed. The tiredness he felt from being up all night had dissipated. He had been talking with her for a month since the incident trying to set things right with her. And now she was here. He walked into the steamed room caused but the hot tub. And sitting there anxiously waiting his return home was Menae Sanchez. Justin quickly undressed out of his hospital greens and joined her in the Jacuzzi style tub. He kissed her and she returned the pleasure of his affection. Justin was swept away by her touch, her smell and her whispers. After a playful hour they returned to the bedroom. Justin went into the kitchen to get a bottle of wine and two glasses that had been chilling in his refrigerator. Leaving Menae sitting bare under the covers. She was relieved to be back with Justin too, someone her own age. She met and dated a lot of older men in her career job at the state department. She never confessed to Justin she thought it was one of her visitor's that night. She didn't know who was causing the ruckus until they had gotten out of there and had gotten into his car. She was sure that it was one of the wives of one of her lovers. Very relieved to know it was Justin's angry ex-girlfriend, Menae was very content for now. She knew with Justin's busy schedule at the hospital he would be a perfect suitor. She had share with him that she stayed away long enough to let things cool off a bit.

The crew went into the boardroom to get things set up for the day. It was Friday and Sidney wanted to shot some film footage at the little jazz club. They had gone by earlier and had spoken with the management/bartender and he was delighted something good was final happening in this area. "You could always count on a brawl but never a big-time filmmaker in here" he said rubbing his dry wooly hair on his head. When they returned just before night had fallen Sidney looked up and saw hand written signs nailed to the outside door coming into the small club that read: The great Jazzman, Friday night from 8pm to 1pm. Mr. Tye Pee. Sidney smiled as he walked in to see the same handwritten sign over the small stage where he stood to play his music.

The wooden floor had been swept and the small wooden tables with two chairs were strategically placed near the dance area had been set in place. "Hello" he said seeing Sidney and the crew coming in. "you gonna be on TV?" a lady asked him moving around the ten or fewer tables. This is my wife Cynthia he said. She's been helping me beautify the place. "Please to meet you Sidney said extending his hand. She was putting a small vase with flowers on the tables and holding a beer she was drinking with her other hand. Looking at her Sidney could see she started early.

They set up their equipment and interviewed a few of the patrons who had arrived early or never left. They were eager for the big show. Bragging rights you know! Sidney ordered a round from the bar and waited for the man of the hour. After it got closer to 8pm and Tye still had not shown. The bartender and Sidney went up some stairs to his small room around the back of the bar. He was laying across the beat-up couch and the smell of alcohol filled the air. "Hey! Hey! You have people waiting for you! the bartender stated harshly shoving Tye's head. The bartender wanted his free publicity and his T.V. spot he told him. You messing up! The room Sidney noticed was hardly big enough to turn around in let alone live. His old jacket was thrown across a tattered chair in the corner. Hey! Hey! hitting him on the shoulder. He moved and turned looking dizzy or sleepy it was hard to tell. He turned again now facing toward them. "Oh, oh I'm sorry, I'm sorry jumping up stumbling across the room with his back to them. "You're suppose to be downstairs at 8:00! Do you want to get paid?" the bartender admonished getting angry because Tye was obviously incapable of performing. Sidney didn't say anything he really didn't know what to say He looked around and saw Tye's horn placed safely on a little table at the end of the couch and walked out. "You have ten minutes or you can get out! the bartender yelled walking out mumbling under his breath. Sidney and he went back down to the small bar. They were playing the jukebox and getting ready for the Jazzman himself. Sidney knew looking at Tye P this night was a bust. Though his crew was having fun shooting footage of the patrons dancing to the beats being played on the jukebox.

They put together a couple live interviews from longtime jazz fans, they told Sidney. The crew were enjoying themselves. There wasn't much room to move at this point. So, Sidney suggested staying around a few more minutes to please the very angry bartender and pack up and leave. Sidney stood looking around for a minute. The bartender was back behind the bar talking to his wife about their trifling tenant. After about twenty minutes Tye P came through the door. The crew quickly unrolled their long electrical cords they had packed away. When Tye got on the stage cheering, laughing, shouting filled the small bar. "Now that's what I'm talking about! Someone expressed very loud from the crowd. Soon a hush came over the room has he put the trumpet to his lips and rocked the house! "I told you that cat can blow! Sidney was astounded. He just shook his head listening to that smooth sound coming from that trumpet. "Just roll it! He yelled over the crowd to his crew. "Roll it."

Winfred Hathaway and I left the restaurant lighthearted and refreshed. We talked as I drove down the highway headed to her home after a wonderful evening of dining together. I pulled up in front of her parent's home and walked her to the door. She was staying there during her visit. "Thanks for a wonderful, wonderful evening William" she said graciously standing at the front door entrance to the house. "My pleasure" I said. She and I hugged each other and a quick kiss on the lips was all it took to say goodnight. She watched from the door as I pulled away. She called later to see that I had made it home safely. She was such a gracious lady and kept her dignity the whole entire night. "Goodnight Winnie" I thought turning off my light at my parent's home for a good night's rest.

Hello son! Katherine voiced very loud across the telephone. "Kat! It's earlier and I had a very late night at the hospital" Justin said. He was grumpy and sleepy and Katherine was in a spirited mood. It was his twenty fourth birthday and she felt like celebrating. "Kat I'll call you back a little later when I wake up!" he replied. "Promise! "I promise hanging up his receiver and going back to sleep. His brother Billy had planned a celebration for him in two weeks. So, he had to tradeoff and pulled a few other shifts to make it work. He and Billy had tried a lot of solutions but being a second-year intern was not affording him a lot of flexible time. Billy had made all the reservations so all he had to do was show up with his date. So, for now all he wanted to do was sleep. Looking at the clock it showed he had been sleeping for five hours but his head felt like only minutes since his last interruption. "Hello! he said waken again by the constant ring of the phone. "Hello Justin" it was a man's voice and it wasn't one he recognized yet. "Hello again Justin repeated clearing his thoughts. "This is David, David Parker". David? he was Billy's dad, no my dad oh his nerves kicked in. "Hello David" he said. "Hope I didn't wake you to early" he said but I did want to wish you a happy birthday son". Justin sat up in bed. He didn't know what to make of this call from David. "Thank you he responded. I didn't know you knew" he confessed. "Well I'm sorry to admit I didn't. Davie told me it was your birthday." He speaks very highly of you son". "Davie? Justin questioned. "He and Billy are down visiting and he looked at the calendar this morning doing breakfast and informed us at the breakfast table it was your birthday, I guessed Billy already knew" David confided. Thank you, Justin replied pausing a moment 'Well be sure to tell them both thank you and hello from me." "I'll do that son" he said again hanging up the line. Justin sat on the side of his bed and realized his dad had just acknowledged him. This was a day he'd always remember. Suddenly his doorbell rang. It was the florist with large bunch of balloons and flowers from Kat. "He called her back at the office and thanked her personally for her gift.

CHAPTER THIRTEEN

A new do

Jessica had called Sidney from her last concert engagement. She wanted him to come and meet her in Chicago before her tour heads overseas to visit the troops. "Honey there's no way I can get to you now. We've made a break through with our subject and I just can't get away, you understand, don't you?" Sidney explained asking. "I miss you babe" Jessica cooed over the loud noises in the phone. "I miss you too. Where are you now? Sidney asked curious about the LOUD music in the background. "A few of us came out to relax at this place called the Underground" she replied. The music slams!" making the sound of an instrument to the beat. "Then I will see you when I return back from here? She yelled over the loud noises. Sidney though Jessica always sounds more British over the phone than in person to him "That's a definite, yes babe" Sidney replied. "Love you Sid" then hanging up before he could respond. Sidney didn't trip his mind was on his documentary.

They had been there several months in Kansas City filming. Jackie one of the camera guys had met him a steady chick that showed him the sights around the city among other things. Everyone was working out. Mr. P. was showing up and performing to crowds that had grown so much they could not fit into the small place. The publicity brought in by the jazzman made the bartender smile A LOT. Tye's idle days were still not enough to keep him from the booze, but when night fell, he was ready to play most nights. They were dancing in the streets.

Some crowds were causing fights. You know those who had drank way too much liquor and were out to ruin a good time. So, for Sidney to continue with his documentary he would have to move this venue to another place.

Where? He had met with Tye on several occasions trying to get a feel for this man of jazz. He had taken him out to eat many times over the months and felt so bad when he saw him scarfing down his meal. It was as if he hadn't eaten in days. That in most cases was probably true. But since he had been playing consistently at the Jazz Spot is what it came to be known as, his meals were coming frequently when he would use his money for food. Sidney sit across the table from Tye watching him hurriedly finish his meal. "So how did you come to be called Tye, is that a birth name? Sidney asked. "Pretty much my name is Tyler" he voiced. He looked in appearance much older. Sidney thought him to be his age around forty but changed his mind after many conversations that he was closer to the age of his younger brother which was twenty-seven. The streets had not been kind to him Sidney concluded. He confirmed his age as being 29 and continued finishing his dessert. "So, who taught you how to play that horn?' Sidney asked "you touched core deep with your music" he added. "I learned to play that instrument almost from birth" he said wiping his eyes to keep emotions back Sidney thought. Talking about this made him a bit emotional. "Are you originally from St. Louis?' Sidney continued to question. "Well let's just say anything before that time I've chosen to forget." He confessed. Sidney pondered his answer. What grade did you complete?" continuing to record his answer in a ledger. "I have gone to college if that's what you're getting to" sounding a bit put out by Sidney's many questions. "Just short of my Bachelor's regrettably, Tye recalled. "It's just all part of this story man" Sidney voiced that I'm trying to convey. No harm intended" he said extending his hand across the table for a shake. Feeling he had asked enough questions and didn't want to frightened him off Sidney closed the ledger and asked. "You've been here for a while do you know where I can get a descent haircut around these parts? "Over on Wilmington and fifth" he responded. "Do you mind walking me over there?" Man! He expressed looking at Sidney "No more probing questions today I promise." Tyler got up from the booth where they were sitting and he and Sidney walked toward the door. "Hey! The waitress behind the register yelled as they left. "It's on the table, and thanks" Sidney responded heading out the door to the barbershop. "We can walk from here man, let's go this way. Walking and talking it wasn't long before they arrived two and a half blocks around the corner. Tyler stood at the door of the barbershop motioning for Sidney to enter. After Sidney entered, he stated in a friendly tone "Come on you said I could get a good cut here, you have to go first" Sidney teased. "If they mess your hair up, I'm not getting in the chair! "Tyler laughed so hard. It was the reaction Sidney was hoping for. "So, you don't trust me?" he asked walking in. "Cut him first! Sidney continued to tease sitting down with a magazine. Smithy the barber nodded for Tyler to sit in his chair. He asked how he wanted it cut and prepared his station getting clippers in hand. The lady barber cutting hair next to him recognized Tyler from the club. "Hey are you the Jazzman from the spot" she said. "Yes, he responded very shyly. "Oh, please let me cut his hair, my girlfriends will not believe this! Smithy looked at Tyler, "it's all right" he said moving over laughing. "Next! Smithy said pointing to his chair. Sidney took the chair and they both laugh. "Well let me in on the joke?' Smithy asked. "Oh, I was just waiting to see how his cut came out, I'm new around here" he confessed. "Oh, don't worry you're in the right place, now a block over and you would be in trouble" they all shared the laugh. "Tye P right?" holding his hand while Sidney snickered to her flirting gestures. "Come over here" she sat him over in the corner and put his head under the water. She took a small package from the shelf and squeezed it into his hair. With plastic gloves she massaged it into his head. "What are you doing?' he asked. "I'm going to make you look like you play" she said "now sit for a few minutes your friend won't mind". Smithy was finishing up Sidney's cut when Tyler was going under the hair dryer. "She's hooking you up man! Smithy teased slapping him the high five while he sat under the dryer.

Sidney could see the change in Tyler's body language. He felt like Tyler's self esteem and image was being rebuilt. What had caused this young man to plummet and end up on the street?" he thought. "Sidney paid for all services including his cut and then asked. "How much longer darling?" keeping the atmosphere lively. "Oh, about an hour" she said moving around quickly to finish. Another client had made her way into the shop for her perm she voiced loudly. "Sidney walked over further away where Smithy was sweeping up in the back and whispered. "Where is downtown from here?" Tye's going to be looking so good tonight I'd better prepare myself". "Way to go man!" Smithy replied giving him directions to the clothing shops near the area. "I'll be back!" Sidney yelled to Tyler under the dryer leaving the shop. "I can walk back home" he yelled. Thanks for everything! "Not on your life and miss this cut you're getting?' he laughed. Then he turned to Smithy "Nice fade man, real nice fade.

Billy and his son had so much fun with his parents David Michael did not want to leave. They had covered so much of Spokane and surrounding area's including Seattle. Billy joked he had to get back to work to rest. They visited the Space needle and rode the Monorail in Seattle. They went to Olympic National Park and watched a mountain bike show in the northern Cascade Mountains. David knew his grandson would like it because he used to take Billy there and he certainly enjoyed it then and now. They went each Sunday to Mt. Nebo's services with his parents. David Michael loved meeting the children his age. Mom even invited some of the children David Michael's age over for what turned out to be a big fun party. But my parents didn't mind. They were enjoying it. They seemed to be reliving my younger days through David Michael. And of course, Mrs. Ann met my son. "My! My, the spitting image! she said holding his hand. She was my favorite Sunday school teacher growing up. Our days were filled with memories, old ones for me and new ones for my son David Michael. Mom and dad were the proudest grandparents there that Sunday when she introduced him to Pastor Hathaway and Pastor Edinberg in morning service. Although Winnie had left the previous week she and I made a standing invitation for a special event they were having at the Ford theater in Washington D.C. in September and I was to be her invited guest. I promised mom they could send for David in about three months. That's when he had another school break. I knew that from seeing his schedule on my electronic calendar. Knowing he would be back in three months made it easier to leave. Though it didn't stop the stream of tears from mom and Davie's eyes as we boarded the plane home.

Sidney went back to his car and following Smithy's direction was soon in the heart of downtown Kansas City. He parked and began walking. About a block or two down the sidewalk he heard some music playing and he stopped at the door. He looked in and went over and took a sit at the bar. There were a few happy hour patrons there is what Sidney surmised looking around the place. He was still on the other side of the tracks but certainly a better neighborhood. The bartender came over after rinsing his glasses and asked. "Can I get you something sir?" looking Sidney over real, good. "Bud beer" Sidney replied. He walked over and put the coaster on the bar and sat the beer down. "You look like a man who needs a glass" he added. "Thanks Sidney responded still looking around this fairly large establishment. We could probably fit the spot in here three times he reasoned assessing a closer inspection. "What kind of music does your establishment have?" Sidney questioned. There were two people playing pool in the corner on a very worn pool table and a jukebox with oldies playing aside of another wall. "Why do you ask? It's early this place gets jumping around 9:00 or 10:00 o'clock" he replied. You're obviously not from here?' he said looking at Sidney. Sidney just shook his head indicating no. "Well come back through a little later tonight" you'll see! Sid finished his beer and got up to leave. "I just might do that" he said. I just might do that! He walked on and went into the men's clothing store and made some purchases and headed back to his car. Stopping again he rented a small apartment that was a few blocks from the barbershop. Sidney noticed the rent sign as he passed going downtown. It was clean. There was a kitchen to prepare meals and a bed to sleep in. "Thank you! The landlord said after he paid her for the entire month's rent. "Thank you, Jesus! She expressed going back closing her door lifting her hands in praise.

Dalmatia had stopped by the station to see Sidney who was still out. She had an invitation Mossy had asked to drop off to Sidney on her way to the university campus today. She could have left it but said she would come back later. She used any excuse to see Sidney. Unaware to Sidney she had become infatuated with him.

Sidney was pleasing surprised when he walked back into the barbershop and saw Tye. "Man, you look good, ten even twenty years younger! Sidney could not believe is eyes. She had dyed his graying hair and cut and trimmed and tapered his sideburns. She left a slight hint of hair to grow around his face line and under his chin. "Watch out Wyton!" "I told you she was hooking him up! Smithy said proud of his assistant in his barbershop. She was very proud of her work too! Tye got up looking at what they were raving about. A haircut couldn't have made that much difference. He stood looking in the mirror. I think it had been years since he saw exactly who he was. He joked to hold back tears. 'Thanks so much and hugged her. Everyone felt the love in the barbershop that moment. Soon the atmosphere was shattered the door opened for a customer who was swearing every four-letter word you could think of! Her ride had made her late for her appointment! she stated coming in for her perm. Sidney tipped the stylist and they left. Tye was still emotional. Sidney knew there was more to this man and he was seeing it right now. Thanks man! I don't know how to repay you for this" what they're paying me at the Spot barely covers the roof over my head" he confessed. "Please, please don't worry about it." Putting his hand around his shoulder and heading to the car. He drove back over to the spot. "Will you be here tonight? he asked Sidney.?" you bet! Sidney pulled the car around back. Tye had this smile fixed on his face he couldn't wipe it off.

He felt good about himself for once in a very long time. Sidney got out too. Tye looked puzzled. "Get your things you're moving" he told him. He stood there puzzled with a questioned look on his face? All I have of value is my Trumpet". "Then get your Trumpet and let's go! Sidney said smiling at him from the car. Tyler ran quickly up the rickety stairs. "Like a child he got back in the car after putting his trumpet carefully in the trunk of the car. Sidney drove about five miles back toward the barbershop passing it coming to this newer apartment complex. "Room 2 is where we want to go" Sidney explained pulling up to the curve. He sat waiting for Sidney to open the trunk and further instructions. Sidney pointed to the door getting out and gave him his key. "Getting out he stood awed. He trusted he'd be safe in that place behind the bar. Key there was no key! Sidney watched him walk up and put the key in the lock and open it. Tyler stood for a moment in disbelief and smiled. It was already furnished. Sidney began taking the trumpet and the clothes from his trunk. Tyler ran back out to help him grabbing his priceless trumpet and both walked in. "How will I pay for this? It's nice, thank you Sidney," he expressed sincerely. "Everything his covered for this month we will talk before I leave" deal? "Deal he said looking around in his bedroom and kitchen. "Oh, and before I forget here's a couple of suits to get you started." Tyler flopped on his couch. No one in a long time had been this kind. "I also noticed there's a store not far maybe a block or two" get some food in here okay?" And I'll be back at around 7:30". "You don't want to be late. "Man, how can I pay you for giving me my dignity back? Embracing Sidney as he left from the apartment. "Thanks man."

CHAPTER FOURTEEN

Should all acquaintance be forgotten be forgot

Dana was putting a beautiful live green plant in her bathroom. She noticed the Turkish tile that lined her gorgeous tub. "This is the perfect spot she thought sitting the lush plant in the suns light next to the tub. She hurried and dressed and headed out the door. Billy and David were going to stop by her office coming in from the airport and she didn't want to miss them. She made her way across the busy morning freeway to the hospital and parked in the garage there. She along with others headed to the hospital hurrying to get on the crowded elevators going down. Getting off the elevator she walked across the lot to the hospital entrance. As Dana got closer to her office after entering the hospital there was a lot of commotion going on. She saw someone being carried off on a gurney. She couldn't imagine who could be coming from her office! She got close enough to see it was Mollie. "Mollie what happened? she asked feverously staying out of the way as they wheeled the gurney quickly through the hallway. She could see blood on the sheets that covered her but couldn't make out the problem. She caught one of the orderlies by the arm. "What's wrong with her? Where's the blood coming from? she asked walking along quickly trying to keep up and out of the way. After confirming she was a doctor of the hospital a male nurse answered "She tried slitting her wrist" he replied moving behind the curtain leaving Dana standing in the hallway stunned. "Please keep me posted" she said handing her card to the receptionist at the nurse's station and moving quickly out of the way has the doctors came running in. Dana went back to her office. Her door was still open and the blood was on her floor. Mollie had left her a note: Dear Dana I can't make them love me. I'm too fat, or not fat enough. I hate me! Mollie." Dana had sat down and called a janitor to come in and clean her office. She was informed that was going to be a day's job at best, and she was added to his long list. She called and rescheduled most of her clients, the ones she could reach my phone. The others she assigned to speak with one of the other psychiatrists on the staff if they so desired. Dana sat out in the hallway and waited for Billy and David. After finding out Mollie was going to be okay, she left going to have breakfast with Billy and her son David.

"Jessica Strassberg" he requested calling her answering service. "Please have her give me a call this is Sidney Owens". "I'll give her the message" the voice came back. Hanging up he drove back to the station to check with the crew on how the editing of the footage they had shot was coming along. He shared with them his day and gave each one time off until 6:30. "We will assemble here get everything ready and head out to the Jazz Spot". He went back to his room he had a full day. Sidney had just lain across the bed closed his eyes and there was a knock on the door. Weary from his busy day he walked and slowly opened the door. "Dal! What a surprise" he said. "Come in, I just came back to the room. "Mossy asked me to drop off this invitation to granddad Owens birthday party Saturday." "Thanks, I almost forgot" he said taking the envelope from her hand. "How are your classes going? Sidney asked Very well, but I was wondering about this story this journalist wrote in a magazine? Sidney sat on the bed and pointed for Dal to sit in the chair. "Where's the magazine? he asked. She took out the magazine and he read the article and began explaining it to Dal when his phone ring? "Hello honey! Oh, hello Jess", just a moment sweetie I've been missing you." putting the receiver down. "Dal let's talk about this another time maybe Saturday okay" leading her to the door shutting it behind her going back getting the phone to talk with his lady fair!

Dana enjoyed breakfast with David and Billy. He caught her up on his trip and said grandma and granddad said hello. "Next weekend mom we will talk more okay?" "Okay" she kissed him and thanked Billy for bringing him by. They were going home to crash from jetlag.

Tyler moved around in his new place. He quickly put the packages Sidney had given him in the closet in his bedroom to look at later. He could hear music from one of the other apartments. It was gospel music and he hummed some familiar ones. Back in the bathroom to shower and then look for a grocery store. He took the packages out and opened it. The two suits where now hanging in the once empty closet. 'Hey cool jeans! I'll put these on" laying them across the bed. There were a couple of shirts and socks. He had everything he needed. He decided on a shirt and hung the other one in the closet to wear with his suit tonight. "Humming to the music he went in and took a long hot shower with soap and a clean towel! "He stopped for a moment he couldn't believe someone did this for him. After he finished his bath, got dressed he went out to find a store. Sidney had left money on the table. He implied it was for his time today on the story. Tyler put the money in his pocket and went out looking around outside trying to decide what direction to go in. He stood in front of his door looking at the shiny key he held in his hand. "Hello young man" Are you my new tenant? An elderly lady asked. It had been a long time since someone addressed him that way. And it felt good Tyler thought. "Yes, ma'am I live right here" he replied. "I need to find a store, what direction should I go in?" he asked reasoning that since she lived here, she'd surely know. "I could tell you, but if you don't mind, I'm headed that way". "Can you drive?' Tyler hadn't driven in a long time and besides he didn't have a car. "I can drive but I'm without car right now" he replied. "Oh, I see, well we will go to this store about two blocks over if you don't mind walking with and old lady." My name is Dorrance Bean by the way". Hello Tyler replied extending his hand "Tyler, ma'am Tyler". Well it's a pleasure meeting a nice young man like you. Rare you know! She turned the corner and continued talking. "Now it's small and it doesn't carry a lot of things like the large store on Vine but it'll do in a pinch! She giggled. "My husband does the driving he's resting now I didn't want to wake him he works so hard keeping up this place." "I needed some baking powder for his cornbread" she shared. "My mother "Tyler said then he stopped. "So, what brings you to Kansas City?" He had never thought about why one day it hopped the train in Saint Louis and came to Kansas City. Just as Tyler was about to come up with an answer she said "Here it is! Walking into the doors of the tiny store. You could hardly walk around in it. It was crowded She quickly got what she needed and stood waiting for Tyler humming her hymns of praise she called it.

Tyler spent about $50.00 on salt and pepper and rice some bacon and other items he needed to sustain him for the week anyway. He paused for a moment looking at the liquor shelve but opted not to purchase any right now after looking over and seeing the elderly lady standing by the counter waiting for him. "Walking back, he'd have plenty enough time to cook dinner before tonight but right now he wasn't hungry. "Thank you, Mrs. Bean" he said opening her door helping her into her apartment. "Oh, just call me Mother Dora that's what everyone else calls me" You take care" closing her door. Tyler went into his apartment. He could hardly believe it. He put the small amount of groceries he purchased in the cabinets. He felt so proud. He went in his bedroom and fell on his bed smiling. "Sid! Wow! He was so grateful for everything. He went to sleep listening to Mother Dora humming as she cooked her cornbread for dinner.

Dal! Did Sidney say he was bringing his crew to the birthday party for granddad?

Mossy asked her while she prepared dinner. He didn't but I'm sure he will they go everywhere together" she said sounding put out. "How do you know?" "I don't but they're in town, too aren't they? "Some of them are your age, he tells us", "wouldn't know! and she left going to her room. "That girl is getting quite a mouth Desmond!" Mossy stated to him. "Can't say anything without her commenting negatively on it! 'What do you mean? Desmond had walked in to get a beer from the refrigerator before dinner and now he was discussing his sister-in-law. "She'll grow out of it" he said hurriedly making his way back to watch the big game on television.

The big day had come for grandfather John Owens birthday celebration. Mossy had decorated her home and instructed the caterers who were coming in as Desmond left where to set up the food. Mossy's brother Slovenia, Henry one of the attorney's in the Owens law firm, and Desmond had already arranged the tables for this affair. With everything in place Desmond left to go into Kansas City to get his grandfather. When Desmond arrived his grandfather was ready. He had on his brown suit and white shirt and silk tie with its' tie-bar across the broad multicolored stripes on it. His shoes were spit shine to a gloss and his handkerchief in his jacket's pocket. "Ready? Grandfather, Desmond asked walking into his small little house that was perfect for him. He could do everything for himself. Just like he wanted it. He didn't want anyone coming in invading his privacy he'd said. And what he eats he can cook himself. He had sold their large home after his wife Amelia died years ago. His grandson Desmond often talked about those visits and running hiding in the basement from his brother Sidney. He had given his favorite grandson Desmond a very nice monetary wedding gift for he and his bride's new home and for all tense and purposes he lived a content life. He got up from his recliner and turned off the news he was watching on the television. John picked up his briefcase that he always carries and his house keys in his hand. Grabbing his hat from the rack by the door. "Let's go, he said smiling as he stepped down the steps of his home. "Easy does it!" Desmond said helping him into the tall Hummer vehicle. "This is something! he said. I can see all over Kansas City from this vehicle" he joked as they rode along the highway. "Well grandfather do you feel any older?" Desmond questioned, "Well son, I tell you, when you reach a certain age in life the years after that all look the same!" And let out a big laugh. "I told Harvey, down at the recreation center where I play cards that I ride in this kind of vehicle all the time". I told him my grandson owns one!" "He's one of those doubting Thomas's saying he'd have to see it first!" John Owens is a very humble but proud man who loves his family. We're almost there! Desmond was getting more excited he had been working on this for his grandfather for a long while. Finding some of his old friends had proven to be a challenge but he and Mostalgia had managed to pull it off. They turned into the long driveway entrance to Langley Estates. "You know every time

I come this way it's prettier and prettier" he told his grandson." The trees are really growing and your landscape is very nice too" he stated. "Grandfather we used that gardener you recommended. "Wilson?" yes grandfather Wilson Hutson". Well I say, he's done a wonderful job, wonderful job, looking around at the huge yard area surrounded by a ranch style wooden fence. Getting closer they could see a crowd out front. Desmond was smiling. They hadn't even started coming when he left. His grandfather looked "what's going on?" looking at Desmond who was showing no indication that something was wrong. "Who are all of these people?" he asked. This was supposed to be a no fuss dinner with his grandson's family as always. Soon it was evident. The Hummer stopped short of the drive way and he was greeted by non other than his old pal Harvey Rollins from the recreation center. "Well now John I guess you were right! he said coming over to the very tall vehicle with John still in it. Mossy had invited all his friends from the recreation center. The vans she told Desmond hurried the guest in and left until time to pick them up. "Hi John, they yelled. There was Sally, and Lillian and Rose. Herbert and his bid partner Collins were there too! Desmond had found a couple of his old retired lawyer buddies Clint Thompkins, and Melvin Barney. "Howdy John, Clint said walking over to shake his hand. "How's life treating you sir? he asked. "Life's good! his grandfather replied. Everyone moved into the patio area that had been designated for this large gathering. The weather was perfect. And the caterers had done an awesome job of preparing a meal for the age of their guest to be served. Desmond and Mossy was pleased they were able to get about forty of Johns current an old friends and bring them together. He was having a wonderful time meeting and greeting each one. "Hi! Hi! Papa! Jordan, Valde and Maggie ran over tugging his pants leg. He was beaming as he picked each one up and held them in his aging arms giving them a kiss on the cheek. All his friends could now see all his stories were true. He does have a wonderful family and he loved them very much. "Come on now let grandfather enjoy his party" Mossy said leading the children to their sitter to play in another part of the massive yard. Soon looking out coming up the driveway were some more cars that surprised even the Owens family. Desmond kept his eyes toward the driveway as the car pulled in. As they began to get out, he noticed it was his dad and mom. "Our flight got delayed hope we're not to late" they said hurrying from the car. "Not at all" Desmond responded hugging them as they walked around to meet the others. He went back and saw another car belonging to his brother Sidney. And he had a friend with him. "MOM! DAD! They turned to see their older son Sidney. "My this is a surprise! Martha replied hugging Sidney. "Hello son". "This is a friend of mind Tyler Parsons the crews on their way he added. What a birthday this was for Mr. John Owens! His Son, and daughter-in-law, His grandsons and his granddaughter-in-law, and the great-grandchildren and of course his many closest dearest friends. Getting together eating and enjoying some soulful jazz with hugs and kisses and much love all around. As we leave this scene John is over showing his friend Harvey the inside of his grandson's Hummer.

CHAPTER FIFTEEN

It's over

Dana sat in her car anxiously waiting for Roger to come. He was meeting her in front of the hospital and she was going to have him follow her to her new home. She sat impatiently watching every light of each car that passed her by. Quickly glancing at her watch, she could see he was a half hour late already from the time they had agreed on meeting and she was getting irritated from waiting. "Ring, ring! "Yes, she said answering her cell phone. "Babe I'm sorry the freeway was backed up on 1-0-5 give me a few more minutes" he explained. I should be there" After Roger called, she settled down and before long up pulled Roger in his service vehicle beside her. He got out and came over to the window. "Hi sweetheart," Hello you, she responded. Then they shared a passionate kiss. 'Wanna get something to eat?" Roger asked "I've been driving from Waterville after getting off the plane and haven't had time to stop and eat. "Where were you coming from sweetheart? "I've been working down in Portsmouth outside of Boston" he replied. Some equipment that only our vendors carry was needed at a hospital there." "That's great Dana replied. "Great for business "But why are we standing in the street talking let's go to a restaurant! Roger stated standing by Dana's car. "Get in your car and follow me" she suggested waiting for him to get in and start his vehicle. Dana made a u turn and headed to the freeway. About a mile down the highway she took and exit off, Roger followed close behind. Then she pulled into this very upscale complex with large townhouse and gorgeous flowing lawns. Roger stopped and blew his horn. Dana waved from her window to keep coming he followed slowly behind her. She then pulled in a driveway and used her garage door opener to elevate the door pulling inside. Roger waited. "Come on in" she yelled getting out and coming over to his car "this is my home". He raised his eyebrows and pulled his car in beside hers getting out and hit the button allowing the garage door to close automatically. "Come in" she said holding his hand leading him in through the garage entrance. "Well I don't have to ask what you have been doing while I was away, he stated "this is fabulous! "What about 3000 square feet?" "Good guess it's 4,500, come in." He walked around looking at her beautiful décor and the spacious rooms. He especially like her big screen television in her den and her luxurious bedroom was fit for a queen. Roger walked over and passionately kissed her again. He picked up her tiny frame and carried her into the den and placed her on the comfy sofa. "Oh, Roger I missed you so much she said as they embrace intimately kissing each other. "I missed you too rubbing her leg upward underneath her skirt. "Hey! I thought you said you were hungry?" "I am! composing himself and getting up from the sofa. "This place is such a turn on" he said heading to the kitchen. "I've prepared dinner get your things from the car while I put it on the table" he tapped her backside as she walked away and he headed out the door to his car whistling. Dana was happy too. She skipped into the bathroom and washed her hands and changed into a more relaxing outfit. Things had already started happening and she like the way it was heading. She went back to the kitchen. The prepared food she had purchased earlier from the restaurant was in the conventional oven. She took it out to put on her best china plates and warmed it before arranging it like the chef had said to make it more inviting. She ran and lit the candles when she saw Roger coming back through the door with a suitcase. "Put it in that bedroom" she said pointing to her master suite. The other room was David's her son. Whistling carrying his suitcase he asked "do I have time for a quick shower before dinner? Sure" she said. That would give her time to prepare a fire in the fireplace. "click! the fireplace was lit. "Modern technology" she said heading back to put the wine on ice.

Ring! Ring! She could hear the water running in the shower everything was ready and she was going to join him and someone's calling. "Hello' hello! who's calling? She asked edgy. "Dana its Mollie." "Oh, Mollie how are you doing?" "I'm alive" she replied Thanks for coming by to see me last week." "Hey what are friends for" she asked. Then Mollie explained about her incident. Fredrick had left her for an even bigger woman. She had gotten too small for his taste. Mollie wore a size eighteen dress. But had very good taste in dressing herself. "I go in next week for my surgery" she told Dana. "For what Mollie? I thought everything was fine now and you had gotten over Fredrick." "That's pass! She replied "I doing this for me!" I'm going in to have bypass surgery! I'm having my stomach stapled and when I get beautiful watch out world!" Dana was happy for Mollie if it's what she wanted. Her life certainly had changed sense her facial surgery and he was in her shower and she was jawing on the phone. "Take care Mollie, we'll talk okay! Goodnight Mollie said hanging up. "Now that's right! The water was still running she quickly remove what little she had on at this point and headed into the shower to join her man before dinner.

No one recognized Tye Pee his first day back after is mini makeover. And he didn't know it was soon to be his last night at the Spot. His new hair-do and clothes made him look like a new man. But as soon as he put that horn up to his lips, they knew he was the jazzman. The small place had become incredibly over crowded and there was brawl after brawl every weekend and the police ended up shutting it down. Tye though his life was over before he begun. After four months of being somebody everything came crashing down. Sidney found him drunk lying in the little shack in back of the bar he didn't even get home to his apartment. "What now Sidney? Where do I go now? He asked looking up at him from the broken-down couch he sat on. Sidney had gone looking for him after the cops had asked everyone to leave. They were nearing the finish of the extended documentary about his life anyway. Sidney was getting ready to head back to Baltimore. He had spent six months working on a piece that was intended to be only two. He and Jessica spoke often and he saw her maybe once when he flew out a couple of days to meet her in New York. He took Tyler back to his apartment, meeting mother Dora as they entered. "Hello Tyler, "I missed you coming in these last nights" she said. He looked horrible and smelled terrible but he smiled said nothing and quickly went inside to bathe. "Excuse me mother Dora I'll talk later closing the door. She continued sitting on her small porch in front of her apartment in her rocking chair watering her very small but colorful flower garden. After a while Sidney came out of his car. He looked bewildered and he appeared tired. "Hello young man" she said. "You're the one who rented the apartment from me aren't you?" looking him from head to toe. "Yes, ma'am Sidney replied. "He's a good man, life as dealt him a bad hand more than once and I was trying to help him out," "Yes I do understand", Mother Dora responded to him. "But I have to get back home and I don't know what's going to happen to him when I leave." Sidney shared sadly. "Well we do what we can" she said "and then turn it over to Jesus." Sidney didn't respond. He as a rule didn't attend church. Maybe once or twice doing his life. But he agreed with Mrs. Bean if it was her belief because really there was really nothing else to do. "I'll be back in a while" he told her. "All right" she said and continued humming her tune. Sidney got into his car and drove downtown to the place he had went by a few months ago. Looking at the newly lighted neon sign on the building. "The Jazz Place". He walked in the floors now were glossy and it had a stage along with some small but attractively set tables close in front. It was arranged to have a very large dance floor and a white baby grand piano flanked in the corner. "Hello, a gentleman greeting him from the bar as he walked in. "My, this place has changed! Sidney said. Then looking closer and so have you! The man laughed. "Oh, you were here a few months ago when I first opened up". Yeah a few things changed" he confirmed. Sidney saw the older gentleman had premed his hair and wore it wavy all over. "What can I get for you today?" he asked. "a beer Sidney replied. He laid the coaster down and brought Sidney a beer "glass, right?" Sidney nodded. "So, how's the entertainment here?" Sidney asked. "Second to none" he said. We're still bringing in a select crowd. Business is good! Sidney hesitated for a minute. I know this great trumpet player who would love to help you bring in business" he remarked. "Trumpet player?" What's his name?" the bartender asked. "His name his Tyler' out of St. Louis. "Oh yeah, I heard about that cat! They say he can really blow". "Yes, nothing like him since the great Armstrong" Sidney voiced. "I heard he had a drinking problem though" missed a few gigs because of it must be pretty serious" he stated. "Sidney knew it was true but he had calmed down remarkable since his new image, new place and a steady income. Wasn't what he was worth by any means but for him his dignity and being able to play his horn to make people happy was rewarding enough. "Well, tell you what give him a chance on my word." Sidney said he knew he was going out on a limb. But it was something about how truly sorrowful Tyler told him he was about messing up is what he called it. After all, his hard work touched Sidney's heart. "Is he still playing over at the spot across the tracks?" he asked. Sidney was feeling pretty good he was still asking questions this was good! No! Sidney replied. "No! I thought you said this cat was good! "Then it must be that other problem got him fired." "No, no nothing like that! Sidney explained. He looked waiting for an explanation. When Sidney finished telling him honestly about the crowds and the brawls and the police closing the place down. Most of it he knew anyway from patrons but had not connected the two. He wanted nothing to do with Tyler or Sidney.

He wouldn't even let Sidney pay for the beer. "It's on me! he said walking to the back-leaving Sidney alone at the bar to walk out. "Now what, he thought? He was returning home in a week. His flight was leaving Kansas heading to Baltimore on Monday morning and he had shared with Jessica he'd be on it. Sidney got back in his car and went back to Tyler's to say goodbye. Mother Bean was still on her porch. "Well how did it go! she asked, looking as if she knew where he went. Strange as it seems Sidney somehow sensed she did anyway. "Nothing!" Sidney replied heartbroken from what the man had said. "You have a few minutes?" she asked. Sidney didn't want to get further involved in this than he already was. What could she possible want? he thought. "A few", he found himself saying. "Just a minute" she said going into her apartment and coming out with her purse. "Get Tyler, tell him to bring his trumpet!" And as Sidney went in to get Tyler telling him what she had asked, he returned to find her sitting in the front sit of his car waiting for them. They got into the car and she pointed them to the highway. Sidney drove for quite a while, fifteen maybe twenty miles down the freeway. He couldn't imagine where this lady was taking them. He didn't know why though he wasn't bothered by her at all. He was content in just following her requests. Soon she motioned for him to exit the freeway. 'Now turn right at the next light" she said to him. "There it is! Sidney and Tyler were very surprised. She had brought them to church. "Come on come on! She replied. Sidney hurried out of the car and ran over to open the passenger side- car door. Tyler got out and stood by the car. 'Get your horn" she yelled and come on! Heading as fast as she could to the door of the very large church. Sidney and Tyler followed. They helped her up the steps and into the sanctuary. They knew it was a weekday. Tuesday to be exact but lots of cars had started to gather in the lot. "Wait! Mother Dora, Sidney said what are we going to do?" "Sit! she said "just sit right there". Pointing to anywhere they wanted to sit in that large sanctuary with two upper decks and a very large stage. Sidney and Tyler quickly sat down and waited to see what Mrs. Bean was doing. She walked over to one of the gentlemen standing up front. "Oh, hello Mother Bean, how are you today?" He asked. He obviously knew her, he hugged her and kissed her on the cheek. Sidney watched like a young man learning his first lesson. Some more men and women were coming in so it got a little noisy and he was distracted from Mrs. Bean's conversation. Then Mrs. Bean came and sat beside them waiting. She told Sidney while he was gone, she had called and talk with Bishop Morrison her pastor. After about twenty minutes everyone had gather into the sanctuary. Sidney thought he was about to be a part of his first church services in a long time. He wouldn't dare asked Mother Dora who was humming one of her praises has she waited. Soon the pastor Sidney guessed asked everyone to stand. They stood and he prayed over the entire group and everyone disassembled to the back of the church through a door at the side of the stage. Then the gentlemen Mother Dora was speaking with came over to greet them. Sidney didn't know why he was so afraid but his knees were shaking. "Hello, he said extending his hand to them. "Mother Bean says we have a talented musician in our midst". He looked at Tyler and then Sidney. "Yes sir, Tyler spoke up. Sidney was already pointing at him anyway. Sidney was a very leader-oriented man but he was in awe of the minister in charge of the music and Mother Dora he felt just like a child again. 'It's nice meeting you he said to Sidney. "Come this way young man" he said beckoning for Tyler to follow him up front. "Please bring your instrument" he told him. Tyler hurried back to where we were sitting and quickly grabbed the tattered case carrying his precious trumpet. Soon the other men and women came from the back room talking and laughing and making noise. Mother Bean just sat smiling and Sidney watched still wondering what was about to take place. He looked with his mouth opened wide they all had instruments. It was the church's Orchestra. There were the stringed instruments violins, basses and a harp. The cellos had their own section on the opposite side. The horns were assembling themselves directly in front of the conductor. Sidney was finally getting the picture. The flutes were closest to the front then the clarinets and oboes. The horns and the bassoons, the trombones, trumpets including the big tuba and the drums. Sidney stood up he couldn't believe his eyes. They were all here for rehearsal for their Sunday services. The conductor asked Tyler some questions and then had him to sit down with a sheet of music on a stand in front of him. Sidney could see him nervously taking his horn from the tattered case. The conductor stood before them and tapped his baton to get everyone's attention. He started them out with a very simple melody to warm up with. Tyler could read music but he was trying to get a feel for this piece. The conductor started a few more times stopping patiently to let Tyler grasp his notes. After a few more attempts he played the entire piece with the horn section only. "Now he said, everyone together!" It was the most beautiful sound Sidney had ever heard. Mother Bean was wiping her tears and Tyler they could see was blending in well. The orchestra went over a few more pieces before ending the rehearsal. "Still holding the attention of his orchestra, the conductor turned to Tyler who was sitting off to the side of the horned section and said. "As you can see, we only have two trumpets in our orchestra, but I would be honored if you would join us as our third trumpeter. Everyone cheered, and clapped their hands. He asked him to move to the section with his group. Sidney was smiling. He could see Tyler had come home. Sidney finally got his story's end. He finally saw the missing part of Tyler's life.

Tyler played for his home church for as long as he could remember. And was very attached to his father. His mother and father brought him up in the church. And he was taught to fear God. He loved to play horned instruments and was first chair in his jr. high and high school band. Tyler played every Sunday with other musicians at the church he and his family attended. When he was a year out of high school his father was killed in and bus accident in Spokane Washington. He was on the bus too but he said God had spared him. But dealing with his father's sudden death was more than he could handle and he moved from home to live with a relative in St. Louis. Trying to forget about the pain of his father he enrolled in college after high school to fulfill his life long dream of his promise to his father. But it became difficult and he felt he had no one to talk to or confide in and he soon dropped out after 3 1/2 years of college. He then began to party and stay out late and in no time drinking liquor. His relative shared with him he had to stop or get out. Well he said he was a grown man and could do what he wanted. So, he left and after a few years of fast life he ended up on the street, no money, homeless and with no place to go. He roamed around Saint Louis he said four about five years until one day he went to get some food from a shelter and the city had closed it down. Hungry and desperate he went into a pawnshop and traded the only thing of value he had an expensive watch his mother had given him for his graduation from high school. He traded it for his trumpet so he could make a living playing at small dives around town and have a few dollars to get a meal. Tyler cried has he shared with Sidney. He knew how to read music and play an instrument before he entered middle school. Cold, hopeless and frantic he hopped a freight train and ended up in Kansas City.

The entire orchestra made him feel welcome. They looked forward to him being a part of their weekly fellowship. He shook each one's hand. Some even shared a hug of love. Tyler got into the car beaming about his new position in the orchestra. Mother Bean was pleased too. "Please keep in touch now! And when you get back to Baltimore young man you find yourself a good church home" she said to Sidney patting him on top of his hand resting on the gears shift. Sidney didn't say yes or no to Mrs. Bean's suggestion though he did join Mother Bean and her husband Lawrence for Sunday services before getting on his flight early Monday morning. She told him Tyler was up late every night practicing his music so that he would be able to play this Sunday with his orchestra. Mother Bean went right up front with the other ladies in white dresses when she entered the sanctuary looking very proud at Tyler sitting in the horn section of the orchestra. Sidney and deacon Bean sat a few rows back listening to what Sidney wrote was the greatest orchestra he had every heard. "That's how Jane Pauley introduced the story on dateline with Sidney Owens as corresponding editor.

CHAPTER SIXTEEN

Okay, fair, is fair

Justin had finally gotten two days off together to spend with Menae. They always had time for an occasional rendezvous. And most were very intimate and passion moments lasting maybe a few hours between breaks at the hospital or maybe a rare night together. Menae was all right with that but Justin wanted more. He wanted to wine her and dine her. And of course, show her off to his friends. He'd love to spend more precious time with her. Take her to classy places. He was so taken with her etiquette, the way she carried herself, she was a lady capital L. Justin said she was the total opposite of Ariel his ex-girlfriend who had to be taught by his mother Katherine. She allowed him to be a total gentleman when out with her. Everything with Ariel his ex-girlfriend had subsided. She was dating someone else and vowed to never speak with Justin or his family again. They sometimes ran into each other in the hallway of the hospital where the two worked and she would turn and continued on her way in another direction. "OKAY fairs, fair. He was feeling great with having time off and had called to invite Menae out for dinner but she hadn't returned his call. He walked around his home anxiously waiting her call. Ring, ring! "Sweetheart I apologize for not getting right back to you but I'm out of town for a few days. I should return Sunday" she said in a soft voice. "Out of town? Darling why didn't you tell me I'm off for a couple of days and I wanted to spend it with you" Justin confessed. "I m so sorry dear I'll make it you to you promise" she replied. Well what are you doing out of town?" flopping down on his sofa. "A meeting dear" one of those boring meetings" I'll tell you all about it when I get back okay sweetie. He sat talking to her for about twenty minutes. "Honey I have an early start in the morning, I have to go to sleep but I will call tomorrow." Menae I miss you! I miss you too". Hanging up leaving Justin all along in his high-rise bachelor pad. "Ring, ring, who could be calling me. Oh, it's just the doorman announcing a visitor. Before long, "Ding, dong. It was his doorbell. It's Franklin, he said he'd come by. Well he sure picked a good night for it, getting up to open the door. "Hey Justin! Franklin how are you. He wasn't alone. He had two young ladies with him "Can we come in?" he asked "Frank man what are you doing?" he asked bringing them in from the hallway. They had been partying somewhere before arriving he guessed. "This is Peaches and Chocolate. "What's your flavor?" he had been drinking. "Sit down before you fall" I told him. The ladies were holding him up. "Mind if I use your restroom? Stumbling in the direction Justin pointed in. Justin went in his kitchen and fixed a stiff pot of coffee and minutes later poured Franklin a cup to drink. Can I eat something? he asked. He was getting sick and nauseous. The only thing Justin had quick to eat was pizza that he had the night before. Peaches hurried and warmed it in the microwave and brought it back to Franklin. He consumed it down quickly and drank a seven up to settle his stomach and finished his cup of black coffee, letting out a loud burp! 'Whew that's better" he said hugging Peaches who up to now hadn't said anything. Justin sat on his chair with the two now vying for Franklin's affection. Franklin man so what are you up to?" Justin asked again. "The Mrs. makes it hard to be around her right now she's got about two weeks before she blows and I'm restless". Why don't you take one of these off my hand, so I'm free to enjoy the other" motioning for him to take Chocolate. Both girls were beautiful and sexy but it's not what Justin had in mine. 'Man, you are crazy! you know that, crazy! Justin shared. Feeling better Franklin took Peaches and went into the guest bedroom and closed the door. Chocolate asked for something to drink. Justin offered her a beer or said he could mix something for her. "No do you have soda?" she asked surprisingly. Sure, Justin smiled and jumped up to get her the soda. She sat and talked while Franklin and Peaches were behind close doors. Do you have any board games? She asked scrabble, bingo or something to past the time? It was obvious they weren't coming out soon. Justin had brought some board games.

Ariel had a love for board games too. He went into the hall closet and brought out some of them. She chose something call connect four. "It's fast and fun" she said. They sat playing and laughing, each took turns winning. May I have that drink now? she asked. She and Justin went into his kitchen and mixed up several concoctions experimenting for taste. No! try this he said getting her to drink from his glass. My turn she said mixing something for Justin. After several drinks they finally settle on a margarita with lots of salt and headed back to the living room. She tickled him as they walked in "I won more games than you Justin! He tickled her back she giggled that tickles she said. Is this your place? "Yes, let me show you! he said proud of it. "You have seen my kitchen, den and living room he said walking her through his spacious home. That room as you know is occupied. "This is very good! she said sipping from her glass. And this is my master suite. Wow! Your bed is gorgeous! Do you ever sleep in it?" she teased very flirtatiously. Kat his mom had recommended a decorator to decorate the place. She had picked out everything for him. 'Thank you I'll have to tell my decorator" he said. And over here is my master bathroom" he acknowledged. "My look at that tub! May I? she asked removing her shoes and stepping in it with her clothes on. She sat down and "there's so much room! and look at the hardware is that brushed pewter? she asked. Kat had obviously picked that too. "Yes, my decorator" he responded. "Okay help me up please" she giggled holding Justin around his neck. He put his hand on the faucet to brace himself while he lifted her from the tub. He had finished his drink and sat the glass on the vanity counter. She was laughing because obviously both had experimented with the liquor and both were a little tipsy. "Ready," he said. "Wait why do they call you Chocolate?' he laughed. You don't look chocolate to me!" they both laughed. "My hair silly! Justin guessed a brunette. "Oh okay, ready! When he braced himself lifting her, he bumped the faucet turning it on and she screamed. "Oh! Oh! Oh! Getting quickly up from the showers cold water shooting from its shower head running in the tub. With Justin's help THEY MANANAGED TO TURN IT OFF. But they were soaked. They stood there dripping and laughing at the incident. He tickled her again. "Stop she said teasing him back with a tickle. Then as he was tickling her, she caught him and held him tight to keep him from continuing. She rubbed up close to him and he kissed her. She kissed him back. Wet clothes went flying everywhere. Justin picked her up and carried her to his bed. He turned back the covers and closed the door.

Billy had called Desmond apologizing for not getting by as promised. He spent time with his friend Winnie Hathaway he explained and the time got away. "Winfred how is the lady these days? Desmond asked. "Oh, Winnie is still Winnie busy lady dealing with all those congressional issues but as you know she can hold her own. "That's the Winnie I know! So, how's Mossy and the children?" Billy asked after explaining why he wasn't coming by for a visit this time. Their good! but you have to come and view the new location of the law firm. We've been there a few months and it was a good move, Desmond affirmed. "You probably have more room than the whole old building you were in?" Billy asked "Yeah! and running water too! he joked. Well man let's see" Billy said looking over his schedule. "You know being a single parent you almost have to live on two planets. The activities, field trips, preparing food, getting him off to school it's a full-time job all by itself" he teased. "How's that going are you handling it okay?" Desmond asked being a father of three active not yet in school toddlers. "You know I'm enjoying it. His mom lightens the load quite a bit when I need it." Billy confessed. "Well that's good". So how is she doing with all this?" I mean coming back and having all this family not to mention Justin your brother." "She seems to be doing just fine," she moved into a bigger place and I have to get by and see it. Court purposes you know, but I'm sure if Dana is living in it it's fabulous" he replied. 'See there's always something! I confided. "Don't get huffed, Desmond replied. I know Jillian is hard to replace but it's been a few years are you seeing someone else yet? he asked. "I know! Almost five years" Billy said sadly. And you're right no one will ever replace Jillian in my heart" "I do date a little. She's a secretary here at the firm. Her name is Annie Clark but there's other's really no bells there" he confided. "Well that's good to know you are seeing someone! I know man, I know! "Okay let's see! Billy said snapping back to reality. "Let's see David gets his next break in two months for about a week. He's spending the summer with my parents this year and boy is he excited". He loved it there". "Speaking of your parents, how are they?" Desmond inquired. "Their wonderful!

"Please give them my love" he said. I will do that man. I'm sure they will appreciate the fact you thought about them" They are off visiting friends in Norfolk mom tells me though I will give them your hello. We finally concluded with rescheduling a visit that I wasn't going to miss.

Back at home Billy went right back to work getting out some briefs he had put aside earlier. He had also done some work on a case that went to trial. But since he was on vacation, he chose to assist Baines a fellow attorney with the pre-trial instead of taking the reigns totally. Ring! Ring! "William Parker?" "Billy my man it's Justin how's things! "Well Justin how does it feel to be another year older?" "Good man, good! "Look you need to make and appointment with me after your shindig to talk about some legal business" I shared. "Legal business?" What is this about?" Justin asked a bit alarmed. "Hey just say, your financial troubles will soon be behind you" Billy responded laughing. "Okay this is sounding good" Justin reasoned. Paying for medical school pretty much emptied the bank not to mention his new lifestyle he was rapidly starting to enjoy. "Anyway, things are all set for this Saturday night! Be there or be square, Billy teased with Justin his younger brother. See you then bro! He said hanging up. Okay back to work. "Annie could you please get me the Murray file Clifford and I are working on" he asked calling from his speakerphone in his office.

Katherine and Ellen had gone shopping earlier in the month for their gowns for Justin's big birthday bash! It was to be held at the Hyatt Imperial room downtown and Katherine was excited. "I wonder if David will be there? she said looking through the gowns at Norfields the elegant posh and did I mention expensive dress boutique in Maine, Ellen Pelsner her best friend asked. "David? David who?" "Oh, he's a friend I knew along time ago' she implying there was no connection. She was not about to tell her the whole truth. "Now! This will surely be a knock out! she said pulling out a chiffon black number by Valentino. "I want this gown to be a show stopper she kept sharing with her shopping buddy Ellen who had settled on a Versace' and was headed to the counter to make her purchase. 'Here it is! She raved. "This is it! Kat voiced. It was elegant black gown by McClintock a form-fitting bodice with a halter neckline with rhinestones that sparkled. "I must try this on! She said going over to the fitting room hurriedly. They were on their lunch hour and time was running short. "Hurry! Hurry Ellen said. "Mason will have a fit if we're late again. She was the boss's secretary where they work. Katherine quickly went into the large mirrored room. She put on the dress and "Oh! Yes, this is it! Pulling her hair up off of the shoulders. "Watch out ladies! She danced around a bit then quickly took it off before Ellen could get back to see it. "You've taken it off already?" she stated coming over to see what it looked like on. "Yes, it's going to be fine" she replied. Kat felt she was going to be the bell of the ball. Well ballroom anyway! Paying for her purchase with her credit card and leaving the store with their lunch in brown bags in hand.

Sidney was finally back in Baltimore. He had met and spoken with Mr. Finister who was very pleased with his story. The finally finished project was due in a month. Sidney was sending a crew of cameramen back to the church to capture the true spirit of the orchestra. He chose a month to give Tyler a chance to really settle in. He was proud of him too. Not really wanting to get involved in too much today he stayed around the station making busy work most of the day. He even did a spot for the noon report for another reporter who was out in the field. J.T. one of the anchors at the station and he were getting together to celebrate the success of the project and Jessica was coming too. Leaving the station headed home Jessica called. "Hello sweetie I can't wait to see you! "The feeling's mutual I'll meet you at your place okay. She didn't answer. "Jessica do you prefer to meet me at my place?" "Yes, you go home, and I'll meet you at your place" she agreed. "Okay sweetheart, see you soon" turning his car heading in a different direction." Sidney was glad she had called he got in late and chose to stay at a hotel near the airport instead of driving home. He hadn't told anyone he was coming home Monday because he had said it so many times over the months and changed his mind due to his story so few would believe him anymore. When he arrived, it was very late so he got a room near the airport and rode into work from there. Walking into his suite FOR THE FIRST TIME SINCE RETURNING TO BALTIMORE he got a big surprise! Someone had been partying and the house was a mess. And that's putting it mildly. His jaw dropped! What the!!! has been going on! He walked over some clothes getting to his telephone. "Ring, ring, "Hello" Jessica answered. "What have you done to my home?" he asked furious about its condition. "Oh, dear I forgot to tell you I had a few friends over while you were gone" Doing what! he screamed and for how long? He added. "Now, now, Sid don't go getting your nerves rattled that's what cleaning people get paid for! She said jokingly. But Sidney wasn't laughing! He slammed the phone down disconnecting the line. He was tired, mad, and angry as he sat looking at his very chic bachelor pad all torn apart. He walked around angrily picking up clothes and emptying ashtrays from each table. Then he dialed asking management to send a cleaning lady to his apartment suite address. He got his coat and walked out the door. He jumped in his car. "Calm down Sidney he had to tell himself after almost hitting two parked cars leaving the lot. He moved quickly across the freeway headed to Jessica's penthouse downtown. Arriving safely, he talked to himself all the way on the elevator. 'Keep your cool Sid". He knocked at the door and stood for about a minute or two no one answered. Jessica! I know you're in there open this dam door! he yelled. Seems everyone opened they're doors in the suites building except Jessica! He knocked again banging this time! "Keep it down! some yelled from down the wide hall. Getting even more frustrated he was about to kick the door when it opened. It was Marty and one or two of the band members. 'Hey mate!" he said seeing it was Sidney. Sidney looked at him and asked, "where is Jessica?" I know she's here I just spoke with her" he stammered. Marty sat back down with another gentlemen who was doing God's knows what with a mirror on the cocktail table. Marty nodded his head toward the bedroom in back. Sidney looked around carefully before preceding down the hall of the four thousand square foot condo. All the doors were shut so he knocked at the first door nothing. Then he knocked at the door that was ajar and it opened. He couldn't believe his eyes! He turned and started to leave but decided to go back to confront her. 'Jessica! calling her by name. "What are you doing? And for how long has this been going on?" His heart was hurting, angry and he was near crying. He had waited for this. He questioned himself. Is that why she acted so funny when I came to see her in New York? He turned and walked out the room and slammed the door. Jessica jumped from the bed slightly dressed running out the door behind him and Bridget followed her OUT THE DOOR. By the time she reached the parking lot Sidney was gone. Bridget never returned either. She walked back into her penthouse crying. "She made me Sidney, she made me! holding her hands over her face weeping into them. What happened darling? Marty asked coming from her kitchen with beer in hand. "I hate you! she said. "I'm in love with Sidney, I shared that with you over and over again! You should not have let him in! she insisted. "You didn't seem to be thinking of him last night or last week or any of the weeks before" came Marty's very British response.

"I hate you! Jessica yelled and stormed into her room. After awhile she came out to find everyone had left including Marty. Jessica was determined to find Sidney so that she could explain. She really missed him but the crowds that were around her influenced her and she fell into the lust of everything going on. The constant partying, and drinking, and yes sex and drugs. "I'm so sorry Sidney I didn't mean to hurt you! she thought sitting in her penthouse suite looking around waiting for the car she had requested. She got up and took a long bath and got dressed. She was headed to find Sidney and win him back at any cost. She went out the back of her penthouse as not to be noticed by anyone. In case Marty and his group were down in the lobby. She had her limo driver take her to Sidney's apartment and told him to leave she was spending the night. The doorman didn't ask questions he knew who she was, and she had been there plenty of times with Sidney and without Sidney. "Good evening Ms. Strassberg he said seeing her come into the building as the limo drove away. "Good evening is Mr. Owens in?" Yes, he is he went up about an hour or two ago" he said. "Thank you, sir, please see that we are not disturbed" she asked handing him a large bill in his hand. She waved as she stepped on the elevator and headed up to win her man's heart back. She knocked lightly on the door before using her key to enter. The maid had been in and the place looked immaculate. The water in his bathroom was running and she walked in and made herself at home. After a while Sidney came walking out of his room with his robe on to see Jessica sitting with her feet upon the sofa eating a bowl of ice cream. "Jessica what are you doing here? he yelled, get out. "Honey you don't mean that! She said "let's talk" "There is nothing to talk about! How could you? how long has it been going on? How long have you been playing me for a fool? Dragging me all over television and from city to city like a little puppy? 'No Sidney you're wrong! Jessica screamed franticly getting up coming toward Sidney. "No please don't you come over here, I never want to touch you again" Go back and sleep with Bridget! He was angry. She ran over to him and he pushed her back against the table. "Jessica, just go! You disgust me! He sat in his chair with his arms folded. She picked herself up and went over to him again, pleading and crying for him to take her back. Get out Jessica! Get out now! He was furious and pushed her again. She fell into the shelf and put a small cut in her forehead. "Please Jessica just go! He pleaded. Then the doorbell rang. She hurried to the door to open it. It was only the maid who had cleaned the room earlier. She had stopped by to see if Mr. Owens needed anything else tonight. "He walked over and said everything was fine. He was speaking only of the suite. The maid looked at the blood on Jessica's face. "Oh, it's just a scratch! Jessica said we're fine closing the door. Trying to be calm he said "Jessica you have to go and go now! gathering her things putting then in her hand and forcing her out the door into the well lighted hallway. "NO! Sidney no! she kicked and screamed. The maid who was coming from another room saw her standing out banging on his door. Walking back over to Jessica she asked, "are you alright madam?" "Oh, just a little misunderstanding" Jessica replied I'm fine". "Here madam, handing her a Kleenex to wipe the blood that was screaming from her forehead now. "Thank you" she said. She noticed other doors were closing back also as the maid made her way down the wide hall. Jessica fumbled around in her purse until she found her key. She opened the door and started to walk in. Sidney quickly grabbed her and was pushing her out the door. She was screaming and kicking as on lookers watched the disagreeing going on at the door. "No Sidney I'm not leaving. "I'll kill you Jessica if you don't leave here now!" he shouted. She had pushed every button Sidney had. She had hurt him, belittled him, and betrayed him with another woman. He was in love and she broke the trust. And right now, he wanted only for her to leave! The other residents had stopped being inconspicuous and were standing in the hall watching Jessica Strassberg scream and beat and kick the door in. She was not going to let Sidney close the door. She scratched him and bit him until he conceded and let her in to at least save some of his dignity and respect in the building. This is certainly going to be front-page news he thought. Residents were taking pictures as the raucous was going on right in front of them. Sidney couldn't believe this was happening. He backed away from the door. She walked in battered and bruised up closing the door behind her sitting on the sofa breathing hard. "Jessica this is foolish and if you won't leave then I will". He quickly put on his clothes and left out the back entrance. He was not going to show his face around this building tonight not after what just happened, so he exited out the back entrance and got in his car leaving Jessica alone in his suite. She dialed someone on the phone and shared she was spending the night at Sidney's not to worry. "Good night! She got ready for bed putting on Sidney's favorite piece of lingerie. He'll cool off" she reasoned lying in bed going to sleep. Tomorrow everything will be normal" After an HOUR Sidney returned passing his doorman who noticed the scratches and bruises as he went hurrying back up to his apartment suite. But after seeing Jessica asleep in his bed he gathered some clothes from the closet and exited back out through the back to hopeful go and get a good night's sleep.

Sidney woke up the next morning. He had stayed in a small motel a few miles from where he lived. It was clean but certainly not what he was used to. All this place could boast about was clean sheets! He gathered his things put them in his car and went looking for some coffee. It was earlier than he had gotten up in a long time, so he really needed his coffee fix. Shivering a bit from the early morning cold because he hadn't brought a jacket he hurried to a coffee shop down the sidewalk about thee blocks. He parked and got out walking in and sat at the bar. The waiter whispered to the cook behind the counter. "Sidney looked as they seem to be whispering about him and all he wanted was coffee and he'd be on his way. The small television was on the news, but he was to far away to make out what story was being run. "Coffee please? he asked getting the waiter behind the counter's attention. He brought the coffee over and put it down and kept staring at Sidney. "Thanks" Sidney said. He was probably looking bad with all his scratches and bruises. He had forgotten his hair comb and other toiletries he used in the morning as well. All he was hoping is that when he gets back home Jessica and everything, she was about is gone, he thought drinking his hot coffee. Feeling uncomfortable about all the stares and whispers he moved over to a table in the corner. Now he was close enough to see the small television screen. "They were now flashing a picture of him saying he was wanted for the murder of the music diva Jessica Strassberg! "What! Sidney couldn't believe it! He jumped up from the small table knocking the cup to the floor! The cup broke and shattered all over the floor, but he didn't stop until he reached his car parked out front. Forgetting he had left his cell phone in his suite he looked franticly for it to call J.T. He had left his overnight bag with dirty clothes and everything in the coffee shop and drove toward his suite. They had the building cordoned off. "There he is! Someone shouted noticing his car pull up. Soon everyone surrounded him was saying it. There he is! Many of the on lookers were holding him so that he couldn't run away. "NOT THAT, That WAS ON HIS MIND. Then a detective he guessed walked over in a gray color suit and asked who he was. "Sidney Owens" he replied. Sidney Owens you're wanted for questioning in the murder of Ms. Jessica Strassberg. They put his hands behind his back cuffing him and another led him to a patrol car "You have the right to remain silent. Anything....

CHAPTER SEVENTEEN

Birthday Bash

Everyone had started arriving at the elegant Hyatt Hotel. Billy had reserved the Imperial Room there for Justin's twenty-seventh birthday party. There were limousines pulling up to the front letting out passengers and the valet was very busy after parking the Lamborghini at the front entrance as he entered. Billy got out of his Jaguar and handed his keys to one of the valets noticing a Mercedes Benz and Maserati pulling in behind him. The valets were very busy with all the invited guest's expensive automobiles. Billy had gotten there early to go over again the menu for the evening and get the live band settled in. Annie Clark had come along with him tonight as his date and she assisted him with last minute details. "Thanks Annie" for all your help,' "It's not a problem you know I like social events" she replied. They moved around the very large ballroom making sure the names were in place for each assigned table and all details were followed. "William I'm going to go and change into my dress for tonight" Annie said seeing a few guests starting to arrive. "That's fine! he responded walking over to give some requested songs of music to the musicians. Hi! Two of Justin intern buddies from work were among the first to arrive. "Hello, Billy replied extending his hand. "I'm William Parker" Justin's older brother." Both looked at each other noticing the difference in nationality right away. "Rob, Charles" they said individually shaking his hand. "Oh, it's a long story! Billy replied. "Get Justin to share it with you." but do enjoy yourselves tonight" he said turning moving away to someone else coming in trying to find their assigned table. Hello! He said again, assisting a couple to their assigned table. After awhile the person who had volunteered to show or escort the guests to their seats had arrived. Katherine Heller and her friend Ellen with her husband Mark "Well hello" Billy stated seeing her come into the ballroom. "I'm William Parker and you must be Katherine! She stopped and looked at him curiously. "Now how would you know that? she asked in a matter of fact tone. "No offense meant but Justin described you to a T." "Oh! she said William Parker, David and Tetra's son?" "Yes, I replied extending my hand. "One in the same I believe" shaking her hand. "I'm so sorry this is my friend Ellen and her husband Mark Pelsner" introducing the guests who had come in with her. Soon another man came over and joined them. She turned and locked arms with him. "This is my date Dan Harold". Please to meet each of you". "May I give you this guest list and you can show the guest their assigned seating?" Billy asked. She had volunteered. he could have hired someone on the Hyatt staff to do it. They were doing everything else! But it was not his job to upset his brother's mother, so he dropped a friendly reminder and walked away. The room started to fill up. Dana and her date Roger who just happened to be in town came in. Katherine now doing what she loved meeting and greeting people gave them their seat assignments and moved to the entrance where a steady flow of guests were coming in. Annie came out looking lovely in her Vera Wang white gown walking around on Billy's arm meeting many of the guests. Her long blonde hair hung to her waist and swayed has she walked arm in arm around the room with him. "Hello! Dana said seeing Annie and Billy walk by their table. "Oh, hi it's good to see you two here! When did you arrive? he asked looking at Dana. "We haven't been here to long' she replied. "You know Roger Haskell?" "We met briefly, pleased to see you again, William Parker" extending the hand. And this is Annie Clark my date for the evening. "Pleased to meet you," Dana said shaking her hand along with Roger. "Might I take this time to say you look lovely! "Thanks Billy so do you" she smiled. Dana wore a gown by J. Purcell with beautiful shimmering diamond earrings to accent her stunning face. Giving a friendly wave they moved on to other guests of his who had come to the party. Katherine moved back to her table walking slowly so that onlookers would get the full affect of her lovely McClintock gown. The rhinestones on its haltered bodice sparkled against the bright lights in the room. She appeared to be floating in mid-air has she crossed the floor heading to sit if only for a moment at her table. Dan and Mark were at the bar getting drinks for their ladies.

The band was all set up and ready to start playing. "Where's the birthday boy!" someone shouted. Billy looked at his watch and he guessed a few other guests looked at their watches also. He should be here, Billy thought looking again at his Rolex on his wrist. The caterers were impatiently standing waiting to serve tables and Justin was late. Then suddenly there was a rush of noise coming from the hallway. "It was the man of the hour 'Justin Parker and date Menae Sanchez walking in fashionably late. Heavy on fashion! Justin was wearing a three-piece cashmere suit with a silk tie. His lovely date delighted herself in a gown by Klein that was royal blue and covered in dazzling rhinestones to the floor. The band struck up the music. "Let the party began! Someone yelled. Billy went over to speak and greet his brother. "Justin! Walking up giving him a big hug. "Thanks, big brother for letting me into your world" he said "sincerely thanks" he whispered as they embraced in front of the now filled room. Billy reached over and extended a hug to his lovely date as well. As soon as the caterers knew the honored guest had arrived, they began serving the meal. The waiters who were serving hoer durves and French Cuvee champagne upon arrival in the foyer for the guests before entering had now moved to the inside of the Imperial ball room. They were putting expensive bottles of Cristal Champagne at each table. And the festivities were in full swing! The waiters hurried around from table to table with fresh greens with vinaigrette dressing for salads. The main menu was a succulent sirloin steak or baked salmon served with diced red potatoes and a bread choice. They moved quickly to get everyone served while those in the partying mood stayed on the dance floor. With everyone still being served a hush of only conversation came over the room as each sat down from dancing. What a great meal sat in front of each one. With a meal served for everyone they ate together enjoying the great meal and conversation. For dessert they served a bowl made from a coconut filled with assorted seasonal fruit, Strawberries, grapes, pineapple, melons. "This IS GREAT! Justin said beginning to enjoy himself more now after eating. Justin requested a dessert sweet called a lemon tart, and what party would be without birthday cake. WOW! Justin got up and thanked his, family and all his guests for coming. He acknowledged his mother Katherine Heller and Billy. "This is my brother William Parker" bringing them both up front and giving each a hug. Billy gave a toast to the birthday boy and the party was underway.

The band played an assorted arrangement of music for the mostly under thirty crowd, though all ages and I mean everyone got into the spirit. 'Come on mom" it's our turn" Justin said coming to her table reaching for her hand. He made his rounds dancing with all the women. Menae didn't mind she danced with the guys who asked, and everyone enjoyed the lively friendly atmosphere of the music. Ellen and Mark were enjoying themselves too. They had shared with Katherine they were hoping for a good time it had been a long time since they were out dancing. Dan wasn't letting anything dampen his spirits he was a live wire dancing with all the young women who said yes to his request for a dance. It was a wonderful party and when the clock struck 12:00 the band had just begun their second set. The bartender had restocked the shelves, and no one was in a hurry to leave. Everyone relaxed and enjoyed themselves to the highest for they knew from the invitations that each invited guest had a reserved room to spend the night. That's right Billy had reserved and paid for a room for each couple or guest of Justin's one hundred guests that attended his very fun and very lively birthday bash!

CHAPTER EIGHTEEN

I'm having a bad dream

Desmond woke up to his telephone ringing. He looked over at his clock that read five thirty. Shaking his head to clear his thoughts he answered hearing. "Desmond, I need you! the voice said. Desmond still a bit sleepy could not distinguish who it was, but asked. Sid is that you?" "Yes Desmond, I'm in trouble" he confided. He now had Desmond's attention. He had just left Kansas City two days ago what could have happened in that short time and to Sidney! "Trouble Sid, what kind of trouble could you possible been in where you need my help?" he questioned. Sidney was always the "squeaky clean one". Trouble can't be that serious Desmond thought. "Desmond I just need you to come to Baltimore please! Okay but you are scaring me what kind of trouble are you in? he kept asking. Sidney couldn't bring himself to say it because he couldn't believe it himself. She was alive when I left her. Alive! He exclaimed. "Where ARE YOU Sidney, are you hurt?" Only his heart and he was so ashamed. He hadn't done this horrible thing to Jessica. He may have felt that way because of what she had become. But he would never hurt her he loved her. He hated the very thing that caused her to betray him, but he'd never kill her. Desmond I'm in jail" he finally said. "Say no more! I'm on my way". I'll call and get the details and I'm on the next plane out" Desmond added "hang in there Sid!" Desmond jumped from his bed and ran into the bathroom turning on the shower. "You're getting up early! Mossy said not being disturbed by the telephone but the showers running water woke her up. Yes! I have to get a flight out to Baltimore, Sidney called." Sidney! he just left is he hurt or something?" "No, at least I don't think so!" Well what's wrong? She questioned. "He says he needs me! he yelled heading into the shower with Mossy still asking questions. "He needs you! she had now moved to the bathroom talking loudly through the shower's door. "Yes, he says he's in trouble and he needs me." What! Mossy teased "a speeding ticket! Probably you no Sidney but he's in jail! He said stepping out of the shower as Mossy finished brushing her teeth. Jail?" she repeated walking in turning on the television and crawling back in bed. Desmond dried off with his big fluffy white bath towel and wrapped it around his waist walking back into the master suite. Mossy had the remote flipping through the channels looking for something of interest when she heard Jessica Strassberg. Desmond was standing at his closet and putting on his underwear deciding what suit he was putting on for today for his flight. "Honey here's some gossip about Sidney's lady-friend she said. "Oh, what premier is she attending now?" he asked buttoning up his shirt. Then she heard Jessica Strassberg was found dead early this morning at the Exclusive Suites Estates the upscale condominiums in Baltimore. A maid coming in to start her daily shift found her lifeless body in one of the bedrooms. Detectives say the apartment belonged to her journalist boyfriend Sidney Owens. He has been arrested on murder charges pending an investigation. Desmond turned around quickly. "Turn it up Mossy! he stated wanting to hear clearly. He stood there in shock and listened to the whole story. Mossy was crying silently sitting in bed. He turned around looking at Mossy and took a deep breath. "Mossy please pack my suitcase, I have some calls to make before my flight." "Please call mom, she probably knows already just let her know I'm find and I'm headed to Baltimore and I will meet Dad there" he kissed his wife and headed to his study

The news was all over the television. Every station from coast to coast was talking about the journalist who's being accused of Jessica Strassberg's murder. All the radio stations were playing her songs. She was a big icon in the music industry. The media had every inch of the story covered. From Sidney's childhood to his work at the local station in Baltimore. And Sidney sat in a Baltimore jail waiting to talk with his lawyer.

"Mother Dorrance, Mother Dorrance, Tyler said running into her apartment. 'Look! look he said turning her television on the news. "Now why are you turning my gospel network" she asked? 'It's Sidney he's in trouble! He spoke very loudly. "Sidney! she sat straight up in her big chair and listened. "I was at home practicing and I had and urge to turn on the set. I talked myself out of it for about an hour" he confessed. But something kept saying turn on the set" he told her. "And when I did, they had Sidney's face all over it. "Oh my God! she said after hearing the charges. "That young man just left here a few days ago and was heading home. See how busy Satan is! she said getting up going to her phone. "Who are you calling Mother Dorrance? Tyler asked. He had run out of his apartment with his trumpet still in his hand. "First I'm calling Bishop Morrison over at the church then I'm calling a prayer meeting! she said dialing her phone.

Desmond called Billy his friend in Maine who was already trying to call him. Desmond asked if he would come to Baltimore. "Let me get David squared away" he said "notify my office and I'll be on a flight out today" he told him. "Thanks man. Billy as well as the whole nation had seen the airing of today's top story that was being televised.

Dalmatia watched crying holding her pillow as she sat in the middle of her bed. She wasn't going to the university, she told Mossy when she came knocking on her door when she didn't see her for breakfast. "Ring, ring, Hello, Mossy said answering her phone. "Mossy this is John, is Desmond in?" he asked. No grandfather John he's on his way to see Sidney! "How are you doing?" she asked. I'm all right I guess" he said. "You sound tired, was Emily by yesterday?" "She was, I didn't sleep well last night, it was probably something I ate" he shared with her. Oh, she replied. Grandfather John I'm not going into the office today Henry and our associates can handle it. Why don't you come and spent the day with me?" she suggested. "Are you sure, I don't want to get in your way" he said. "I'll pick you up in and hour okay." Okay! John said happily. He was so worried after he heard the story that started airing at about five o'clock, he thought he couldn't think about anything else. And she knew for him to worry like that wasn't good.

Dana was up getting breakfast when Billy came to her door. She looked at her watch. it was now 6:30 and she still had on her robe. She walked over and looked at the monitor that records the entrance of her home. Seeing who it was she opened the door. "Hi, did something happen?" You're here early" allowing them to enter. "Why are you two out at this hour in the morning?" she asked puzzled. "Good morning Dana" Billy said coming in and standing in her foyer. David gave a groggy hi and had gone to his room and got into bed. "I apologize for coming before I called but this is an emergency! "What happen! What happen! She asked going over to the sofa in her den. "Apparently you haven't had the news on." I haven't Billy just tell me! she insisted. "Jessica Strassberg was found dead last night. he acknowledged. "Jessica Strassberg the singer! Yes, he said. AND!!! She was the girlfriend of Desmond's brother Sidney and they have arrested Sidney Owens as a suspect in the murder" What! oh my God! She got up pacing around her house. She looked in on David and came back. "So, you're going to help Desmond?" she said rubbing her fingers through her hair and thinking back. "Yes Dana" she sat on a chair and started to cry. "Billy came over and hugged her "Don't cry Dana" I'm sure Desmond wouldn't have call if he were not sure of his innocence" he told her. "I know but so many lives will be effected." I'm so sorry, please give Desmond my love" she said sitting up wiping her eyes then added, "I do understand." Billy got up from the sofa "Right now I can't say how long I'll be gone, but I'll call everyday and speak with David". We've gotten use to talking with each other and I don't want to lose that" he affirmed. "Okay" she said wiping her eyes. He went in David's room and kneeled by his bed and gave his sleeping son a big hug. Getting up he then looked around for a moment quietly. Dana came in to see him standing over in the corner praying as not to disturb David from his sleep. She returned to the den and waited turning on the large screen television. After a while he came out of the bedroom. "Dana, I have to go; I have a plane to catch, if you need anything you call me" he was wiping back tears too. Dana walked him out through the living rooms foyer and they embraced connecting regarding the situation. Then he walked out and Dana closed the door. Billy had contacted his office and let them know where he was. He would call Annie later when she got in and refer his clients to other associates and brief them on the cases he was working on. For now, he was headed to the airport on a flight to Baltimore to meet his best friend. He wanted to see him but not this way. He thought also about Dana and what she must be feeling after losing her parents this way. He parked his car in long-term parking he could always change later if needed and walked in to board his flight.

Justin was sitting at home after a short shift at the hospital when his doorman called up notifying him, he had a visitor. It was Chocolate and she was by herself. "Send her up he said. 'He hadn't really spoken with her since she Franklin and Peaches crashed in a month or two ago. "Come in he said seeing her at the door. "Hi do you remember me?" she asked shyly. "Yes, I do Justin said showing her in to the chic den of his home. "Have a sit." "thank you, "So what brings you by? he asked. "I came by to apologize for few a weeks ago" she said. "Well there was nothing to apologize for" Justin responded we're both adults! "For just dropping in on you and disturbing your tranquility" she stated. "Oh, don't worry about it" Justin said "can I get you something to drink? It was only about 1:15 in the afternoon. "Soda or coffee I mean! "Nothing for me, I just finished lunch and got up the nerve when I saw you come into the building to come over." "I'm headed back to work" "Oh do you work around here he asked curiously. That wasn't discussed in their last meeting. "Two blocks that way" she said pointing with her hand. "I work at the West Maine Bank." "Bank huh! Justin teased. "And what do you do for the bank?" thinking she was making it up. "I'm the branch manager for this particular branch" she shared looking again at her watch. 'AND you saw me come into the building from two blocks away?" he teased looking at her. "No silly, I bought a suite in this building. I was so impressed when I saw yours. I came over here first thing that Monday morning and acquired one for myself. I have been trying to come over before now but you never seem to be in" she said getting up from his sofa. "My schedule at the hospital is rather hectic to say the least." But I'm glad you caught me. "And I guess I should say "Welcome neighbor". "Thanks! she said heading to the door. "Oh, and the name is Rae" walking out leaving Justin to stand and wonder about all he had gotten wrong about his girl. He'd have to pay her a visit in the very near future to apologize too!

Desmond was the first of the three to arrive at the jail in Baltimore. His dad Leron Owens wasn't to far behind him. Desmond had got all of the legalities out of the way and was waiting to see his brother when is dad came up. "Hello son giving him a big fatherly hug "Have you seen him yet?" No dad I'm waiting though I know they have not formerly charged him with murder! Leron sat back hard on the wooden bench behind him. He put his head down, how could this have happened" I had spoke with Sidney and he was so pleased with that project he had in Kansas and now this" he shook his head. "I know dad, I called William Parker to come also." Desmond shared seeing the state his dad was in thought it best if he just stay in the background. Desmond knew he wasn't going to keep him away. So, he was going to ask Billy to be his brother's attorney. "William Parker? Someone I know? he asked. "Yes, dad Billy" oh little Billy. yeah! well I guess he's all grown up now, just like you." he took a deep breath. I'm getting older now son. But I never thought I'd see this day! "My own son." Leron was clearly shaken by this incident. Desmond I' going down the hall where I can call your mother to let her know I have arrived." She's been calling my cell phone constantly. So, when you get in please let me know" he said walking off toward a quieter area to call. Desmond was sitting waiting and getting very impatient of waiting for them to bring Sidney out. Hey man! Desmond was reading some legal papers and was startled when Billy came and tapped him on the shoulder. "Oh, thanks for coming" he said getting up to embrace his friend. "So, have you spoken with him yet?" "No, I've been waiting about and hour. They have not formerly charged him now so I don't think there's going to be a problem getting bail. "Right! Billy said the wheels had begun to roll around in his head. Mr. Owens" an officer said "you may come this way" leading them into an integration room. Desmond and Billy walked behind the officer. He stopped and opened the door. "Who are you? he asked stopping Billy short of going in. "William Parker one of his attorneys" he replied showing his identification of proof. "Come on in" looking at Desmond for confirmation. They sat down and then Sidney came through another door. His hair was dry and looked scruffy. His five o' clock shadow was almost a beard and he looked forlorn in that orange jumpsuit. He walked in ashamed to face his brother. "Are you all right?" Desmond asked grabbing his hand before the embrace. "His look said it all. He just wanted to be out of this place. "You remember Billy" he asked him. Sidney shook his head indicating yes. 'I'm so sorry you had to come here for me" he finally said. But I called you because I didn't do this," I have never killed anyone in my life" he said. "Good! Desmond put both feet on the floor and sat up tall. Billy took out a tablet and began to ask questions. "Okay Sid, run us through what happened that night. Desmond turned his small recorder on. The homicide detectives were walking pass the glass window as they sat and talked about that night. Sidney told them about how he came and found his place in a mess and went over to Jessica's to confront her. But said he left her at her place with her band members and a lady friend. About and hour or so Jessica came back to my place. How she got there I don't know. When I got out of my shower she was sitting on my sofa, Sidney informed them. We scuffled because I was trying to make her leave and she wouldn't leave. Then what happened? Billy asked. "Things escalated and moved outside the door. "Were there any witnesses to this? Desmond asked. "Yes! Unfortunately, all up and down the hall they were coming out looking" So this got pretty serious?" It did get very serious but not death serious. She just wanted in and I was saying no! So then what happened. After I saw she was not going to go away, I conceded and let her in. "Did you two talk then? No, but I told her if she didn't leave I would and so I packed a bag but when I got to my car, I found out I had left it. "Where did you go? About a mile or two down the street from where I live. "Were you there all night?" "No, I had left my apartment in such a haste I didn't take any clothes so I came back to the apartment to find Jessica asleep in my bed." I got the packed bag and left. I didn't know about a murder until I heard it the next day on television. Desmond got up and was moving around. "How did you know she was sleeping when you came back? Because Jessica snores, and she was snoring loudly! he added. Now looking at his police report they say she had bruises all over her body? Billy informed reading from the documents in front of him. "It was probably from all the kicking and clawing she was doing to come in earlier but she was alive when I left, he concluded. Soon someone knocked on the door opening it. "He had an overnight styled bag in his hand" He introduced himself as one of the homicide detectives on the case. "Do you recognize this bag? he asked Sidney. "Yes, it's my overnight bag" he replied. Someone came and turned it in." "I must have left it the morning I came back in that coffee shop" he remembered. 'Well it was full of clothes with Jessica Strassberg's blood on them. "You are now formerly charge for the death of Jessica Strassberg. Taking him from the room to book him. Desmond and Billy looked on "We have our work cut out!" Billy stated looking at Desmond.

CHAPTER NINETEEN

New friends/old problems

Dana had taken her son Billy out to Boothbay Harbor for Windjammer Days. He had brought his best friend Tommy along and they were enjoying watching the boat races as they walked into the resort. The sails of the sailboats had beautiful colors ranging in various shapes and sizes. "Look over there, Tommy, at that one! They ran along the beach pointing and oweying and ahhh-ing at what they saw. There were small fishing boats sailing by also. Dana had promised they would even go swimming in the area that was designated on the big Atlantic river. She stayed close to the two young boys and they ran looking at all the exciting things going on at the large resort village. It was a beautiful July day and she was sporting her short-shorts and big straw hat to cover her from the hot sun. "Slow down she said every now and then when they got to far ahead along the beaches shore. There were vendors out with wares to sale. David and Tommy had purchased some silly character hats and put them on their heads. They had so much fun picking them out from the many choices they had to choose from laughing the entire time. "They walked and looked far down the beaches shore. "Anyone hunger?" Dana asked of the two boys. But they were so excited looking at the races going on now she didn't force the question. They found some bleachers and watched with the crowds of town folk as well as the many visitors that had come to Booth Bay to enjoy the great coastal shores. "Howdy, hello" Dana replied. "Is this sit taken? he asked looking at a space next to Dana. "Oh no, she moved over a bit and the stranger took a sit next to her on the bleachers. "My name is Rusty" he said extending his hand to her. 'Dana" she replied shaking his hand. "Nice day isn't it?" "It sure is! She replied. "This is so wonderful do you come here often?" he asked still making conversation. Dana had run around with the boys most of the day so it was good to have some one to talk with. "Maybe two or three times a month when weather permits" she said. "So, you're a native here." "I guess you could say that" she responded. "Me too!" They sat talking while the boys enjoyed the windjammer races. Each would pick the windjammer they thought was going to win and jump up YEAH! When it won. After the races ended Rusty turned to Dana "have you eaten?" "I haven't but I was just about to round up the boys and do that." "Oh, these are your boys?" he asked surprised, he thought Dana was by herself. David and Tommy were sitting down front on the bleachers. Dana made her way down from the bleachers upper level. "Mom can we just get a hotdog and go swimming please! Please! David asked anxious to get in the water. "This must be your son" Rusty said looking at Dana. Brilliant deduction Dana reasoned since Tommy big blue eyes and ash blonde hair was a sure give away. "Hello young man shaking the boy's hands. 'This is Tommy and my son David" she responded. "Hi, David said pausing a moment remembering his manners. "But can we please! "All right" she conceded. "There's a great place to eat that's right near the swimming hole." "Can you boys swim? Rusty asked in a teasing way. "Like a fish! Tommy replied. "Come on! grabbing Dana's hand and pulling her to the other side of the resort, through crowds of people. David and Tommy ran ahead. He just kept saying keep going we're almost there! Dana had her hand on her head holding the straw hat. She didn't want to lose it or have the breeze blow it off her head as she made her way through all those people. 'There it is! WOW! Tommy look! It was a big swimming hole made on the side of the mountain and there were slides that went into the water below! Wheee! They could hear and see the young children their age and older having fun. "Come on Dana! come on! David had gotten her hand. "Wait we still have not eaten" she said. "We're not hungry Dana! The boys said together. Dana knew they should be she was. They had been there since nine o clock in the morning and it was nearing noon. "Look why don't you go and find a place near the pool and I will get hamburgers and hotdogs for everyone, sounds good! Rusty suggested.

"Thanks! Dana replied with Tommy on one hand and David on the other pulling her to the entrance gate to enter the huge water hole. Thanking the kind stranger again she went in and found a spot where she thought was a great view to watch the boys from all angles. She laid her little blanket on the grassy area and both boys shed their shorts with their trunks underneath and took off to the hole. Dana watched them jump into the water and start having fun. 'Dana, Dana she heard them scream watch this every time they'd get to the top coming down. They would slide down this mountain formed in the shape of a slide. She could see they were having so much fun. Soon Dana looked up to see Rusty walking around looking for her. His hands were filled with boxes and a carry tray with drinks she guessed. Standing up and raising her hands flailing them in the air she called out to him. "Rusty, Rusty I'm over here. After a while he finally heard her through the crowds an headed her way. Rusty! He waved at the boys after he had put all the food he had purchased down on the blanket. Dana moved over to allow him to sit down. "What did you buy?" she asked. Well, you know boys, they never know what they don't want. 'Thanks" she said getting a hamburger for herself. As she and Rusty were eating and having conversations about anything her cell phone rang. "Hello" Hello Dana this is Billy". "Oh, Billy how are things going out there" she asked. "Oh, we're just getting started but it looks like I'm going to be here for a while! Oh, she sighed. "How's David can I speak with him". "Oh, Billy he's in the water. I brought he and Tommy out to Boothbay and their off swimming. "Oh good! lucky for him he's having fun". "Boy is he having fun he's old enough to come to the other side now" she acknowledged. "I'll have him call you tonight". 'That's' fine just call my room at the Baltimore Sheraton okay". I will" she replied. And give him my love also". Bye, bye. "I'm sorry, Dana said now turning her attention back to Rusty. "That was important". "Now what were you saying, you're just a ranch boy?' what exactly does that mean?' Dana asked as she and Rusty enjoyed their burgers, cokes and fries. The boys were still having fun and were asking to come back before they left. Dana finally got them to settle for a bit and eat their hog dogs before returning again for just a few more minutes and then we're leaving after a couple of hours. "Thank you so much Rusty" I would have never thought to bring him to this side of the cove". He had a wonderful time and so did I," Dana admitted. "It was a pleasure meeting you." "Likewise," he said with his country accent. He helped Dana gather up the trash and she folded her blanket and everyone headed from the hole. "Next time I'm going to" the boys were making plans for their return visit. As they approached the cars in the lot Dana stopped and thanked Rusty again for a wonderful time. He helped her put the blankets and wet towels bundled up tight in the heavy tote into the trunk of her car. The boys ran and got into the back seat. "Thanks, Rusty! they yelled shutting the car doors. Dana gave Rusty one of her business cards. "Thanks" he said and stood waving as she and the boys pulled away putting the top down in her sporty little Porsche.

David Parker had gotten wind that his son had the Jessica Strassberg case. "Dad I was just about to call. Desmond asked me to take the case. Conflict of interest you know". "Oh, son, are you sure you're ready for this?" 'Dad honestly I don't know" I have contemplated it and certainly prayed about it." "Well who else is on the team of lawyers with you?" his dad asked. "Right now, it's just Desmond and I, Mr. Owens Desmond's dad is here for legal advice and helping us with our strategy." He's pretty torn up. "Oh, I can only imagine David said. "I'm praying for you and the whole family. "You've looked over it, so how do you think it's going to weigh out?" David his dad asked. "Well we have to prove he was not at the scene when Jessica was murdered that's the first thing'. 'What are they saying caused her death?" "Coroner reports shows she was smothered probably with bed pillow but I have my crime investigator Rory Blake looking into it as we speak. "Son, if you need me don't hesitate to call". "Oh, don't worry that's a given" Billy replied. I'll be in touch" his dad said disconnecting the line. Rory had been looking around again helping Billy and Desmond build their case. He had spoken with the small motel owner that was at the desk the night Sidney came in to rent a room. But since one could come and go without having to come through the lobby, he had no way of knowing if Sidney was there all night. The doorman in his building said he saw Sidney come back home at 5:30 the first time and then he left for about and hour or so coming back around 6:30 he remembered because it was the time, he eats dinner. And he was finishing his dinner around 7:30 when Ms. Strassberg came in going up to his suite. And he didn't see either of them until around 9:00 p.m. "Mr. Owens came back through the front door I hadn't seen him leave though. I don't miss much!" he confessed. He could have gone out another way." "And I never saw either of them again that night" Rory was noting all this down as he looked around the very large foyer of the exclusive suites ground floor. "Is there another way one might get out without passing this way? he asked. "There's a back entrance for the residents. We have a lot of high-profile residents living here he said. Most want their privacy". "Thanks! Before I leave" he said I'll just look around in back. "Oh, one last question how did Ms. Strassberg get here that night." "Limo dropped her off and pulled away. Thanks, Rory responded heading out to the back of the building.

Tetra and David were at service Sunday morning when their son called to tell them that things were still not going well in the investigation and to just pray for a break through on the case. Tetra being a mother and David of course a lawyer but a father as well was feeling the frustrations and anxiety this case was bringing. During alter call both got down on their knees before God and thanked him with tears streaming from their faces.

Both knew that if anything was going to be done in any direction it would be through God. After the church service was over, they arrived home to find a message on their answering machine from their son Billy. There was another person they needed to contact regarding Jessica Strassberg's murder. And right now, he seems to be eluding us but thank God we have hope. It may not have been a landslide decision but for David and Tetra it was and answer to prayer. They rejoiced right there in their home every time they thought about it.

Rory had gone thoroughly over the scene with his investigative team but he felt he needed to check another lead out that had come to his attention. He took his forensics investigator with him. He wanted to try and get some prints off of the back-exit door. Finding it wasn't easy. He learned only the residents knew exactly where the door was and unless they showed their guest how to get to it goes undetected. 'Thanks Rory said after being shown by the security where the back-exit door was located in the building. It was clearly visible from down underneath the garage of the large building's structure. After forensics had taken any prints, they could gather especially on the doors knob and surrounding area near the back-exit door, they requested a list of names for everyone in the building. After getting the list and all the evidence he needed he headed back to the station to speak with Billy and Desmond, Sidney's lawyers.

Friday night and Dana was sitting reading a good book and thinking about Roger who she had not seen for about a month. He called everyday and was just so busy he said but couldn't wait until the time when he came back her way. Since Billy was still away in Baltimore Roger would certainly meet her son David. She wondered what David would think of Roger? Would he even like him since he's become so attached to his dad Billy? 'Ring! Ring! "Hello! "Howdy! Hello Dana said again. "This is Rusty, how are you?" he said. She as surprised he called. They had exchanged numbers but it was a friendly gesture to say thank you. "Hi, she said again a bit startled. "I never expected to hear from you! How are you doing?" "I'm wonderful! he said in this happy over the top tone. But it was contagious. "Sooo, why are you calling?" Dana asked getting into the spirit of the call. "I was wondering if you and the boys wanted to come out to the ranch this Saturday?" "The ranch? Dana questioned. Yeah! They can ride the ponies, and hayrides and lots of fun here!" "Are you kidding me?" She still didn't believe this man she had met bout three weeks or so ago. "I told you I was just and old ranch boy!" Rusty looked to be in his late forties is what Dana figured. She hadn't given it much thought sense she knew she'd never see him again. But he seemed very intelligent and easy to hold a conversation with. "That sounds wonderful, but where is this ranch?" Dana asked curiously. "Well, it's a ways out but I can give you directions which aren't hard to find at all" he said convincingly. Dana had run out of places to take David. Children their age tend to bore quickly of things. Except for Boothbay and Dana was wore out from that overcrowded scene. "Sounds fun! She replied. He proceeded in giving her direction with his country twang. "See you tomorrow" she said. "Okay! bring your chaps! He teased disconnecting the line. "What am I getting myself into Dana thought with the psychiatric mind. "David! David, she said sitting right next to the intercom that was in every room. David was in the den playing his video game and didn't hear her speaking.

"DAVID! She spoke even louder. "Yes Dana, he replied lying on the floor in front of the television's huge screen. "Call Tommy and see if he can or wants to come with us tomorrow for an outing. David and Tommy went everywhere together. Tommy had and older brother and a much younger sister so his mother was glad he and David chose to be best friends. Billy spent time with Tommy's family too. He jumped up and began dialing the phone. He didn't like ever being by himself he liked having his own company which was mostly Tommy. He was kinda sad he said when he went to live with his dad because he had to change schools. He liked staying with his dad but he missed some of his old friends from the previous school. Davie easily made new friends at the private school his dad had enrolled him in and things were looking up. But it was till a distance from where Dana lives. "He didn't miss Tommy they were together all the time. Billy and Dana promised. "Where are we going Dana? He yelled from the other room still on the phone with Tommy. "Are we going to Boothbay?" "No! it's a surprise", she said. And David use the intercom and stop yelling I can hear you just fine." "Okay, turning his attention back to the call. "Well are you coming Tommy?" "Dana! Are we picking Tommy up or does his parents have to bring him here?" "We will stop by around 8:00 a.m. tomorrow morning tell him to please let Lily know. "Okay" see you tomorrow and Dana says wear blue jeans bye". He hung up the phone and ran into the living room where Dana was reading on her chaise. 'Where we going Dana?" he was now excited. The word surprise made David excited and asked Dana all evening until she shared her surprise with him.

David and Desmond were hoping they could clear Sidney of the murder without going to trial but things were not turning out that way. Desmond met with Sidney everyday and was convinced he had not done this horrible thing to Jessica. But he wasn't the one that would need convincing at this point it would be a jury. Rory had done a thorough investigative job and they had put together some credible witnesses. Even the ones who had seen the scuffle in the hall prove to be helpful. Her limo service was stalling on getting the names to them of which driver was driving Jessica that particular night. The evidence Rory had collected from the back-exit door had lots of prints. All the fingerprints they were able to match with the residents of the building including Jessica's prints but there was another unidentified set of fingerprints that was giving them trouble. They had no record. So, getting that information from her limo service was vital. Desmond had just got off the phone from speaking with them when Rory came in. 'Are you two ready to hear this?" They both looked up waiting. "The limo driver who supposedly was driving Jessica that evening is now in the morgue! He was found shot in his hotel room last night by a co-worker who was picking him up for his shift. Desmond and Billy looked at each other in shock! This could be a break they later thought. Somebody is trying to cover his tracks. "But was he the other prints you pulled from the exit door in the back of the building. "No! The prints are still a mystery Rory concluded, "our man is still out there somewhere" he reasoned. Well I'm headed to go and talk to the co-worker who found the limo driver" shaking their hands and leaving.

Desmond went down to speak with his brother. Sidney had written a letter to a friend and asked if Desmond would mail it. How are you holding up brother? he asked seeing this was causing him much stress. He had lost weight from his already thin frame. "I'm all right I guess" he said. "Hang in there, I'm not giving up on you! Desmond affirmed to his brother embracing him. He was feeling the anxiety but was not going to let Sidney know it. Their dad had gone back home for a few days for some rest Desmond hoped. This ordeal was proving to be a bit much for the aging Owens.

They sat back in their seats. "Sidney did Jessica usually have the same limo drivers when she was at home? Desmond asked. "Most of the time they tried to keep the same one" he replied. "There were times when I have ridden with her and another driver was used but it was rare". "I remember her regular driver's name was Vance and occasionally they would use Michael? "Desmond put is head down. Why?" why do you ask Sidney inquired. Because, Michael Messner was found dead in his hotel room last night we were told. "He's the one who was driving Jessica that night Sidney remembered. Because when I went to her apartment to confront her about the mess in my suite, he was standing out by his limo smoking a cigarette" Sidney informed Desmond. "We exchanged hello's and I went up. "All right" Desmond said getting up to leave "hang in there!

CHAPTER TWENTY

Prayer, price, promise

Mother Dorrance had gathered everyone into her small apartment. It was her quilting circle. They were not there for quilting they were coming together to pray. Mother Dorrance said she had declared and all out war against Satan and he would be defeated. Tyler was heading out to orchestra practice and stopped in as he always did to let her know he was heading out. Mr. Bean her husband had helped him fix up and old car he had and had taken him to get all the things he needed to be legal. Tyler was finally feeling like his life was coming back together. He had been hired at one of the music stores that the church owned and was doing very well. He also worked helping Mr. Bean with the up keep of the complex which cover his rent. Being close to his old neighborhood he often ran into some of the people from the little jazz spot that recognized him. But he was determined to pull himself out of that lifestyle. He certainly had not been perfect since getting his break in the orchestra he'd messed up more than once but he was surrounded with people who love him and wanted only the best for him. The church has a ministry that helps those with rehabilitation needs and they loved and encouraged him through the alcoholism. He had even planned a trip back home to see his family whom he had disowned in his mind for so many years.

"Mother Dora I'm headed to the church" he said coming in speaking to all the ladies sitting around the room. 'Okay God bless you! she replied. "Drive careful." She gave him a hug and he was on his way.

"Now Alene you read the scripture and then we're going to pray. I've been watching that trial on TV and I'm just sick and tired of that devil and his mess! Hallelujah! They shouted. Alene read from Chronicles 7: 14 with power and authority in her voice, "If my people...and when she finished all you could hear for the next hour was a pouring out to God. With praises of thanksgiving filling the entire room.

Tyler had arrived at practice early and sat out in the parking lot looking at the mail he had gotten that day. He sat reading his mail he had received which he hurriedly past as he went into his apartment after work. Looking through it again there was a letter address to him. And to his surprise it was a letter from Sidney Owens. His heart felt so heavy with grief for him. Sidney had helped him and there was nothing he could do to help him out of this situation.

He slowly opened the envelope and took out the single page letter. "Dear Tyler, I know by now you and all the world have seen the mess I'm in. I want you to know I didn't do this. I have been wrongly accused. But that's not why I'm writing. I'm writing to thank you for helping me see." Tyler was confused he didn't understand what help had he been to Sidney. Sidney did everything for him. But he continued reading. "We go through life thinking we've arrived when we attain so much wealth and we keep buying into it over and over again. But you've shown me a man's worth when he has nothing at all" Even though I have attained status none of it can get me out of this place". So please thank God for me because through you I see a higher power". Please remember me in your prayers and give my love to Mother Dora." Love Sidney. Tyler sat in his car praying and weeping to God on Sidney's behalf. He was taught to pray long ago. His parents brought him up in the church and his learned prayer life had been instilled in his heart. It had kept him all those years that he had turned his back on God, he sat thinking. Someone came over and tapped on his window to let him know they were ready to start practice. He looked around to see he was surrounded by a full parking lot of cars as he sat praying undisturbed.

Dana was just pulling up to Tommy's parent's home and he was waiting with the door opened looking for them. Dana had called Lily earlier to let her know she was on her way. Tommy's mother Lilly was up waiting also so they wouldn't disturb the rest of the household that early on a Saturday. Dana spoke briefly with Lily letting her know where they were going and about when to expect them back. She waved from the door as Dana pulled away with the boys jumping up in the back seat because the surprise Billy was holding had spilled over to Tommy and they were in hysterics. Dana drove along the highway with the boys asking questions that she really didn't have answer to yet. "How much longer Dana? David asked as she sped down the highway. Rusty had told her it was about fifteen miles from Boothbay. So, she figured they had about another five or so miles to go. As she drove along, she looked over and saw a little fruit-stand on the side of the highway. She pulled over to give her self a relief from all the questions. "You think five and six year old's have questions. Try taking two twelve-year old's to a ranch to ride horses! "Are we here? One of them asked as Dana pulled the car off the rode. "Not yet, would you boys like some strawberries? She asked. She couldn't believe the energy these two young men had. David is so quiet and reserved when he's alone but with Tommy he is a bundle of noisy energy. The two boys jumped out of the car and Dana followed. She let them both pick out a basket of strawberries and she chose some bunches of grapes. "Okay you boys get back in the car while I pay for our purchases, and we can be on our way" she shared with them. They took all that energy back into the car. "Well! the old timer said "your boys are sure happy bout something! Taking the money from Dana and getting her change. "Yes, we're on our way to Double H. Ranch", have you heard of it?" she asked. "Double H Ranch! He laughed, who hasn't heard about it? That's Rusty's place about five miles up the road on your right you can't miss it!" he said putting her grapes in a plastic bag. "Have fun!" he waved as she pulled off. Dana felt better now apparently, she was the only one in Maine that had not heard about this place. She drove on. The strawberries had calmed the boys a bit. Now they were finding the various shapes that the strawberries had grown in to before entering the tiny basket. "Look Tommy, look how big this one is! After about ten minutes Dana saw a very large wooden sign that READ Double H Ranch exit. She slowed down and turned into the dusty road. It was wide enough for two cars going in the opposite direction she thought. But her car was going to need a good detailing from all the dust. She drove along the dusty road. "Look, look! They were starting to see cattle scattered all over and there were lots of them! Dana smiled oh! She thought this is what he meant about a ranch boy. "Look Dana, they saw a couple of cowhands twirling a rope over their head riding after a calf, is how Dana explained it to the boys. They're called cowhands!" she added. After about two or three miles she came upon a very big fenced yard and large wooden gate. It was made of large wooden post the size of an average tree's trunk and it surrounded this massive area. The beautiful green grass lay stretched out toward the huge gorgeous ranch house. "How could something so beautiful be hidden back here Dana thought? It seemed to be an oasis in the desert. She slowed down as a man on a horse came riding toward the car. "Howdy ma'am may I help you?" The boys were just amazed watching the cattle and everything else going on around them. "Look David! he whispered the man was on the side of the car where Tommy was sitting and the horse looked big! he thought. "Hi, Dana responded timidly "Rusty Higgins invited us?" he didn't ask anymore questions he just beckoned "Right this way. Leading Dana and the boys up to the main house he called it. Seeing the car coming up closer to the house Dana saw Rusty standing out on the very wide driveway. "Park here" he told her. She could hardly get the car in gear before the boys wanted out of the back seat. The excitement was more than they could bear from the back seat of a Porsche.

Mossy spoke everyday with her husband keeping him abreast of things at home. He trusted she and Henry could handle things at the law firm so Mossy told him not to worry. "Sweetheart you just concentrate on Sidney now we're fine and the firm is fine! Did you speak with Henry about Allenbee?" Yes, I spoke with him last evening did something else come up regarding it? "No! he wanted to run some questions by you about the settlement and I wanted to make sure he had gotten in touch with you." How's your clothes holding up?" she asked since he had not expected to be there four weeks now she thought. "I'm fine we have all the services here at the hotel so my clothes are holding up fine dear." "How are my children?" "Oh, Desmond their growing and I'm seeing new things everyday." She said but don't worry the video camera is working overtime." I've even taught Dal and Janie to use it. Janie was the children's sitter. "Jordan decided to use grandfather's shoes for his action figures boats." What! Desmond laughed. "Grandfather was resting. I've put him up in the guest room until you get back. "He's taking this pretty hard though he won't admit it, Mossy shared with her husband about his grandfather. He had gone to sleep in the den so I woke him and helped him to lay down for a nap it was around noon I'd said." He left his shoes by the chair in the family room. Jordan decided his action men needed a boat to get over on the other side of the river to fish for food. And so, he put them all in grandfather's spit shine shoes and sent them across the pool. Dal thought it was so funny" she was in the pool laughing with the twins letting them jump in and out and didn't notice what Jordan was doing until it was too late. But Janie as some great footage with Jordan running back into the house crying after the shoes were out of his reach in the water." Desmond and his wife shared a few more laughs together before saying their good-nights. "Okay let me talk with Vlade now" taking a turn with each one. She missed him but knew the purpose in which he had gone there, so she kept her spirits positive for him. "Honey, I love you and give my love to Sidney. "Oh, and Desmond can he receive letters there?" Dal wants to write him! she said which surprised her even as she said it. "Sure! He's only been accused not his privileges taken away! he said. "He'd love that dear "Goodnight sweetheart" Goodnight.

"Welcome! Rusty said seeing Dana and the boys getting out of the car. I'm so glad you decided to come". Do come in leading Dana into the house. The boys had run over to the fence watching the cowpokes wrangle a calf. "Can we just stand right here? David asked not wanting to go in and miss the excitement. "Sure! "Corky keep and eye on them I wouldn't want them wandering off yet until they learn the place". "Thanks, Rusty! They said in unison standing on the lower railing of the large wooden fence that surrounded the ponies. And what a place it was. "What's that over there? they asked Corky pointing?" "That's the barn and that over there is the stables. "The stables?" Is that where the horses are? Tommy asked. "They sure are young one! Corky replied. "Let's walk a bit." Corky took them around the huge ranch. They walked and rode on a golf cart looking thing, is how David described it to Dana after returning back to the main house. They saw

Rusty's large swimming pool and the tennis courts. Rusty's ranch was the biggest thing Tommy had ever seen he believed. The boys stayed outside with Corky and Dana and Rusty went into his elegant ranch home. The entrance had a big leather saddle on a beautiful oak wood stand. There were lasso and ropes hanging from the ceiling. It looked so Rusty, Dana thought. The living room was elegantly country with plaids and flower prints blending to make a gorgeous motif. In his kitchen there were pots painted with flowers hanging from the island in the center of the room. "It was breath taking Dana believed. "You're not going to tell me you did all this by yourself?" she asked regarding his home's décor. All three rooms opened up into the other to form a great room and the style of each complimented the other. "No! he said that's all Donna! He said with a smile as big as his heart, Dana reasoned. Donna?" she questioned moving back to the living area to sit down. "My wife' Rusty said. "Oh Rusty, I sorry you didn't tell me you had a wife? I shouldn't be walking all around in her house! She explained. "Oh, that's all right, she isn't here' he stated sadly. "Where is she Rusty?" "Donna is in a care hospital' he confessed. She has this rare disease that doctors have been trying to cure for years" he said. We moved out here from Texas for the climate and she was alright for a while and then she got sick again and had to be hospitalized." "I'm so sorry to hear that" Dana responded. "How long has she been ill Rusty? He had sat down on the leather chair still talking. "Donna's been sick now for about five years. And she's been in the hospital two of the five" he said. I go by everyday and spent time with her I love her so much". I hate to see her suffer." And we've looked at everything they have to offer. Some days I think I'll just bring her home because she's doing so well and the next day, I'm unable to see her for one thing and then another" he added wiping his eyes. "Hey! We didn't come here to talk about me lets go out and see what the boys have been up to," walking out the door with Dana following.

'Hey Dana! Dana you have to see the ponies? David yelled seeing them walk out. They all walked out to the stables. The hay on the barn floor was worth Tommy and David reaching down to pick some up and put it into the horse's mouths has they walked from stall to stall. "Can we rub them? Tommy asked reaching over into the stall. Yeah!

'They're all-pretty gentle when being rubbed" Rusty replied. Corky had the riding ponies ready for the boys and Sugar who Rusty requested was waiting for Dana. "As they walked out from the stalls the boys saw the ponies. "I want this one! they both shouted running to one of the ponies. "That one David is "Patches" and Tommy you have "Smokey". They stood looking at the ponies with big grins on their faces. They looked so big David thought. "But look at those two!" they replied speaking of "Sugar and Coco" the horses Rusty and Dana were going to ride. "Let's go can we go! They were jumping up and down. "Corky why don't you show the boys how to mount after you brief then on the horses saddle and I'll get Dana in some proper clothes for riding" Rusty suggested going back to the main house. The boys had on their jeans and t-shirts and Dan had worn her very tight designer jeans and tennis shoes. She stood watching Corky patiently answer all of the boy's questions about the ranch and the ponies. She looked over and saw Rusty coming back from the cart with something in his hand. "What's this? she asked as he handed her a beautiful riding outfit. "Rusty? Is this your wife's," "No, I bought it hoping she'd be able to ride again like we use to, but that was a while ago. I was supposed to have taken it back to the store but I couldn't it felt like I was giving up on her" he confessed. Dana looked at the beautiful white soft leather chap styled pants and short top vest trim with sparkling rhinestone braids. "This is very nice are you sure you want to part with it?" "I've fallen in love with it and I haven't even tried it on" she said teasing of course. "Right over there! He pointed "Is where you can change, I'll get the horse ready" and walked off. "Dana looked again at the entire outfit as she went into this outside dressing room to change. "Cowboys here have got it good, she thought looking around the large changing room in the stables. After getting dressed she walked out. Rusty was standing there holding a pair of white cowboy boots. Dana smiled, walking out with tennis shoes that was playing havoc on the outfit. The boots fit perfectly. "Now those are yours" he said. "What do you mean? Dana questioned. "Every cowboy or cowgirl needs a good pair of boots that fit! He chided now holding the horse's bridle in his hand. "How did you know what size to buy?" she asked preparing to get into the saddle. "Well when we were at Boothbay, I just happen to observe your shoe size from your sandals that you were wearing when you took them off as we sat on the blanket talking." Rusty? Thanks, she said kissing him on the cheek. She looked like she had stepped off of the cover of Rodeo Riders magazine.

Corky and the boys had already left on the trail. They couldn't wait for Dana they were too excited. Rusty helped Dana into the saddled horse Sugar and he got on Coco and headed down the trail. "You ride well have you ridden before? he asked.

"When I was younger! she remembered "my grandparents had a farm in Oregon". Granddad would let me ride when we went there for visits." But it was nothing like what you have here". She shared. Maybe once upon a time, I've heard stories but I can't remember it every being a ranch like this" she confided. "Well riding a horse is like riding a bicycle once you learn you don't forget". he responded riding at a click clop pace along the designed trail. They went on riding and talking for about and hour maybe two. When they arrived back the boys where learning to ride around in a fenced area. "Look Dana! David was riding around and round without assistance. "Corky said we could learn how to do tricks and everything! Can we Dana? They were both yelling as Rusty and Dana rode up toward the stables. Both dismounted from the horses and stood watching the boys take turns riding the ponies and becoming more familiar with them. 'He's pretty good! Rusty said speaking of David whose confidence had grown a lot since starting to learn the animals better.

"Thanks for a wonderful day but we must get back". Dana said standing still watching Corky instruct the boys. "I understand, Rusty replied gathering the bridles an heading into the stables. All right boys we must go! She yelled out to them going into the stables to change and get ready to leave. "Okay, just one more ride! They yelled changing now it was Tommy's turn to ride around again. After Dana had changed and Rusty had convince her to please keep the outfit, he had given her she put it in the car and waited for the boys who were out watching Corky catch cattle using his rope. "Rusty this has been a wonderful day. The boys had a great time and so did I" she shared as they sat on his outside patio giving David and Tommy a few more minutes on the ranch.

"Well I'm glad it was good for me too! He smiled. This place gets pretty quiet out here sometimes!" Rusty admitted. Dana figured Rusty to be about late forty's early fifties. She wasn't going to ask it would come up soon if they saw each other again. Soon the boys were back in the car. Dana shook Rusty's hand and the boys thanked him for everything including those great juicy burgers his cook Mavis made for them. 'Dana! Corky said we can come out and get riding lessons and learn tricks can we Dana?" was the request all the way home. When Tommy got out at his house, he asked David Michael to call him because he was going right in and asked his mom and dad about taking lessons. Though Dana was tired she had a wonderful day. She didn't know if she would see Rusty again. She felt sadness for him because of his wife. And the time she spent with him today was memorable she thought sitting out on his patio preparing to leave the ranch.

"Thanks, Corky for all your help! Rusty acknowledged to his faithful ranch hand. "I enjoyed it boss, I always do!

Justin had become the ultimate bachelor. He had purchased a new two-seater convertible Beamer with his newly found wealth. He didn't approve of what Franklin his friend was doing but it was his life. They often partied together. Franklin a biochemist who worked at Unisom Technologies a huge conglomerate world- wide company was a party animal. From Monday to Thursday he was a devoted husband and a career-oriented man but Friday nights got the best of him and he usually yield to any temptation. He had chosen the bank where Rae worked for all his dates most of the time. They all knew him and his wife. They banked there. He'd come in with her or without her and was just as friendly all the time. When she delivered their baby, he came in giving out caramel pops on Monday and Friday he was picking up his date from the parking lot of the same building. Some women have no scruples, I guess! And it doesn't hurt that his account was pretty impressive too. Franklin well, he was just a dog! And some women have dated him more than once! His rules were he never dates the same one two weeks in a row. If Mrs. Ostrowski didn't know about it, he said, if wouldn't hurt. Justin had started getting a lot of excuses from Menae, she wasn't always available for him. His schedule was so hectic at the hospital anyway so his wanderings were kept at bay and close to home. But instead of wandering off he started spending more time with his resident now lover Rae. Rae unlike the others was shunned aside that night for Peaches. Whose real name was Allison by the way. It was a joke for the girls changing their names when dating Franklin in case Pamela his wife found out. So, after her brief encounter with Franklin Rae met the man of her dreams. She had set her heart on marrying Justin Parker. Sure, she knew he needed to sow a few oats but she would wait she felt he was worth it. He was cute, and smart and successful and, well I can't tell you everything! Except, he was now her target. He loved taking Menae out to a luxurious dinner and wine and dine her showing her off to his many friends and colleagues. She was gorgeous with long red loose curls that hung down her back. She spoke so soft and sultry and her beautiful red lips and flawless baby soft skin hooked him in every time. While he found a different kind of contentment with Rae who was sexy in her own right and down to earth and laughed and put her dark brown hair up in a scrunchy, and let him run with Franklin and still would care ever so gently for him and his needs. He had the best of both worlds one would say. "Menae are you coming by tonight? Justin asked calling from the hospital on his break. He had not seen her in two weeks and he longed for her touch. "Justin I will be there! Have the wine chilled" she suggested. "We are staying in, tonight right?" 'Yes! Justin confirmed I have an early morning" he affirmed. "And I do understand sweetie, I'll see you around seven," she agreed. "Cool! Disconnecting the cell line and spinning off doing a dance. He was so busy all day but every moment he only thought of his evening with Menae. He had called and caught up with the Baltimore case from Billy and was ready to spend an evening with his girl. When he got home, he noticed she was already there! She was an hour early. He hurried over and clicked on the light over his front door. That's to let Rae know he was not to be disturbed. Then he took the chilled bottle of Dom Perigeron from the refrigerator. She hearing him coming in stood in his bedroom door with her lingerie on and he did all he could to keep his clothes on until he reached the room. One sentence of Latin and "Here we go again!

When he got up the next morning, she was gone but had left him a note. Sweetheart I'll call you later, love Menae. Justin wasn't sure when she left everything after they finished the bottle of wine for him was blank. And he had to sit and watch this surgical procedure for about and hour with a splitting headache. And sure, enough as not to be disturbed by anyone he went that evening to Rae's apartment. And she nursed his headache and prepared his dinner and let him rest in her bed as long as he wanted too.

CHAPTER TWENTY-ONE

A new look

Rory had helped Billy and Desmond put together a good case. (solid well we will leave that to interpretation.) But they still needed to find that limo driver whose fingerprints were on the exit door leaving Sidney's condominium. Rory interviewed all the witnesses over again which were a lot. Most lived in the building and the interview process took a while. They interviewed every limo driver who had every driven Jessica Strassberg around before. Everyone was cleared. Lawyer David Parker called his son in Baltimore. "Billy how's it going?' I've been watching the investigation unfold on television, he shared. "Unless we find that limo driver, we'll be heading to court next week" Billy confessed. Wherever that man is hiding, its good." we have looked all over for him" he shared with his dad. We have turned over everything trying to locate him". "Son I'll tell you what, let me send you somebody that has a keen sense when it comes to locating someone. I'll get on the phone with him and if he's available I'll call and let you know when he'll be there. "Thanks dad, we sure could use it" Billy replied. And dad, Desmond's holding up well." You tell him we're praying for him and you as well son". Thanks again dad! Good-bye".

Two days and countless hours had gone by when "Hello" the man acknowledged walking into the address location on the piece of paper he was holding in his hand. "I'm looking for William Parker or Desmond Owens? He stated. Billy had stepped out to speak with the prosecutor. "You must be Masony?" Desmond said. 'Yes, he responded.

'I'm Desmond Owens pleased to make your acquaintance" again extending his hand to him. They had met briefly at a celebration Mrs. Parker had given for Billy years ago. Masony had put on some pounds over the years. And his hair was always gray it just appeared slightly thinner now, Desmond thought has he looked upon the aged private eye. 'Please have a sit". Billy is with the prosecutor right now" but I can catch you up to speed."

Desmond started Masony at the beginning and shared with him what they needed from his investigation. He gave him Rory Clark's number for any additional questions. Masony said he was pretty familiar with the case from following it in the media. "He was on it". Just has Desmond had finished briefing Masony Billy walked in. "Well look who's here! 'How are you Masony?" Billy said affectionately but loudly coming over to embrace him. "How's your wife?" "She's good! Masony replied smiling. "It's sure good to see you! and I see married life is agreeing with you he added patting Masony on his now protruding stomach. He smiled and greeted him back with an embrace.

Desmond have you briefed Masony on the case yet?" Yes, we were just finishing up when you came in. "How did things go at the prosecutor's office? Well they think they have a pretty strong case because Sidney does not have an alibi for the night of the murder. But if we could locate the man who left the fingerprints on that exit door we have a fighting chance". And I'm thinking that as long as there's a possibility there is still hope" Billy explained. Have you had lunch yet? He asked turning to Masony. "No, I haven't your dad said time was of the essence so I headed right over after I got off the plane." "Good we haven't either, 'Let's go! holding Masony and Desmond around their shoulders heading them toward the door for lunch and to talk strategy.

Dana finally said yes to David's constant asking for pony riding lessons. He would go everyday after school for two weeks and then and an occasional Saturday. Cory had said they could be in the beginner's rodeo halftime show and they were determined to do their best. Lily and Dana took turns taking the boys during the week. And Dana would take them on the weekends. She was spending more time with

Rusty even seeing him almost everyday for two weeks. One Saturday she came but he was at the hospital visiting his wife and she sat out by the pool. Taking a dip in the water every now and then until the boy's session had ended. She felt so sorrow for him he was such a devoted husband. He shared with her about all the attempts he and his wife had gone through over the years to make her well. He was a caring man and loved children. But because of his wife's illness she could never conceive. Dana had gathered the boys up and was heading out when he was pulling up the dusty path. "Howdy! He said stopping the car. "Rusty! You should have seen us we were standing on the ponies today! David said shouting across the car. Corky says we can take the ropes off next week." "That's great! The boys were speaking of the safety rope that's used during practice session to keep them from falling and hurting themselves. "Well I'll have to make a point to be here next time" he told them. "Okay bye! And they sat back down taking their heads from the windows. "Did you ride out today?" he asked Dana sitting behind the wheel. "No, I decided to read a good book by the pool and swim a few laps, she replied. "Well I'm glad you felt comfortable enough to come and be here when I'm not". That makes me feel good! he shared in his country accent and big smile. With a wave of hands Dana and the boys pulled away.

When she arrived home, Roger was sitting out front. David was spending the rest of the weekend with Tommy and she was going to spend a quite day at home going over some paperwork she had brought from the office. 'Well hi! I wasn't expecting you lifting the garage door going in and getting out of the car. She went to the door and Roger pulled into the garage and she let it down with her remote. "He walked over and they embraced at the front door. "So! I wasn't expecting you until next week" what are you doing here?" "I made an early delivery to my client that's due next week and came to see my girl"! "You sound so lonely the last I time I spoke with you!" You broke my heart, he said picking her up in his arms dangling her legs off the floor. "Oh, aren't you sweet. They shared an intimate kiss. Then he put her down and picked up his luggage from the porch and went into the house. "Where's David, looking around not seeing him in his usual spot in front of the television. "He's at Tommy's for the weekend Dana informed him. "Great! Then we can go out dancing" Dancing! That was not on Dana's agenda. She and Roger had been together quite a while now at least a year and she still felt like they were dating for the first time. She felt they always had to entertain one another and she wanted to move pass that. He on the other hand wanted to always go places and he loved dancing and that was all right sometimes. It often got hindered when David was there. Dana had to be full time mommy since Billy was off in Baltimore and she was starting to like it a lot. And there were Saturdays when she would go out with Roger but was home in bed by 1:00 and that had caused a few discussions too. So, tonight was one of the free nights that Roger loved! No David. Okay, but where are we going?" she asked not really wanting to go but would make the sacrifice for her lover. "Let's go back to that place we had our first date" I want to remember when I fell in love with you" he said holding her hand. Sounds wonderful let me take a shower and you can find something in the refrigerator if you're hungry and I'll be out soon. "We can watch a good movie together before we go out" she explained heading into her bedroom. She turned on her shower and went over to her closet to pick out the outfit to wear tonight for dancing. "This will be fun she said picking out a dress with lots of swing in the skirt and a sexy haltered bodice top. She then stepped into her shower for a long shower from the day. She wasn't thinking about dancing today her mind was on the ranch and Rusty. How lonely he must be in the big house all by himself. She was thinking about how caring he was with David and Tommy when they ask that 100th question or how thoughtful he was when he met her at Boothbay. She stood with the water running down her body and her thoughts so far away from her home. Then she felt his hands on her and he kissed her on the back of her neck. "Oh, Rusty she thought loudly. His embrace was starting to feel so real. "It's wrong, it's wrong" she said and it came out loud. WHAT! oh honey, I was just thinking when did you slipped into my shower? She asked Roger who was now standing behind her in the large shower. She turned and kissed him and continued the moment with Roger!

Well how did it go today?" Rusty asked Corky as they sat down for dinner. It went well the boys are anxious to learn and I think they will be ready for the opening day rodeo, Corky believed. Well son, I think I'm falling in love with her" he confessed. She's easy to talk to and so understanding. I don't think she will move toward me not after I told her about Donna." But you, better than anyone know how I love Donna" he affirmed to Corky. "Yes Rusty, I know" he replied shaking his head. Corky was his son from another woman in Texas that he had befriended for a time after Donna had been ill for about a year. But he vowed never to leave Donna. Corky's mom stayed around hoping that Donna's illness would be fatal and allow her to have Rusty for she loved him. But year after year she was his other woman until Donna found out about the affair. Donna asked Rusty to move to Maine using her health as the reason. Rusty never told Donna about Corky the child he had from the affair. Corky's mother gave up all hope of Rusty leaving Donna and over time met and married someone else, but Corky stayed Rusty's secret love child and the child moved with him, lying to Donna that he belonged to one of his ranch hands. Donna found out years later about Corky but at the risk of losing Rusty she never let him know she knew.

Masony got right to his snooping. He had spoken with Rory Clark the crime scene investigator working with Billy and Desmond, and they went over to see the murder scene again. "Look, is that a surveillance camera Masony said noticing it had been turned around and hardly noticed at all. The one on the other side was very visible and it's what Rory had used to this point. "it sure is! How could I have missed that?" he asked himself feeling a bit silly. But Masony has been doing investigative work so long he had an innate quality for finding evidence and David Parker knew it. Masony didn't move as fast as he use to and he had his own style of questioning but bottom line he got results.

After checking with the security camera angle regarding the video from camera B in the parking garage they were looking for some additional footage. The camera had now been corrected to its right position so they went through the video footage of those days again looking for something they may have missed from camera A's range site. Masony wanted to talk again to the limo driver who found his deceased co-worker that morning. Rory gave him the limo services address and Masony put it in his pocket for later. "STOP! "That right there! Rory said pointing. "Now that's different look at the tire marks left on the garage floor". They sat watching but everything else was the same as was in the previous camera footage. "I'm going to stop back by the condo and then go over and speak with the driver" he shared leaving Rory's office. Masony went back over and using a visible solution like used in fingerprinting the car tracks became visible again. He took a photo of the car's tracks and would compare them to see what car made that type of track. The tracks were very close to the backstairs of Sidney's condo. On to the next appointment he had for himself. When Masony arrived, he was told the limo driver was out on and assignment, picking up some high-profile person coming into town and wouldn't check in until tomorrow. "thanks" Masony said moving away from the counter slowly. Masony wanted a closer look at this man. He eased his way into their locker area without being seen. That was a feat in itself.! He reached into his pocket pulling out a tool to open the locker. Looking into his locker he quickly noticed he was a fan of Jessica Strassberg. Her pictures her taped all over the inside. It looked like a typical man's locker, a few girly pin-ups and a clean uniform. He moved a few things around and noticed something out of the ordinary but dismissed it has not having any worth to the case. Knowing Masony he would keep it in mind. Masony's style was sit and wait and that's what he did. The next day he waited outside of the limo business. Rory had given him a picture of the driver. After about an hour Masony spotted him. He came in to check in though he was continuing the same assignment until the client left town or had no further need for their services. When he left not yet wearing his work uniform Masony followed him. He buzzed in and out of traffic arriving at what Masony guessed his residence. After and half hour or so he left dressed in a uniform for work locking his door and driving away. Masony looked around before going up to the apartment door knocking. He took out his very small tool and with a few clicks he was in. "Strange" he thought looking around did I open the right door? He carefully went out again and looked at the number on the apartment and slowly went back inside he hoped undetected. "It was very feminine Masony thought looking around the neat apartment. "Umm now that item that was in the locker makes sense" he reasoned. He went through the closet and back in the corner were lots of woman's clothing. Maybe he's married or lives with a woman I'd better be careful he thought moving around looking at his watch. Then he saw a picture of a woman and Ms. Strassberg over on the night table. "Ummm! Suddenly he heard someone coming whistling as they approached the door. Where in the world could a man of Masony's size hide? He couldn't get under the bed. He'd had to take his chances in the closet. He stood there amidst the women's clothing listening. "Here it is, he had forgotten his wallet, Masony heard the voice say and then he heard the door close and finally silence. "Wheww! That was close". Masony made his way back to his car he'd have to regroup and looked forward to and evening of rest he hoped.

The crime scene investigators determined the tire tracks were the same kind that was on the limousine that drove Ms. Strassberg around. But the supposed driver was in the morgue and days had turned into weeks and now months had past and Sidney Owens was now on trial for the murder of his starlet lover Jessica Strassberg.

Will the court come to order! Those words rang out early in the morning. Sidney dressed in a navy blue Alfani suit sitting at the defendant's table with William Parker and Desmond Owens as his attorneys. Sitting directly behind Sidney in the courtroom was his parents Mr. and Mrs. Leron Owens. Mostalgia who had come to spend a few days with her husband and David and Tetra Parker Billy's parents were also present. The prosecutor sat with this confident look on his face regarding the many witnesses he had gathered who put Sidney at the scene earlier that night. After things got settled the bailiff call the court to order. "Please rise! The honorable Judge Calvin Bottley presiding" with everyone on there feet the judge walked in and took his seat on his bench. This court is now in session!" The prosecutor was up first for his opening statement. He pointed at Sidney as he accused him of luring Jessica back into his apartment and maliciously and with out forethought put a pillow over her head and smothered her to death. He went on painting a grim picture of that night pointing out the fact that several witnesses had saw him brutally pushing and hitting her in the hallway. Sidney Owens could only sit and listen wiping tears making their way down his face. Then the prosecutor turned to the jury that had been chosen. I ask that you render the only verdict possible, guilty in the first degree! Looking over at the defendant's table before taking his seat. Then it came time for Billy's opening statement. "Lady's and gentlemen of the jury you see sitting before you a wrongfully accused man. Mr. Owens was in love with the victim. His every waking moment was thinking about her. Martha Owens rolled her eyes has he spoke. She was showing fatigue as well as worry, but kept it under control for his father's sake she expressed to her son Desmond. "He had left his penthouse suite after he couldn't get Jessica Strassberg to leave to end the argument" he went on to say. He felt bad about the scene at his door. Which by the way was him pushing the door to keep her out? He never hit her at all". To save his dignity from all those on lookers he chose to leave from the back-exit door. Now wouldn't you think that if he was the one who murdered her, he wouldn't have drove up to the building when he heard the news?" Sidney Owens left home alone without anything in his hand"." The surveillance camera on the property proved that statement. The bruises found on her body could have come from her kicking at the door he admits but it does not prove he murdered her. Until that night he and the defendant were in love and contemplating marriage" Billy had the courtroom quiet as he caused pondering with each spoken statement. "They argued about the condition his suite was in when he arrived". We have a housekeeper who will testify about the condition Ms. Strassberg and her fiends left his suite in days before he even arrived". I trust after you go over all the evidence you will search your hearts and fine a not guilty verdict for my client Sidney Owens". Billy went back and sat down. Desmond extended his hand to him shaking it in agreement of his opening statement. David Parker nodded at his son and smiled proudly.

CHAPTER TWENTY-TWO

Reaping what you sow

Dana and Roger were having a great time dancing and meeting some friends from the hospital where she worked. They drank, laughed and partied until early in the morning. She was enjoying her night out not having to worry about David Michael, who was probably sound asleep dreaming of the rodeo he would be riding in soon? Roger and Dana took a break from the dance floor and sat having drinks at their intimate little table over in the corner. They were sitting close and holding hands while whispering sweet nothings in each other's ear when a gentleman walked up and spoke to Roger. "Hello Roger, he stated in a matter of fact tone. "Oh heeehello" Roger's very surprised stuttered response came. 'Funny seeing you in here! the man stated, I thought I saw you dancing but I said no can't be! So, my curiosity got the best of me and here I am! He said standing over them as he spoke. Again, Roger's response was flawed. This eloquent sounding man who spoke in front of crowds for a living stammered and stuttered through his whole conversation with this gentleman. "I, I, was ah just in town doing some business this weekend and ah I thought I'd take in some dancing". "This is Dana, a friend from ah the hospital" he said finally ending this labored reply. 'Please to me you. My name is Arthur Miles extending his hand. Roger had turned white as a sheet. "Well Roger I was just here on business with Joan and we're going back home tomorrow night" he shared with him. When they looked over at the table where he was pointing, Dana could see the lady waving across the less crowded room. "Good seeing you! he said walking away. Dana nodded in agreement and Roger's face showed a look of shock, though that's putting it mildly.

"And old friend?" Dana asked because he had not said a word since Arthur left their table. "Someone I know" he said sadly. All the wind was gone from his sails. When the deejay called the finally song everyone went onto the dance floor. With the room crowded Roger asked if they could leave now. Confused but she would ask questions later when they got home, Dana agreed and walked out to her car and headed home. "Well, now do you want to tell me what that was all about?" she asked. Roger seemed to have gotten his legs back under him. 'He's my competition" was his quick reply. "You know I'm here early this month, I'm usually not here this week, and I wish to God I wasn't" he mumbled under his breath. "Boy, you guys are sure fierce competitors" Dana said as Roger drove them back to her home. Her playful advances the rest of the evening only brought her kind rejections that eventually turned into sleep. When she awoke that Sunday morning Roger had left.

Justin was headed into his building when he heard someone calling him. "Justin, hi Justin! He could see this young boy coming toward him yelling his name. On closer inspection he could see it was one of Ariel brothers. "I was just saying hi! The young boy ten maybe eleven replied. "Well, hi Fletcher how have you been?" "Fine! was his response but Justin could see he really wasn't a least not by appearances anyway. 'Where are you headed so far from home Justin asked?" "I'm coming from school" he said. "From school! Justin said surprised. "Our school was over crowded and some of us got bussed to other schools out of the area we live in. I missed my bus today so I'm walking home". He didn't say it in a way that was complaining. Justin figured he's probably done it before. "Hey I was just about to eat would you like to go with me, I'll take you home after we eat If it's alright" he suggested.

"Yep he said without thought. Unless things had changed at home, he really had nothing to go home to. He was the youngest one and was often left alone until the older ones returned from school. So, he probably chose to walk home to waste time. Justin was headed into his exclusive building but changed plans and headed back to his car.

'Come on he said. "Oh, Justin you have a new car! "Yes, I do". "It's nice! Thank you" clicking his remote to open the car's doors. Justin and Fletcher went to the pizza house and had pizza and played video games and talked. Fletcher said he liked the school he was attending but some of his subjects he could use extra attention in. Adelle his older sister helped him a lot when she could. But he said she has lots of homework too. After Justin had eaten his fill and Fletcher had stuffed himself with pizza and fun Justin and he left the pizza house to take Fletcher home. They talked all the way down the highway enjoying each other's company. 'Thanks Justin, that was fun! Fletcher said pulling up to his house. For me too sport! He affirmed walking into the house with him. "Fletcher! Where have you been?' his sister asked running over to him". "I'm sorry he was with me. I should have made him call" Justin said apologizing for making her worry. "Oh, hi Justin the other's said in unison after they looked up from the small television screen they were gathered around. Adelle was in the kitchen trying to prepare a meal. "I'm not hungry, he said Justin and I had pizza" Fletcher replied. "Oh, Fletcher you're lucky! Another told him. "Justin felt so bad. Ariel probably had not come yet this month or even at all anymore but he couldn't ask. "Okay he said rubbing Fletcher's head "home safe and sound". Thanks, Justin, for everything! I missed you! he acknowledged by hugging him around his waist knowing it was a chance meeting today. Justin was almost in tears. He handed Adelle one of Billy's business cards and a hundred-dollar bill. "Call and make an appointment with this attorney". 'He's out of town now but when he gets back, I'll call and let you know" he told her standing at the door. "And I will call you every week until he returns okay! She really understood, and was so glad for the help. "Thanks Justin" she said closing the door. Justin got in his car and dialed for delivery of three large pizzas and drinks to their address as he pulled away.

Day after day they returned to the courtroom. The prosecutor was calling witness after witness who saw the confrontation going on in the hallway in front of Sidney's door at the Exclusive Suites. The maid also testified she heard Sidney say he was going to kill her if she didn't leave. "This was a big blow to the defense team of Sidney Owens.

It had been two weeks of testimony and Bridget Childs was due to testified this week. She had flown in from Paris and was sitting in the courtroom when it was called into session. With all formalities out of the way Bridget took the stand. Please raise your right hand and state your name "Jessica Childs." "Do you swear to tell the truth and nothing but so help you God." "I do" she replied. You may be seated. The prosecutor walked and stood in front of the jury looking at each one as he questioned the witness. "Do you know this defendant?" he asked. "Yes! she responded with her French accent. "How do you know Sidney Owens? "I met him through Jessica" she again responded. "Jessica Strassberg? Prosecutor clarified. Yes! Now what are you to Jessica Strassberg? "We're good friends" How long have you known Ms. Strassberg?' "Jessica and I lived in Paris together before she came to the states" she said. I see" he replies, moving back behind the desk in the courtroom. "Now when was the last time you saw Jessica alive?" "The night she was murdered" she said wiping the corner of her eye. Sidney was hearing some things for the first time sitting quietly over in the defendant's chair. "I was with her at her condo when Sidney stormed in! she acknowledged. "She jumped up and ran behind him! that's the last time I saw her alive! she screamed looking at Sidney angrily. The court was in a buzz. "Order! Order! Order in the court! The judge said beating his gavel down hard. "Resume" he announced after silence had once again been reached. "Did the defendant see you that night?" Yes! Bridget replied. And, where were you?" he asked allowing her to calm. "I was in the bedroom with Jessica when he walked in". "Jessica screamed and jump up running after him and I followed". She told me she was going to get him back and I left her place and went back to my hotel". she confirmed. The prosecutor continued to question the witness she was proving to be quite a credible friend. "Thank you, he said turning to look at the jury. "No further questions. "Your witness" he said allowing Billy to cross exam. "Isn't it true that you and Jessica Strassberg were lovers!" WHAT! oh my! came from the people sitting in the courtroom. Order! Order! The judge was pounding his gavel and the courtroom was now out of control! I object! could be hear from the prosecutor. Order! Giving his gavel another solid bang. "Another outburst and I will hold this entire court in contempt" he stated. "Objection sustained the witness may answer the question".

"Yes", there was now a hush in the room though heads were turning and whispers ever so slightly could be heard. "So, might you being a rejected lover want revenge?" 'NO! No! she screamed I would never harm Jessica I loved her! "No further questions" Billy replied returning to his seat.

When Dana woke up and found Roger gone, she was surprised. He always stayed the weekend with her when he came. He had in the last three months been coming once a month. It was usually at the months end but she had missed him and had expressed that to him over the phone. To her surprise he had come a week earlier than planned. "I hope that man wasn't someone he answers to and he wasn't supposed to be in town" she thought to herself as she dialed his number. 'Ring, ring," "you have reached the cell phone of Roger Haskell please leave a message" Dana left a message for him to call back and she sat waiting getting some paperwork finished she had brought home from her office. Three hours went by and he still had not called. "Dana tried again but still only reaching his voicemail. Frustrated and a bit upset she dialed Rusty at the ranch. She figured she'd talk to him and it would get her mind off the phone call she was waiting for. "Hello." Hello may I speak with Rusty Higgins? she asked his housekeeper. "Just one moment I'll see if Mister Higgins is in, please hold! "Hello, came his voice. "Hi Rusty" Dana said after hearing his voice. "Well Howdy do! He joked. Just got back from town a bit ago" he shared. "How's Donna?" Dana asked figuring that's why he was in town. "Oh, today was a normal day! she felt pretty good. We got a chance to walk outside on the grounds today". He added. "Oh, that's good so she's up and walking Rusty?" "oh no, I wished that was so" I pushed her around in her wheelchair". "So, what's your day been like?" he inquired changing subject to her. "Today, I just sat around and did paperwork I brought home from the office". "You sit around with David is he alright? he asked laughing hard. "No, David's visiting Tommy this weekend so it's really my weekend to rest" she confessed. "I guess those boys are a handful, but I enjoy every minute with them" he said laughing as he and Dana shared moments of their day. As she sat talking her phone was letting her know she had another call. "Rusty, can you hold I have another call? clicking over hoping it was Roger. But it was David saying he was on his way home from Tommy's. She clicked back over and continued talking to Rusty who was enjoying her conversation as well. "Rusty thanks for the company I really needed someone to talk too" she confessed. "Well, thank you for putting up with an old coot like me! he said laughing which at a point gets contagious. He could make anyone laugh she thought. Tonight, it was just what she needed. "I have to get David's, dinner ready he's on his way home". "Well tell him I said howdy," "I will Rusty goodnight! David had come home and shared about his day with Tommy, called and spoke with his dad in Baltimore, finished his homework had dinner and Dana still sat waiting for Roger to call. Dana had even spoken briefly with Billy finding out how things were going with the trial. She shared she had been following it with the news media like everyone else. She just wanted to hear what he had to say regarding the case.

After David her son had gone to bed Dana showered and got into bed. She looked over and saw Roger's briefcase he had forgotten in his haste to leave, she guessed. "But why was he in such a hurry to leave and why hadn't he called. She got up from her bed and put the case by her bedside and got back into bed. "Look in it! Her thoughts kept saying. She had never even noticed it sitting there until now. He always came in with his case. 'No! self-talking before she laid down on her pillow. "Open it" her thoughts kept saying. After a few more indecisive moments she got up and opened it. She saw a lot of medical papers for the equipment that he sold. She recognized them from having to sign a few of them whenever new equipment was delivered. "He's going to need this! she said why doesn't he call he's probably going crazy thinking he's left it somewhere else, she sat thinking. She took a chance and sat dialing his cell number again but still only getting a recording. She started to close the case and lay back down but decided to look in the zippered pocket. Reaching in she pulled out some pictures. One was of Roger a lady and four children. It looked a lot like a family photo. The others were separate photos of the children. She turned it over and each one said to daddy love and the child's name. "Roger never mentioned he was married. We have been dating for almost two years, a year and four months to be exact and he never said he was ever married or had children. And she was right the photograph had

Haskell's family photo and the year. He was with me then "What's going on she thought.

The next days in the trial were pretty intense as witness after witness pointed all the evidence against Sidney for murder. But Billy was fighting back and they were holding fast. One television station there even announced they were making ground over the prosecutor's case. But nothing still had been concluded. Masony had now started to use his own tactic's to solving the case. He felt it rested with the limo driver but couldn't get any evidence on him and he had no record or prints for Vance Sullivan. Masony bought a tracking device and attached it to Vance's private car and his limo he drove. He followed him to a lot of sleazy places and gay bars when he was not driving the limo. One day Masony decide to get Rory and take him over for another look at Vance's place. He explained to him that something seemed funny. He never saw a woman come from his place but the closet was full on woman's clothing. Now there were lots of women coming in and going out on certain nights but that still did not explain for Masony the clothing in the closet. Rory was known to go against the grain to solve a case so they went in again for a closer inspection of the apartment. The place was neat, immaculately kept. They walked through out looking into drawers and cabinets but found nothing. Then Masony went into the bathroom and one could only imagine what they found. Makeup, glue, a moustache, ect "We got it! Collecting samples of the found evidence taking photographs and leaving from the apartment.

Mother Dorrance had purchased the bus tickets earlier that day and had packed her suitcase headed to Baltimore. She was determined to be there to see Sidney walk from that courtroom a free man! She had been keeping a close eye on the case between prayer services at her home she said. She had her church praying and everyone down at the super market that could get a prayer through, she said she wanted them to pray. She was determined to put the devil out of business! "Tyler are you ready? I don't want to miss that bus! It's going to take us three full days I'm told so we have to leave now". "Okay I'm ready" bringing slowly out his suitcase that had seen its better years. "Bean, you ready?" calling her husband by his last name. He was taking them to the bus station. "Now Bean I got this cellular phone and the number I put on the Frigidaire". "Call if you need me otherwise, I'll call you everyday. "All right Dora, how many times you gonna go over this stuff?" They got their luggage in the car and headed to the greyhound bus station downtown.

Dana finally went to sleep after tossing and turning with what she had found in Roger's briefcase. When she woke up the next day and got David off to school, headed for her office, there was still not one message from Roger of any kind. She at least expected an apology. She had put the briefcase in her trunk in case he came by her office to get it but it was noon and she still had not heard from him. She looked at her schedule and she didn't have another client until tomorrow at nine a.m. She called and asked Lily to pick up David from school and she'd be in touch. She was going to drive to Waterville about fifty or sixty miles away and would pick up David as soon as she returned. She called her friend Mollie to ride along with her. Mollie agreed but she had to get things squared away with a trade off from one of her co-workers. Dana spoke with Mollie's supervisor. Mollie had already taken to much time off with her past incident. But with a vouch from Dana, they were on their way. "Mollie you look good! Dana said trying to make herself feel better she guessed, keeping conversation cheery. Mollie had lost around 40 pounds and wore a size fourteen dress now and looked very stylish. She did have more self- confidence about herself Dana thought as they talked riding along down the highway. But Dana had one thing on her mind and that was finding Roger Haskell. The main office was located in Waterville she knew that someone should be able to tell a doctor Williams where he was. She and Mollie had delightful conversations on the ride down ranging from work to men to clothing and anything in between. After a quick fifty miles Dana exited from the freeway and turned corner after corner locating the address to the large hospital supply retailer. She parked and walked in and was greeted by the receptionist at the front desk. "Hello" "I'm Dr. Dana Williams may I speak with a Roger Haskell?" she asked. The receptionist looked as if scanning a schedule. "Roger is in the field right now would you like to leave a message?" handing her a pen and pad on which to write. "No that won't be necessary' she said getting ready to leave. "Hello! Dana turned to see the man from the dance place coming from the wide hallway a few feet away. "Arthur! He said, we met Saturday night in Portland. I'm just headed out for lunch have you been helped?". "Oh, she wanted Roger! The receptionist replied. "I told her he was in the field". "Roger! He asked candidly is there something I can help you with, I'm his brother-in law dearie? He smiled mocking her. He had seen them together in the dance cafe place and that's why Roger had left in such a hurry. Dana had the picture now! "He left this at my house" she said tossing the briefcase on the floor at his feet to the condescending man. "Dearie, you're not the first, my sister puts up with Roger" she thinks he'll change" And they have four children an another on the way"." He's not going anywhere our family owns this business! he confirmed. Dana didn't know why she was standing here listening to this weasel of a man with her friend Mollie waiting in her car. "Look! he said "chalk it up to a lesson learned" and turned around and started walking back down the hall with the briefcase. Oh, and dearie! "I'll see that he gets it! He yelled as Dana huffed out of the building.

Rory Clark and Masony couldn't wait to get the evidence to Billy and Desmond. They had made a big discovery about the limo driver Vance Sullivan after following him for about two months. And the break came when they searched his apartment. The trial was in its third month and the toll of it was wearing on everyone. Mossy was flying back out to Baltimore to be with her husband and then flying home to spend time with her children. Grandpa John was doing better since he had the little ones as he called them to keep him busy. Brenda would come every other day and take him to the recreation hall which allowed him to spend time with his friends. He had a very good balance in his life and that took some of the stress off of the Owens especially Desmond he loved his grandfather so much. So, when Masony and Rory walked in and handed them the photographs they had taken at Vance's apartment it all made sense. Billy began to share with Desmond his thoughts but the trick was to get him to tell on himself! And with this news they were ready to go back in court again.

Tetra had a message on her phone when she arrived at the Center Tuesday morning. It was a very faint voice. She soon recognized it to be Mrs. Scroogins across the street. She put her purse and tote bag down quickly and hurried back out the Center's door. Hurrying across the parking lot she soon knocked at her door. "No one answered. She had just been at the church last night at her women's meeting, Tetra remembered while standing at the door. Mrs. Mattie Scroggins taught in one of the ministry circles at the church and they simply loved her teaching style. She taught the women who were widowed. She herself was ninety years old. The church had given her a big 90th celebration and one of the local channels did a big story on her life. "Plain, and understandable is what she would say. That's all I know! Not getting an answer Tetra realized she had not brought her purse so she ran back across the lot again and quickly picked it up. "Good morning! James said sounding cheery ready to start his morning. "Good morning! She returned the greeting heading for the door. "Where's the fire?" he asked teasing her. "I didn't get an answer from mother Scroggins when I knocked on her door! she told him heading out with him close behind. "I came back for my key! She stood there fiddling with the knob. Her hand was shaking so she couldn't get it in its lock. James took the key and opened the door and walked in. "Mother Scroggins! Tetra called not wanted to startle her. "No answer. "Mother Scroggins! She said louder opening her bedroom door. She looked and saw her lying peacefully in her bed. "She's still asleep, she turned and whispered to James. She tipped toed up closer to her bed and touched her shoulder and it was cold. "No! no! she fell to her knees crying. James touched Tetra's shoulder to comfort her. Mrs. Scroggins had her worn out bible lying on her bed beside her. And has she always said she would someday be gone home with the Lord.

Dana didn't say much all the way home. Mollie did most of the talking. 'That didn't take long?" Mollie said sitting on the passenger side of the car. "He wasn't there he was in the field." Dana responded. Mollie didn't know any of the stories, she only knew what Dana had shared and they were going to return his briefcase. And until now Dana didn't know the whole story either. She had spent two years of her life with this man and now she found out he was married. "How could he! she thought riding home with her friend along the highway. Dana posed herself on being in control. She counseled people on their feelings; it was her job as a psychiatrist. Roger had done this to her! Countless hours she had spent thinking about him and loving him and waiting on him hoping in marriage one day with him and he's married all ready with children, four plus children to be exact!" And not only was her head tripping but her heart was broken too. She loved this man! She took Mollie back to her car. "Thanks, girlfriend, for the company! she told her. Dana really didn't contribute much at all riding back she was quiet with her voice but her thoughts were screaming out! "See you tomorrow lunch?" Mollie asked. "Call me at the office, my appointments run all day" but if not tomorrow this week promise! She affirmed to her friend. She left going to get David from Tommy's house. He was so excited about how well he achieved one of the trick rides Corky had taught him for the soon coming Rodeo show. "Dana was confused and sad but she had to be strong for her son. She couldn't let Roger break her down like this. This came out of left field. "how could he do this! She kept saying over and over again. She took David by a fast food restaurant of his choice and headed home. "Dana you're quiet is everything okay?' Davie asked eating his fries in the car.

She was so close to tears but no she couldn't, surely not in front of David. "I'm just a bit tired, she implied "as a matter of fact I'm going to turn in early tonight sweetie". After arriving home, she took her briefcase from the car and left instructions for David Michael to go to bed no later that 9:30 because it was a school night. And she went into her room and cried herself to sleep.

CHAPTER TWENTY-THREE

Saying good-bye

Justin walked up to his apartment whistling with an arm full of assorted flowers from his favorite florist for Rae. He put the key in the door and "Menae! I didn't expect to see you? I know baby but I missed you." "I haven't spoken with you in 4 weeks and you know that's to long for me." "But I see you were thinking about me you brought flowers" she said taking them from his hand. "Always! he said kissing her as they stood in the middle of the room. "Let me put these in water. "Where are the vases sweetheart?" "Try under the sink in the kitchen, he replied. Justin didn't know he had a housekeeper. "Sweetheart want to go to Frattello's tonight?' she asked. "Dinner, dancing and friendly conversation?' helping him take of his jacket and hang it in the front closet. "With whom?" he asked. He liked going out with Menae but everything she did was over the top including their lovemaking. He wanted to wine and dine her and get to know her and have intimate time alone with her! Just her! It always involved friends or hurried intimacy and he was growing to tired of it and moved away from her. But he still could not resist his sex appeal and she knew it. She went into the kitchen and prepared them some cocktails. Then she went into the den and turned on the television set and sat watching it while Justin took his shower after just coming in from the hospital. His schedule had improved tremendously for the better. But his time off now was spent with Rae unless Menae came by are called. Calling him had failed so now Menae had started dropping by unexpectedly and uninvited. Do you know what that can do to a bachelor's life? He was surprised that he was able to shower and change into his relaxing clothes without being attacked by his houseguest who was sitting ever so quietly in the den waiting for him to return. "Menae, what are you watching? he asked entering the room". A game show silly" she teased. "He looked at the television screen, "game show uh? "is this mine?' speaking of the other cocktail glass sitting on the table with its salty rim. Yes sweetie". She took both feet and put them on the cocktail table. Her already short skirt went up even higher. Justin looked and took a deep breath. "Justin! she asked could you please get us some more drinks? "There's a pitcher full already made in the refrigerator" she cooed. Justin looked over at her long legs going up to her almost invisible shirt and turned going into the kitchen. "So, who are we meeting tonight Menae? he yelled from the other room. "Just a group from the office you know Fred and Wilma" she teased again. "Here you go" handing her the pitcher of Margaritas she had made earlier. "Thanks babe reaching over to kiss him exposing her top behind the haltered bodice blouse she was wearing. Justin sit the pitcher on the table and a saucer filled with salt aside of it. Then he sat back down flipping through the channels. Why did you turn it?' she questioned putting her hand on his thigh. He turned it back to the channel they were watching and sat back and relaxed as they watched a special presentation on the television. Soon both noticed they had finished the entire pitcher of the delicious drink.

Menae had gotten frisky and Justin no longer mined that she had come by uninvited. After an hour or so they showered and got dressed for the evening. Leaving the building Menae and Justin ran into Rae coming into the building. Menae didn't know who she was but Rae knew she was the other woman in Justin's life. Justin gave her an uncomfortable hello as they passed in the foyer on the ground floor. 'Nice dress! Rae said as they passed. Menae just threw her hair back smiled and kept walking.

They had covered quite a few miles in their three-day journey by bus. The Greyhound bus was on the outskirts of Kentucky and heading into West Virginia and had stopped to give everyone a stretch break from the already long ride. "Mother Dorrance are you, all right? Tyler asked. She had gotten off the bus and sat in the terminal getting some breeze from the air that was blowing by. "oh, I'm fine, I was just sitting her feeling the breeze and praying" she told him. "Okay, I'm going to go over and get us something hot to eat at that hamburger stand over there". Some of the others had gone over, I'm sure we have time," saying nothing she just shook her head. He ran across the street and stood in line. Every one of the other people was from the bus he noticed. He ordered two burgers and two sodas for him and mother Dorrance, that in his calculation should cost around ten bucks and maybe some change. After a while they called him to the window giving him a bill of about thirty dollars. "This is not my order. I only ordered two burgers and two cokes he affirmed. "Right but the other's riding with you ordered and said you were paying". "And look around since you're the only one here you have to pay! Tyler stood silent for a moment. His first thought was to refuse to pay for it and just walk away. The person behind the counter knew it was their mistake he came over after the other people. Now the two workers behind the counter stood and waited to see what Tyler was going to do. "Then Tyler thought about his past. "How much did you say it was?" counting out the money. He realized how thankful he was to be able to pay for anything. He smiled and took his order back across the street and he and Mother Dorrance enjoyed those juicy homemade burgers before heading on their journey.

After getting David off to school Dana poured herself into her work. She was really doing a disservice to her patients today her mind was on Roger and her heart was hurting. She made her way through lunch with Mollie though clear to Mollie something was wrong. "It is Roger isn't it?" she continued to ask across the lunch table at the bistro. "I'm trying to forget him Mollie, please don't bring his name up again! "I told you! I told you he was just like all the rest of those dogs!" Mollie sounded out. Dana let her express her feelings through the rest of their lunch time together. Somehow letting someone share her pain made her feel better. "This stuff works! She smiled to herself. After lunch she lunged back into her paperwork. She had two more patients to see after lunch and her day was free" she thought. "Hey you! calling Rusty who for once had answered the phone. "Well where have you been?" he asked. Dana had locked herself away from everything except David. She had purposely not been going to pick up David at the ranch and two maybe three weeks had passed. She still had not heard from that coward Roger but her hurting heart was allowing her some good days. She talked everyday with Mollie as a venting tool and she felt so much better! Mollie understood her pain and her hurt. 'Oh, just busy with work! She responded. Well! are you coming to the big rodeo this Saturday?" "It's this Saturday?' then she remembered hearing David tell his dad about it. He mentioned that it was this Saturday as they sat talking long distant on the phone. "I guess I am," she replied. I couldn't miss my son's debut at the rodeo." "She was determined not to let her hurting heart get her down. "I guess I'll see you Saturday" she told Rusty. "What time does the boys have to be there?" They should be here around eight o' clock but the rodeo doesn't start until noon." Rusty replied. Okay! She said, he'll be there! Hanging up to finish her workday. She picked up David Michael from school. Stopped by and picked up his custom-made cowboy suit that had to be fitted from the tailor's shop and headed home for a good night's rest. Dana had fooled herself all day and that night again after three weeks she still cried herself to sleep and Roger still had not called to apologize to her.

Tetra was the first one to arrive at the church. She sat silently in the pews looking at Mother Scroggins chair that had been draped over in black satin fabric. She thought of the first time she met this precious woman about ten years ago. She sat unable to control the tears though she knew Mrs. Scroggins wouldn't won't her tears and she was in a better place. David walked in to consol her. He had been out showing the florist and the funeral directors where to bring and place the vanloads of flowers that had come in memory of this precious woman. Mt. Nebo was very large and the whole front area near the stage was covered in every imaginable flower one could think off. David sat down beside her and put his arm around her and she wept silently. "She was like a mother to me" Tetra wept only loud enough that David could hear her. The crowds had just started coming in. "But Tetra darling you know that this is not our home". She always told us her time here would soon be over" "You said last night when you walked her home and helped her to bed that she seemed a bit distant." David reminded her 'But honey I thought it was nothing a good night's rest couldn't cure. "She went home peaceable dear" she was tired and her work here was done". I know David she's in a better place but I miss her smile, I miss her conversations and her morning hello's when I come to work". "Then a strong breeze came in and blew some of the large flower arrangements over. "Tetra jumped up with David and ran to stand them up right. "Now where did that come from? she asked seeing all the doors to the outside were closed. "Oh, I think that's just Mother Scroggins continuing her flight home" David reasoned with a big smile looking up. "You are probably right dear" Tetra responded going back to her seat. Her Son and his wife came and her grandchildren. They had started coming regularly to visit her with their dad after the property she had sold to the church was turned into an overflow parking lot for the congregation. She loved those grandchildren. His wife was ready to leave as soon as it was over, she shared with Tetra not knowing who she was speaking with. There were so many people there it looked like a convention of saints. The lines to express condolences were long. The mass choir sang all of her favorite songs. And Tetra read and wrote the eulogy that brought lots of tears to her as well as the listeners. She and Mrs. Scroggins had shared so much together about their lives and she tried to tell it all in the very short time allotted to her for Mrs. Mattie Scroggins was a remarkable lady. Her son sat next to David and Tetra. He got up and expressed words to the Parker family and Mt. Nebo church of his appreciation and love they had shown to his mother. He thanked everyone for making her golden years on this earth worth living. And he wept as he read Matthew 25: 21 Well done... When Dr. Hathaway, got up to give her finally message he called it. He said there is really nothing I can add. Just look around this room Mother Scroggins life speaks for itself" But she did leave this message on an answering machine for all of us who are left behind: "Jesus is alive and well! Now you all go and tell somebody that Jesus is alive and well!

CHAPTER TWENTY-FOUR

Things are coming together

Justin went over to somehow apologize to Rae the next day for what she had seen. "Come in" she said answering her door. Leaning toward her to kiss her cheek he says "I'm sorry you had to run in to me last night that was not my intention." "Okay so why are you telling me this, you're grown! ignoring his advance closing the door as he came in. She was obviously upset. He thought maybe it was to soon to be coming over. But he didn't want a scene like the one with Ariel and he had let her know everything up front. Somehow he guessed it didn't stop the twinge she was feeling. "Look it's fine I'm going out myself tonight" she said, moving around a vase she had on her table. "So where are you going?" he asked hugging her from behind kissing her neck. "She liked it but her goal was marriage and committed real love. "With friends!" she replied moving away from him. He let her go and sat on her sofa and turned on the television watching the sports channel. "So what time are you leaving?" "I don't know probably around nine" Rae responded. Nine! "That late, it's only six now". I know! but you know how we do it besides I haven't started getting dressed either" she replied. He sat still longer. Rae hummed around in her bedroom getting things ready for her evening, she told him. "Rae" she turned to see him standing in the bedroom door. "Let me take you out to dinner before you go out!" "I promise I will have you back by 8:30 and you will still have time to be with your friends," he pleaded. She didn't answer or turn around she was smiling. 'Come on Rae, we can leave at 6:30 and I'll have you back by 8:30 he said again to clarify his promise.

After a few minutes of composing her smiling Rae conceded. "You'd better! she turned around. He ran over and kissed her and headed out the door down one floor to get ready. She made up herself especially beautiful for she was going to fight for her man! She put on a form fitting black dress that accented her shapely body. Her hair she put up off her shoulders and the beautiful handset diamond earrings Justin had given her were sparkling against her smile. He wasted no time in coming back dressed dapper in a sky-blue suede jacket that matched his sexy eyes. "Let's go our reservation are for 7:00. "Rae you are gorgeous! he said leading her out of the door. Riding over to the restaurant in his car Justin could not stop complimenting her on her look her hairstyle, and sweetheart I love your perfume! Justin felt he had lots of ground to make up. He was still feeling bad about her seeing him with Menae. Even though she knew he was seeing someone else flaunting it in her face was not anything he ever wanted to be part of. "Just not my style! He told Franklin. Justin had got reservations at "Latitude." Billy his brother had share with him about the very posh restaurant down by the shoreline. He drove for about thirty minutes. "Are you sure we're going to be able to eat an get back home before nine?" Rae questioned still playing the role. She was right where she wanted to be, but she wanted a commitment and that she knew would take time. Though things right now were heading in the right direction. "Don't worry I will, but you will have so much fun with me you won't think of anyone else" he replied. Before long they pulled up to the front of the restaurant. A valet hurried over and opened the door. Justin handed him the keys and went over and opened the passenger door of his Beamer helping Rae out. He noticed her tiny feet in her high heel slip-on shoe. Everything about her intrigued him tonight. "Wow! She exclaimed looking at the large pillars of the building. It looked like something right out of Rome she thought to herself. 'Have you been here before?" she asked as they walked in. "No, he explained my brother told me about this place and I wanted to share it with you." Rae felt so special. He has brought her to a place where he hadn't even brought HER! she reasoned. "Mr. Parker?" right this way. Wow! That sure had a great sound to it "Mr. Parker". Rae was taking it all in. This place was magnificent even Justin wooed a little. He had been to some nice places with Menae and Franklin for that matter. But this place was a hidden treasure along

Portland Maine's beautiful coastal shoreline. The maitre de led them to a beautiful small intimate table in the corner. It was almost off to itself very cozy and warm. The mood was flowing with the dimmed sparkle of hundreds of tiny lights and soft music greeted them upon entering. "It looked like a lover's paradise Rae thought walking in. "Thank you, Justin said giving him something in his hand for the table's placement with a smile. After he had pulled the chair out for his lady fair and sat down in comfort, he began to enjoy a wonderful quiet evening with his resident lover. "Justin this is awesome" she told him. "All for you, I really feel bad about last night and I am sorry". "Shhh, She whispered putting her finger over his lips. "I except your apology" she affirmed and leaned over and kissed him. As they sat enjoying the atmosphere in the room their waiter came over. "Justin ordered a bottle of wine and some seafood appetizers to start. The dancing there was very slow and intimate. The elegantly played classical romantic music fit right in with the large glowing fireplace that flanked the dance floor centered in the middle. The stringed musicians embodied each piece with sheer sophistication. And the very mature crowd in this place made Justin stick out his chest to be a part. After a shared dance they ordered their entrees of lobster and it came with lots of side dishes. "Justin loved eating good food and this food was prepared excellently he admitted. "How's your dinner? he asked Rae, "it's wonderful just like you" she flirted. They sat holding hands and flirting back and forth with one another and with more conversation they shared their likes and dislikes. They talked about college and friends old and new. They were being so lovable with one another that Rae forgot all about the time. When the two decided to talk about leaving it was already past nine o' clock. "I'm sorry honey, it's past the time I said I would have you back home." "It's all right this time" she explained. She didn't really want to leave this place" she whispered as he embraced her on the dance floor. Justin thought she was speaking of the posh restaurant. But she meant his arms where he was holding her so close and dancing the night away. Justin soon realized, "Time is nothing, timing is everything!

Mother Dorrance and Tyler had reached their destination. They got a cab and asked to be taken to the nearest hotel to the downtown area courthouse. "I'll do my best but this place is crowded" the cab driver responded. "There is a big trial and we have been mobbed with media and outside visitors" he added. 'Exactly what are you looking for, price wise? he asked looking at the two sitting in his back sit. "Mother Dorrance had on her flower print dress and her lace knit pink hat. He also noticed the suitcase the two had stored in his trunk. Tyler wore one of the suits Sidney had purchased him almost a year ago now and except for both needing to be pressed they were fine. But he didn't think Hyatt fine, or Embassy fine but that's where they were. "Are you sure?" he asked as they got out and he put the luggage and suitcase on the front near the Embassy's door. Tyler handed him the fair. He wasn't sure either but he had learned not to question Mother Dorrance when she was about the Lord's business. They walked in. Tyler had put his suitcase on top of her rolling luggage the young adult group of her church had given her one Mother's Day a few years ago. She never had a reason to use it UNTIL NOW! She walked up to the counter. "May I help you?" A lady seeing them come over to the counter hurried over and asked as she stood in front of them. "Yes, I need two rooms please, Mrs.Dorrance requested. The lady looked at her and turned to whisper to another man behind the counter. "Two rooms?" she repeated. Yes, Mother Dorrance said standing patiently waiting for the next question. The woman cleared her throat. "How long will you be staying?" she asked. "I really don't know," Mother Dorrance replied. "Well let me explain! Our hotel is quite full at this time due to the high-profile trial going on, I'm sure you have heard about it". So, most of our lower price rooms are already taken or have been booked well in advance." "Yes, I'm still listening" Mother Dorrance replied. The woman huffed and continued. The only rooms we have available at this time are $199.00 dollars a night! She looked straight at Mother Dorrance. She had put her purse on the counter to open it. "AND! if you don't know how long you're going to stay we will need to secure it with a credit card! Mother Dorrance turned and looked at Tyler who was probably as tired as she was and this woman was going through this long spill. She had already judged them by their outward appearance and knew with certainty they couldn't afford this place. "Excuse me" Mother Dorrance replied and walked back and sit down still looking in her purse. The man and woman were laughing quietly to themselves and Tyler he wasn't saying anything he was just praying. Two more people had come up and stood in line. She kept searching with her head down. She was taking out papers laying them on the chair beside her. "Madam I have to help these other people if you're not ready! She stated for her patients with this matter had grown thin. "By all means don't keep them waiting I do understand." Mother Dorrance suggested to her lifting her head from its bowed position. The lady quickly helped the other guest that were standing in line and Mother Dorrance finally found whatever it was that was hidden away in her purse. She walked back up to the counter. "I'm sorry the rooms for $199.09 are gone now. She smirked "If you want any two rooms, they will start at 239.00 and up. Mother Dorrance just smiled "Thank you for being so patient with and old lady" she said. The lady looked at her puzzled. "It takes us a lot longer to do things and think things out sometimes" she added.

"We will take whatever rooms you have left dear I just need to rest!" she explained putting her gold American Express card on the counter. "Ma'am, she said softly clearing her throat. "I will need to see your identification". Mother Dorrance showed the lady her I.D. And the bellman took their luggage up to the two adjoining suites of this luxurious hotel and they showered and rested very well in the rooms that where now costing $179.00 a night.

Masony and Rory Clark had pieced together what they thought was the motive to kill Jessica Strassberg. The witnesses were being questioned and cross-examined for the better part of the day. The judge called an adjournment until 1:00 at which time they would reconvene. Desmond walked out in front of the courthouse to get some air. Billy was in talking with Sidney about the afternoon session and people were going out of the building for a lunch break quickly as to be back on time. "Hello, someone said walking up to him. "Hello Desmond replied a little stunned his reflex was to extend his hand to the stranger and get back in the building or courtroom before the media bombarded him. "I'm the jazz man" he said. "Okay Desmond said thinking Tyler was just another quack wanting to ask questions. "I'm a friend of Sidney's and I came down here to see him! he quickly said and it got Desmond's attention. Desmond a little hesitant pulled him over to the side of the wall. "You know Sidney, my brother?' Desmond didn't recognize him from the short visit at his home for his grandfather's birthday party. "Oh, now I remember" he said. "Are you here alone?" "No actually I came to accompanied Mother Dorrance. "We've been here four days now trying to get in but I guess it's virtually impossible. We were expecting this trial to be over but it hasn't yet! he replied pointing at Mother Dorrance sitting as close as she could get to the huge building flanked with media people and on lookers. "Well where are you two staying. He's pretty down right now so knowing he has friends that are here to support him will surely lift his spirit". "We're at the Embassy" he told him. 'The Embassy Suites around the corner?" Desmond questioned. 'How long will you be here?" I don't know, Mother Dorrance says she's not leaving until Sidney walks out free! "If you fly out before this trial is over give me a call" handing him his business card. "Oh, we didn't fly we rode the gray dog" he teased with a laugh. "Okay! I'd better get back inside before I'm spotted ". "Nice to see you again" turning hurriedly going back into the building.

Billy was in the room when Desmond came back. They had delivered their lunches and Billy was eating and talking on his cell phone to his son. "Hope to see you to son goodbye,' disconnecting his phone. "So, are we ready for this afternoon?' Desmond asked Billy. "Well Masony thinks this is going to work. I ran it by dad and he says if it does Sidney will walk out of here a free man!" "Now all I have to do his pull it off! He acknowledged. Speaking of Sidney, he's pretty down. He says this as lasted longer than he could have imagined it would." It's wearing on him Desmond, another night in that jail he says will probably send him in sane! "You might want to speak with him before we reconvene this afternoon" Billy suggested as his attorney. Desmond sat picking at his lunch his appetite was shot, he had not had a good meal since the day Sidney went to jail. Desmond missed his family, his wife and his home. He longed for his tranquil life again with his infrequent calls from his brother to say hello! After returning again to the jail he took a deep breath and asked the bailiff to bring Sidney out so that he could speak with him before court reconvenes. Billy had gone to take care of other matters with Rory and Masony. Desmond sat in the small room waiting. Sidney came in with the shackles on his hands and feet. He hugged him so hard they both cried on one another shoulders.

Desmond pulled out his handkerchief and first wiped Sidney's tears then his own. "Be strong brother" he said. 'We are going to get you out of this place! Sidney just nodded. "Look, up Desmond said raising his head with his chin. I saw a friend of yours from Kansas! "Kansas? Sidney's mind wasn't thinking about anyone who knew him except his brother or some other family member. So, he wasn't the least bit interested. Wouldn't you like to know who he is?' he asked trying to get at least a smile.

From Kansas?' Sidney thought, I don't know. "Does the name Tyler ring a bell! "Tyler, Tyler, you mean Tyler Parson the Jazz Man! "Yes, one in the same! "WHERE! Where did you see him?" the bailiff peaked his head around the corner hearing the loud speaking. "Right here outside this building! Desmond confirmed. I didn't know him. "It was by accident I went outside to get some air and he saw me" Well it does work! Sidney murmured to himself. What? Desmond asked "prayer" Sidney said quietly "prayer". "Where is he?' was he alone here?' he questioned not giving Desmond time to answer. "No! he finally got through despite Sidney's questions. He was with an elderly lady Mother umm I don't recall the name. "Mother Dorrance! she came all the way here" Sidney said. "They came by Greyhound bus! "That's almost three days on the road Desmond!" Sidney said in amazement. "Please make sure where ever she's staying or what ever she needs you get it for her! Promise me Des! "I will, I will. And Desmond can you get them in the courtroom one day I'd love to see them". "Sidney you're asking the impossible with a trial of this magnitude, but I'll see what I can do." Desmond could see how much it would mean to him. Billy came in and said, lets get ready! Sidney hugged his brother and said "nothing is impossible with God!"

CHAPTER TWENTY-FIVE

Not a bad day after all

The big day was here the rodeo was in town! David was excited and up early Saturday morning with his cowboy boots on and ready to go. "Come on Dana we're going to be late" David said standing by the front door holding his cowboy suit and sporting the boots and hat. "Child it's only 6:00 am you are not going to be late! "But remember we have to pick up Tommy! He explained. Tommy is probably still sleep and you should be sleeping too". "Look, David we will leave in an hour and that will still get you there in plenty enough time" she told him sitting down to have a cup of coffee and read the newspaper. David went back into the den and flopped on the sofa and went to sleep. Dana put away David's breakfast dishes then sat and read her newspaper thoroughly, had breakfast along with her coffee, got dressed before tapping David's shoulder. "Get up cow poke time to hit the trail" she said waking him from sleep he could have gotten in his bed. "he jumped straight up. "I'm ready! After they had secured the other half of the Rango gang they were on their way. Tommy's parents were coming at noon with his younger sibling to watch her big brother ride a horse. "Mom did you remember the video camera, I promised dad I would ask you to video it". "Oh, you did! "Will you Dana please?" "Sure, David I'll do my best to capture some footage for him to enjoy" she affirmed. Yes, I brought the camera". They rode along singing songs of the old west and discussing the event they were participating in. When they arrived at the farm Corky the young man who stayed at the ranch and Rusty was standing out front. "Well you boys ready?'

"Pile in" Rusty told em. "Where are we going?" Dana asked. The rodeo is about 8 to 10 miles up the road," Rusty informed her. "Oh, I'd better call Lily and give her directions" Dana replied. "It's best to leave your car here and pile in with us. Those roads are pretty tough on a delicate little car like that," Rusty suggested. He had a Ford two-ton pick up with a seat in the rear. David and Tommy got in the back and Dana sat between Rusty and Corky in the front seat. "Let's go! They were off again. Dana had gotten Lily on the phone, and passed on the directions to where the rodeo was going to be held. But the further they went along the highway there were signs everywhere giving specific details on how to get there. Bareback riding, saddle Bronc riding, steer roping, COME TO THE BIG RODEO! 5 miles take the next exit. They saw so many people coming into the ranch where the rodeo was being held. Many were getting ready for the rodeo events as they drove in down the rode heading to Bar S Ranch. People were moving around all over the place. There were venders setting up their booths and smoky links and barbeque signs all over. They moved around looking at all the rodeo had to offer. Dana purchased her a cowboy hat to match her boots she was wearing. Corky took the boys over to warm up while Dana and Rusty just walked around meeting and greeting his friends and some associates in the ranching business. "Howdy Rusty, extending his hand. "How do Bart" he responded. "This here is Dana Williams," "Please to meet you!" she said. Rusty and Bart shared a few words and they moved on making their way to where the podium was. Little did Dana know Rusty was presiding over the rodeo this year. "Well little darling I've got some things to do before this rodeo begins. "I'll see you later. Unless you want to sit in the booth with me" he replied. "Oh, I'll be fine!" Dana shared looking around at the hundreds of people that had start gathering on the dusty grounds of the ranch. They had hayrides for the young and the young at heart. She stood in line and rode around on a big hay covered wagon looking at where some of the events were being held. After her hayride Dana stopped to observe some young men practicing their calf roping skills. But she still hadn't run into the boys. She stood watching as the young boy roped the calf's neck pulling him down and tying his legs together. She clapped as she moved on through the crowd. Then she heard the announcement that the Rodeo had officially begun. She smiled recognizing the voice coming over the speaker was Rusty. People were running and walking to get to the bleacher area for the barrel racing. The little girls dressed in raw hide vests looked like Dale Evans in their cute little outfits were introduced together. Then they all went back to the bleacher area sitting to hear their name called. Each girl would ride the pony as fast as she could around a barrel trying not to knock it down. Dana was amazed many times. Some of the young girls were pretty good, she thought. And the winner is "Amanda Lafton" could be heard through the applause of the people. "Uh, she's one of the favorites I had picked, Dana said to a lady sitting next to her. Dana waited anxiously for David and Tommy's event. Event after event she moved from saddle bronc riding to bull riding before she spotted Lily and her husband with the younger sibling of Tommy. "Hi guys, their event is going to be right here, she said moving over to allow them space on the lower level of the bleachers that was filling up very fast. After the announcement of all the participants names, "David Parker" and Tommy McCormick" will be team 1. They took a bow. They looked so handsome Dana thought as both stood along with the other teams for the team roping competition. This event requires two contestants to work together, "Okay, let's do this! And they walked around the ring tipping their hats. The crowd cheered. "Hi! Tommy, hi David. Tommy's little sister said waving sitting on her mother's lap. They had to rope a calf as a team. They mounted their horses and the calf was let out to run around the fenced ring. Their challenge was to try and rope him taking as little time off the clock as possible. They had their lassos in the air twirling them over their heads. The crowd watched in silence as the two circled around and around. "Got it! Letting go of his lasso. Tommy secured the calves neck with his rope. Tommy was good at lassoing he was a natural, Corky acknowledged during one practice session to his mom Lily. The calf still put up a fight. He was too strong and almost pulled Tommy from his horse as he rode around trying to allow David time to rope his legs. "Come on David you can do it! he shouted. Dana was nervous. She knew how hard he had practiced. One more time around the clock was ticking. 'Hey! David shouted turning is lassoed rope a loose. The rope caught one of the calf's hind legs and down he came. They quickly dismounted securing the calf and threw their arms in the air! 'Bravo! Hey! Shouts came from the crowd. Corky clapped and laughed. He was very proud of his first students of rodeo. Fans and parents were jumping up and down cheering the boy's success. Dana had forgotten about the video camcorder she had in her hand. She sat back down and steadied her camera view. The announcers loud strong voice came across the speakers over the crowd's heads. "The time to beat is 4 minutes six seconds! He announced. The crowd applauded loudly as the boys stood next to the downed calf grinning from ear to ear. They were as proud as can be walking around with their third-place ribbon vowing to get first place next year. They had fun watching the steer wrestling and steer roping from the older cowboys. And of course, everyone's favorite the rodeo clowns toward the days end. Rusty came over and joined the group during this time and everyone enjoyed a good laugh seeing the clowns try to out smart the bulls! What a fun day Dana thought as she looked around the ranch that was earlier bustling with rodeo fans had faded to just a few ranch hands that were getting the animals set for the night. "Well did you all enjoy yourselves? Rusty asked Dana and the boys as they rode back to his ranch in his truck. Tommy had stayed with Dana he was not ready to leave with his family earlier that day. I sure did! Tommy replied. "Look Rusty! David said again showing off his ribbon. "My! That's good roping! he replied, mighty good roping! Dana hoped she had gotten some good camera footage for David to share with his dad Billy. WITH ALL SHE WAS GOING THROUGH RIGHT NOW WITH ROGER her day had lots of laughter and enjoyment. She had a wonderful time at her first ever Rodeo too!

Adelle was thankful for the money Justin was sending her every month. And it did make things much better. However, when he asked her about two months later, she confessed she still had to work to keep food on the table and it was causing her to miss a few days of school sometimes. She felt bad telling him. She knew it was not his responsibility. But Justin insisted on knowing and had stopped by to give her money for her and the boys every month. Her mother was still wasting the money the county gave her for the children and Adelle would do what she could with what was left after her mother had squandered it away. She would never bring herself to call Justin. He had made up his mind as to what he was going to do and was glad she allowed him to help them. He made it a point to stop by every month with help for the children until Billy his attorney brother came back from out of state. Justin wanted to know they had enough to eat. But even Justin didn't expect the trial to last this long. From speaking with his brother Sidney's lawyer, he certainly didn't expect to be gone for this length of time. Not that the money he gave the children every month was a burden he wanted more for Adelle and the boys. Besides twice Ariel spotted who she thought was him just leaving the children's apartment. They had passed each other on the residential street leading to it. She had almost caught him. Somehow Adelle managed to keep his help a secret from her suspecting sister. Adelle reasoned she was looking out for her younger brothers. She knew Ariel's help was needed but she had other responsibilities now. They had already lost and older brother Malcolm to the system and she still had her hands full with three growing active brothers who sometimes didn't have the stylish clothes and society wants but now certainly had more than enough to eat. She told Ariel their mother was being more responsible with the money and that put Ariel at ease on that matter. Adelle worked her minimum wage job went to school and had the responsible of her siblings at seventeen. So, she kept quiet about Justin's help. As he pulled away from their apartment, he passed Ariel coming up the road. Whew! that was close he thought she'd surely pitch a fit if she knew I was helping them too. So, feeling a little close for comfort Justin called and explained to Billy the situation and what he wanted to do. "I see Billy shared. I'll get another one of the attorneys at the firm to handle this matter for you. "Thanks Billy. By the way how are things going with the trial?" 'Well we have been leveling the field. It's been pretty even up to this point. It seems to be coming down to a creditability issue on Sidney's part. He doesn't have an alibi for that night. But hopefully today things will turn around". The media is certainly giving the trial a front row seat" Justin expressed. Yes, that seems to be the case when you have a celebrity involved." 'Look I have to go but I will call and have Annie make an appointment with one of the other attorneys. Take care!

Come to order! Sounded out across the courtroom. "The honorable Judge Calvin Bottley presiding. It had been a long ten months. And week after week Sidney returned to the courtroom to fight the allegation that he had murdered his lover the very popular music diva Jessica Strassberg. The prosecutor sat smug and confidant that he had made his case as revealed in the media. While Billy and Desmond were hoping what they were about to do today would turn the case in their favor. Call your next witness! The judge declared looking at William Parker. The courtroom was full. Sidney parents had come again after a brief return home. Bridget Childs sit waiting to see Jessica's murderer pay for what he had done. Rory Clark and Masony were near in case they were needed. But in their seats were Tyler Parsons and Dorrance Bean. They had been coming everyday of the trial for weeks now seating in those seats Desmond had made available that belonged to Rory and Masony. And though Mother Bean never complained she was tired. "Billy stood up. "I'd like to recall Vance Sullivan to the stand". Everyone looked around whispering. "Order! the judge said giving his gavel a pound. Vance was surprise he thought he had done his part. Now what do they want he thought approaching the bench. "Please raise your right hand and state your name! "Vance Sullivan." Do you swear to tell the hold truth and nothing but so help you God," "I do" You may be seated? Vance sat down looking nervously around, he didn't expect to be called again. 'Vance Sullivan, Billy repeated walking toward him. Is that your birth name? "Yes' he said very confidently. "Billy looked at Desmond. "Is this the name given you at birth? "Objection your Honor!" he's badgering the witness came from the prosecutor. "Sustained, that question as already been satisfied the judge explained. The courtroom was quiet. "I'll rephrase it your honor! The judge nodded his approval. "May I ask? Billy continued, "The mustache and beard is it yours or did you purchase it?" the courtroom was again buzzing. "Order! Order! The judge said pounding continually with his gavel. The prosecutor was shouting what kind of questioned is that?" QUIET IN THE COURT! Quiet, quiet, or I will hold you all in contempt" the judge voiced loudly, pounding his gavel. After and explanation at a sidebar the judge got his court back in order. "You're walking a thin line Parker", he conveyed to Billy regarding the point he was trying to make. Vance had started now to sweat. "You may answer the question" the judge said looking at him. "Remember you're under oath. "No! He said quietly. Would you repeat that so the jury can hear you!" Billy replied pacing across in front of him. "NO! he said and waited for the next shoe to fall! "Then may I inquire regarding your hair?' "Objection! The judge looked at the prosecutor and he quickly sat down. "No! came again from the witness. Everyone looked shocked what was he looking for? What point was the attorney trying to make? "That's that old devil!" Mother Dorrance whispered to Tyler. "Now! Billy said holding his hand on the rail in front of the jury. "I'll ask this question again! "What is your birth name? All eyes were now on the witness who blurted out Vanessa! "My name is Vanessa and I loved her! But she always went back to him every time. All I wanted was for her to leave his place with me! I didn't mean to hurt her!" she cried out in tears. "No further questions" Billy said sitting down, shaking Desmond's hand and giving a sigh of relief. Bridget sat with her jawed dropped she thought she was the only one. In closing arguments Billy later explained that Vanessa was in love with Jessica and they became friends and then lovers. Vanessa disguised herself and got a job working at the limo company under the name of Vance Sullivan to be near her. Masony found out later Vance was her twin brother who had died at birth. Vanessa took Jessica everywhere. Jessica was what you call a free spirit. Her limo was often a bedroom for them she confessed and Vance (Vanessa) being her sole driver in town knew and saw a lot that went on in Jessica's life. But in spite of everything she was madly in love with her. Her feelings got the best of her when Sidney was gone and she had Jessica all to herself she thought. But that night after Michael had dropped Jessica off at Sidney's Vanessa got really upset. She only killed Michael days later when he threatens to tell the police that Vance had taken the limo from him after he had dropped Jessica off at the suites that night. She became really upset and in a jealous rage went over to bring Jessica back. Vanessa was so upset and went over after Jessica called to say she was staying with Sidney. The doorman didn't see her because Jessica let here in through the back-exit door. Vanessa convinced her she only wanted to talk. Which was probably true. However, Vanessa's attention was to persuade Jessica to leave and come back to her. But Jessica said no! Which upset her even more and she smothered her with one of Sidney's pillows in Sidney's bed. It was her fingerprints we found on the knob of the exit door. But Vance kept getting in the way. We were looking for a man. After closing arguments by both attorneys, the jury was sent out to deliberate. Even with Sullivan's confession it took about five hours for them to render a verdict of not guilty of murder for Sidney Owens. What a day that was!

All the hugs and kisses were shared around the room as each left the courtroom. "That was quite a risk you took Parker! The judge acknowledged leaving the courtroom heading to his chambers. Desmond was smiling and hugging Mossy. His mom and dad were crying and hugging him first and then Sidney. Martha went over and hugged attorney Billy Parker. Thanks Billy, that was a terrific job! Leron said shaking his hand. Sidney had hugged all his family and went over to Mother Dorrance and Tyler. "Mom and Dad this lady and young man loves me! he said. They came all the way from Kansas to be here! Martha hugged her and Tyler while still hearing the story of their meeting with Sidney. Billy looked across the room at the man Sidney was introducing. He looked familiar and he searched his mind trying to place him. With his mind focused on the trial little was thought regarding Sidney's friends who had joined sort of speaking. Many others were coming up in the courtroom to shake his hand and congratulate him on a fine job. Martha thanked everyone for they're support from the bottom of her heart. "Well son Mother Dorrance said to Sidney "I have to be getting back home" you take care now' she told him again. "I will mother Dorrance, I will. Embracing her with tears flowing down their faces. "And Tyler! Billy turned and looked. He walked over to him. "Tyler? Tyler Parsons?" 'William Parker!" "Billy! it is you! Everyone was now wondering what was going on. "Wonders never cease! he said. The two stood looking at one another remembering a bond they once shared. They took a moment standing outside the courtroom to explain to everyone how they knew each other. "Small world! Sidney said small world! "Let's go celebrate! Everyone stayed around talking while Sidney's paperwork was being process for him to leave. They all went out to eat Billy, Desmond and Mostalgia, Sidney, their parents, and of course Mother Dorrance and Tyler Parsons, Billy's dear friend.

When mother Dorrance and Tyler went down the next day to check out of their rooms everyone greeted them and gave Mother Dorrance hugs. They had gotten use to her coming around sharing the word with them every morning. "Goodbye! Mother Dorrance" could be heard from the maid up to the chef at the hotel restaurant where she ate most of her meals. She slowly walked up to the desk. Mrs. Bean how was your stay with us? Kathy asked smiling from behind the counter. "Oh, it was wonderful! she smiled to, "my husband Lawrence may not think so after he gets this bill!" she snickered. "Oh Mrs. Bean I thought you knew, Owens law firm as paid in full all of your services here". And that limo out front is here to take you and Tyler to the airport". Airport! She exclaimed shaking her head. "Now who wouldn't serve a God like that? she stated walking out smiling and waving goodbye with her bible under her arm.

CHAPTER TWENTY-SIX

Winner takes all

Dana was in her office when she got the news regarding the trial. 'Hey! She said jumping up and down with the receiver in her hand. Mollie had called to give her the news. Dana! Dana! Justin came running in, did you hear? Did you hear?' "Yes, she said. Mollie I'll talk later someone is in my office," she then hung up So! did you see Billy's interview on television? Justin asked. I haven't been near a television set all day I've been so busy. I watched something about it at noon, but the verdict still had not come in!" Dana replied. "I did see the interview and he looked great. I was bragging and sticking out my chest! Justin said strutting around Dana's office. "Where's my nephew we have to go out and celebrate!" "I'll be heading out to get him when I leave here, Dana shared. "That is wonderful news! He won his first big case. Ring! Ring! Hello! Dana! Dad won his case! David yelled very excited. "I know honey, I know." That means he will be home soon! It sure does dear". Billy had been gone a long time almost a year nine months to be exact. But he was now coming back home for good, not just another short visit. Dana was spending a lot of time at the ranch, David loved it and was becoming a regular cowboy. Corky was teaching him a lot about being a rancher. But mostly he rode the horses and learn to care for them. Dana had promised Rusty she'd stop by after she got David Michael from school. But Billy was coming home and the first thing he said was, he wanted to see his son. She'd have to call and let Rusty know she wasn't coming. Rusty enjoyed her company. But didn't push himself on her and always enjoyed talking with her about his wife

Donna. Dana suspected he was really falling for her. Rusty was fifty-eight years old and Dana was thirty-five and she enjoyed spending time with him too. He certainly helped her feel better when Roger left her and went back to his wife she guessed. Dana finally got around to telling him what happened because it was affecting her and he sensed something was wrong anyway. Rusty didn't ask or expect anything from her except conversations. They just rode horses are talked during the time they spent together. They did have an occasional swim with the boys and played water games in the warmer months. "Ring! Ring! "I gotta go! call me when Billy gets in, we'll do something together to celebrate" Justin said kissing Dana on her forehead and heading back to the emergency department where he was now an intern. "Hello Dana, "Billy, congratulations," "Thanks, it was a hard-fought battle" I'm exhausted but I would love to see my son! "are you going to be home tonight?" 'I'm sure, He can't wait to see you either" Dana voiced. "I'll come by after I leave the airport, if that's alright?' Knowing she was seeing Roger. "That's fine I'll let David know, see you soon! Dana hung up and called Rusty. He wasn't in so she left a message with his housekeeper and left work for the day.

Adele was walking home from school. She was tired and had loads of books in her backpack. She had spoken with her counselor earlier today and he shared there was still a chance she could go to college once she graduates. He also told her she would have to really buckle down and focus on her classes to bring her grades up and looking forward a very good possibility does exist. Adele was glad to hear that. She was trying very hard but her younger brothers were her responsibility and she had to help them first. Her mom was not pulling her weight at all, she was still drinking and partying. Adele hurried along thinking as not to be late for her job at the Burger hut. That kept the boys in decent clothing and shoes anyway. The county gave their mom money but she would just waste it down at the local bar. She walked along and came upon a man painting a house. "Hello" he said as she walked by". Hello! Adele replied. nice house! "Yes, it could be". I'm here over and over again fixing windows and doors, just painting over that graffiti they put all on the walls" he told her. "Can I look in it? "Sure, he said. It's not in very good condition yet, just waiting for someone to move in." He kept painting while she went in. It had four bedrooms and a living room and a cute little kitchen. Adele imagined it all fixed up. But there's no way she could afford it. "That sure would be nice mister". she told him coming out the door. "Are you selling it?" "No! My wife wants to keep it but I'd love to rent it to a good family". "Rent! She knew they were renting their small apartment. Though it only had two bedrooms hardly any space at all for the five of them to live. She stood looking she still had a long way to walk. She had stayed after school to finish a homework assignment with a tutor and missed her bus. She promised the boys she'd get a car first if they got some money. "Thanks mister, but I can't afford this house". Well would you live in it if you could afford it?" Sure, she told him but we only pay $545.00 in the apartment and this house has double the space. "Well I think you can afford it that's exactly the monthly rent payment on this house" he told her. "Really! Mister will you be here tomorrow I'm going to tell my mom about this house. "I'll be right here dear" You have a good day! She ran off leaping and jumping. Thirty minutes later she was finally home. She was tired but now she had something to work for a better home for her brothers to grow up in and room to stretch out. They were growing and needed more space. Wow! she could have her own room she thought sitting down looking at the mail. Mom wouldn't have to come up with any money it cost the same as this run-down place.

She continued looking through the mail, "light bill, water bill, and then she saw a letter she opened it. "Oh no she thought, we have to move mom has not been paying rent! Now where do we go? Her hopes had faded. She thought of calling Ariel. But she had just stopped by last week and she is now pregnant so they surely couldn't go to her place. She started to cry. Then she saw a letter addressed from the law firm on the card Justin had given her. She remembered it because every night she looked at it hoping it would get them out of this place. She ripped it open and read it. In it was a letter with an appointment for tomorrow at 4:00. Good, she could get there and back before work. "Work! That's right jumping up getting ready and heading to the Burger Hut.

Dana! Dana! Dad is here! David ran over and hugged Billy. "My I think you've grown about two are three inches since I've been gone". "Boy!

I missed you dad" I missed you too son". Dana stood in the hallway door and watched the two embracing and talking. Billy looked up to see Dana smiling at them. "Hello Dana." "Hi again Billy" coming over and gently giving him a hug. "Congratulations dad!" David had him by the hand leading him to the family room. "Dad all the kids at school was telling me to tell you congratulations. Jimmy told me his mom watched the whole trial everyday on some cable channel I forgot!" Dad do you want to see the video from the rodeo! Dad I. "David, I'm going to hear and see everything you did while I was gone. But tonight, I just wanted to see you! I'm really exhausted but nothing a good night's rest in our own bed want cure, he shared rubbing David's curly locks on his head. Dana I was in such a hurry when I came before I forgot to tell you that you have a very nice home". Thanks Billy I really like it. 'Okay dad! David Michael said holding back emotions spinning in his head. "I know you're tired but you have to see this biology test grade! David jumped up and ran to his room to get it. "He's so excited you're home. He called me twice in an hour to see when I was coming to picking in up from Tommy's. "Good! so he has been seeing Tommy?" I really want that to be a constant in his life no matter where we go. "Your childhood friends share a special bond he smiled. At this moment David saw only his dad "See dad! showing off is A+ grade on the test. "Very good son. He stood holding something behind his back smiling. Dana just shook her head. And dad here it is! Showing off his ribbon he won at the rodeo. WOW! Billy exclaimed very impressive! I am very proud of all your accomplishments son, very proud!" Billy hugged him and David went back into his room. After talking a while with Dana while David Michael busied his-self in his bedroom, Billy got up and shared it was time to go. Okay dad, he yelled over the intercom. I'm putting some other clothes Dana bought me in an overnight bag". 'That young man! She acknowledged "Dana I know he's your son too. But I thank you for allowing me to concentrate on what I needed to do with the trial and know David was in good, loving hands." Thank you for trusting me! she said. They gently embraced and said their goodnights. David left with his Dad and Dana sat in her beautiful spacious townhouse alone.

Adele left running to catch her bus at 3:00. School for her ended at 2:45 and she was headed to her appointment at the law firm. It would take her two bus changes to get downtown on time. What had Justin set up for her she thought? Maybe he's going to help me go to college or something in the future. Her mind was going in every direction possible. I wonder if there will even be enough for a car after a house and food. "That's first thing she said house and food. And the boys and I will be happy. Should I tell Ariel?" No! Not yet anyway. She hates Justin for leaving her. But he was always nice to us. "I don't know what happened but I do know he asked this person to send me this letter. So, I'm going to see what he has to say. Ariel has Kevin now and we have nothing! She rode until it was time to get the other bus that would eventually get her downtown. She took out her book and started to read one of her assignments. It seemed to make time go faster and the bus ride didn't seem as long she thought sitting there looking out the bus's windows. She was still thinking about that house she had seen that day. She would have a room for all her brothers. Maybe she could even quit the job at the Burger Hut. Then she would have more time to concentrate on her homework assignments. She was usually so tired when she got home that assignments were either missed or prepared with just enough content to turn it in. Tired most mornings it was important for her to keep the job so that the boys could come by and get free meals when she was working. "She didn't know what to expect her wishes were running high. The boys had shared with her that Jesus could do anything. She didn't know what they were talking about because she didn't go with them on Sunday mornings when a bus brightly painted with smiling children all over it would come through the neighborhood picking children up for Sunday school. She allowed her younger brothers to go with some other children in the neighborhood that talked about how much fun they had there. So, Fletcher often repeated what he heard the Sunday school teacher say. They would go and come back around noon. The church fed them and had given them each a bible they could read. Fletcher's was full of pictures. He was still in elementary school. Riggin, and Hanson were in middle school and they enjoyed it and went most Sundays if she wasn't to tired to get their clothes ready in time. They told Adelle the pastor was a real nice lady.

For a young girl Adelle had a lot of responsibility laid on her shoulders because her mother was so irresponsible. No one ever said what drove her mother to be that way. Though the boys looked up to Adelle and counted on her to be there for them since Ariel their older sister had left home. She rode on looking at the sights of the city. She saw all the car lots of cars. They came in all sizes and colors. She only needed one! She thought as the bus kept riding by. She sat remembering how the boys were so happy the day she came home one day with her drivers' certificate from school. She could get her license but there was no rush because she had no way of getting a car anyway. So why bother? she reasoned. Then looking up she saw her stop. The big bus pulled to the corner and stopped to let the passengers off. She stepped off and looked around. She took out the letter and looked again at the address. A block that way she said crossing at the green light on the corner. Soon she arrived in front of this beautiful glass front building. The large windowed glass was tinted dark so looking in you could only see your reflection. But she noticed once inside she could see the people and the cars outside on the street walking and driving by. The foyer of this magnificent building was huge as she stood looking up in the air turning around in a circle. After about a minute or two to take it all in she stopped turning and went over to the receptionist desk. "May I help you?" Yes, I'm here to see". Adele hesitated she had forgotten the gentleman's name who sent the letter. But she remembered the business card Justin had given here. She had it memorized. "William Parker! She replied. "Just one moment" she said looking down her schedule of listing. "Your name please? "Adele Hodges" she said still looking awed by the beautiful water fountain over in the building's corner. "Ms. Hodges, you may go up now." "Take the elevator to the third floor" she told her pointing in the direction of the elevator's location. "Thanks! And off she went. When she got to third floor and stepped off the elevator. She saw the names embossed on the large doors. "That's it she said. "Morgan Jeffery." She opened the large door and went in. She again walked up to another receptionist desk. "I'm here to see a Morgan Jeffery, she replied. "Adele Hodges?" she asked. "Yes! She smiled. "This way getting up to escort her to Jeffery's office. When she walked in Mr. Jeffery's was speaking with Billy. They gave the receptionist the okay and she went back to her desk. "Hello, Billy said coming over I'm

William Parker and this is Morgan Jeffery." "Hi" Adele said shyly. Have a sit please. Morgan got up and left his office. "I didn't think I'd be here Billy told her. I've been out of town for a while and I was going to have Mr. Jeffery handle this for me." "Do you have any idea why you're here" he asked. "No! Justin gave me your business card and said someone will get in touch with me". I got a letter that said I should come today". "Oh, that's fine, that's not a problem. Billy could see she was getting nervous. "He held out Morgan's candy jar sitting on his desk. 'Have one! Thanks, she said reaching for a red one from the jar. Let's go down the hall to my office so that Mr. Jeffery can get his office back! he said smiling as the two walked out and around to his office. "It was very nice to she thought as she took her seat looking around. "Now! Billy said. Trying to get his thoughts together and remembering what Justin had shared about the family. "Okay what's your brothers names. She gave him all their names and the spelling of each. He also took down birthdays and any pertinent information he needed. Billy didn't tell her he knew Justin. She surely couldn't figure it out by looking. He was mixed with black and Justin was Caucasian but they shared the same Caucasian father that Billy grew up with. Besides Justin wanted to do this without his name being involved and that was all right too. "Your name dear? "Adele Hodges. And I'm seventeen and a half. "well you're close to graduating! Billy replied looking at some additional paperwork he had acquired to put her at ease as he filled out papers, he needed for her. "Yes! I hope so". "Well! I hope you go on to college and be whatever you want to be! He said smiling at her across the big desk of his office. "I would love to but I have my brothers to think about! she told him. 'Billy knew the situation at home from speaking with Justin so he didn't pry. He only wanted the names of the children in the household so it could accurately give an amount to sustain them. "Now you know there are some very good colleges right here in Maine. You wouldn't have to leave home" Billy suggested. "This made her smile. She hadn't thought about that. She only knew she couldn't leave her brothers. "Tell you what when you graduate high school come and see me! "deal! He said extending his hand to shake hers. She was smiling from ear to ear. Billy's heart was heavy as he thought of this child having this responsibility but hopeful this gift from Justin will lighten her load tremendously, he thought. His grandparents had left everyone a share of their huge fortune that was well in the millions so money wasn't an issue for the Parkers. After he had finish writing he looked up. You seem like a very intelligent young lady. And you have been very responsible with the small amount of money you have had to live off of. So, I'm going to help you and your brothers" he shared with her. "Why? She asked sincerely. "Someone loves you Adele" he replied. Someone? she asked questioning what he said. "Jesus" Billy replied knowing his limits of being careful with religion in the workplace. He was a partner in the firm) Adele smiled she had heard her brothers talk about Jesus. "Do you know him?" she asked. "I certainly do" Billy responded smiling. My brothers talk about him too Adele shared. Billy nodded I understand. "Now you have shown yourself to very responsible for a young lady your age. And I have put together for you a trust fund" he told her explaining everything as he went along. "Do you understand everything I've said so far?" Please stop me or ask questions if you don't understand". She was smiling and nodding her head it meant she could get a bigger house for the boys! What is the first thing you would do if you had the money? he asked. He wanted to find out exactly how mature she was. "shopping, theme parks, was what he expected to hear' from her because all she talked about was caring for her brothers. "Mr. Parker, the first thing I have to do is get a house to live in." Adele stated. Then she went on to tell her story. Billy was almost in tears as she shared it. How long do you have to find a home?" he asked looking at her winkled brow of concern. "About a week! Maybe two. She said quickly but continued to speak. "But I saw a really nice house and the man said I could rent it for the same amount as mom use to pay in our apartment". So, when she gets home, I'm going to tell her". "When did you see this house?" the other day" she said proudly. Billy knew that meant her mom didn't come home to her children everyday either. "Well young lady, because I believe you're doing a wonderful job with your brothers and I see here from the attendance report they are attending school regularly. "That's good. "Do you think you could handle the family's finances? "I do! she said honestly, I work at the Burger Hut and I use that money to keep us in decent clothes" she answered. "Where is this house you're looking at? Adele came prepared because she was going by on her way back home to make sure no one had rented it. She took a piece of paper from her backpack. Here it is! "Thanks, he wrote down the address and handed it back to her. "That's it for now. I will send you a letter in the mail. You should receive it in two days and it will be addressed to you." "I really feel you are intelligent enough to handle this" Billy confided." Please feel free to call me if you have any questions at all." he smiled. "Thank you, sir, she said leaving his office she was sad. "Here, now keep your head up" Billy said smiling. It's not bad. "Please take some candy to your brothers." Giving her two hands full in her backpack from his desk. She felt a little better and walked out.

Dana had been spending a lot more time out at the ranch. David Michael and Billy were busy catching up on things. Besides after everything had got settled, he and David moved into his grandparents 60+ thousand square feet renovated estate. One day as Rusty and Dana was heading out for a ride, his wife called. She had never called before when she was there that Dana knew of anyway. "Rusty! Mrs. Donna is on the phone to speak with you! the housekeeper yelled. "I'll be right there! He hurried to get the phone in the barn. After about twenty minutes he came back. Sorry about that, I never know when it's an emergency he explained. "Oh, I understand" Dana said mounting her horse. Rusty mounted and off they rode. Dana rode ahead flirting innocently with Rusty. Taking his hat from his head and hugging him as she rode beside him. He was surprised but he enjoyed her company and the attention. She knew he loved his wife so he was not going to make the first move on her though he thought about it many times, she knew that. They had spent a lot of time together since their meeting at Boothbay. They rode on along the trail with Dana making flirtatious advances. Soon it was time to turn back. Dana stopped and dismounted from her horse and tied him on one of the small trees along the trail. She took a blanket from his saddle. "Let's sit for a while before we go back, she smiled. Rusty dismounted and after tying his horse he laid down next to her on the blanket with his hands under his head and a straw twig between his teeth. "Tell me Rusty, what would you do if you lost Donna?" she asked. This was the type of conversations they had all the time. "Oh, I don't know! he said." I don't think about it! it saddens me to much" he replied. She picked at his graying hair on his head. "I told you I was an old man he said making light of himself.

Dana laughed. She wanted this man. Her mind was saying no he's got a wife. But he had not been with her in three years intimately anyway. She longed for a man's touch. Roger left so abruptly. But this was the same situation he's married. "Rusty picked up another straw of grass and rub it down her face. It disrupted her thoughts and she smiled pushing him playfully. "Well now what would you do if you didn't know about Donna?" he posed to her. "I don't know, things would be less complicated'. "Oh, you mean in the case of Roger?" "Yes, but I think you're different. You were honest! That snake took advantage of my love!" "Love! Rusty said holding her hand. "I'd never do that darling! She lay down beside him bracing herself on one hand looking into his face. There was a silent moment then their heads met. Dana was kissing Rusty and he was kissing her back and to them it felt right. She tried to talk to herself but his strong hands now holding her consumed any thoughts of letting go. They were enjoying each other's love. And we'll just close the curtain on this chapter to allow your imagination to write it's ending.

CHAPTER TWENTY-SEVEN

Isn't it lovely?

•

Justin had come home the past few months to find notes left by Menae. She was sure he should have been home according to his schedule but upon her arrival his suite was empty of his presence. Justin was whistling again and dancing again but to a different tune. He was spending his time with Rae. As a matter of fact, he was taking her out to the gathering Billy had planned for the family and close friends to celebrate is victory in the trial. The invites had been sent out and the newly hired staff for the estate was in place to get everything ready. "Annie had assured Billy all the flower arrangements he had ordered were to be delivered on Friday and she would be there to oversee that all was well. Annie cared for Billy more than he for her. It's not that he didn't care for her they dated though it wasn't exclusively her every time. You know how it goes. "Money, good looks, charming and did I say Money! Let me explain, looking at William Parker was like looking at "I pass for white, Geary Dourdan" with billions! But Annie was most frequent. And she would be the one escorting Billy to his gathering tonight. He was busy at the office tying up the lose ends of the trust fund he had put together for Adele's family. He had also called and spoke with the owner of the property Adele was interested in. Since getting back from Baltimore he had not really gotten involved in another high-profile case opting to take some time off since he was now a partner in the prestige law firm. He asked Reverend Morris the gentleman who owned the house to install new appliances and new carpeting, and whatever else was needed throughout and send him the bill. "I'll get right on it, Mr. Parker" he replied. And God Bless you son! He added before getting off the phone.

Dana the mother of his son had not shown any love interest in him since that horrible first date they had after his fiancée die. But their relationship had grown civil and they shared outings with their son David every now and then. Dana was not going to let Billy hurt her any more is how she stated it. But she knew she would always have a hidden love for him deep inside her heart. Billy felt bad when he recalled that date. He admits he was trying to get over losing Jillian and he was having a difficult time at it. Blaming her for the hurt she caused to Jillian when she took their son years ago. "He explained he needed someone to blame and she was there! Dana never attempted to reconcile with him again. Then of course there was Roger! It took her a long time to share with Billy about Roger. But after a few visits to her home to get David and general conversation he knew that for her that ship had sailed. And tonight, the family was getting together. His good friends from the law office were coming as well as Desmond and his family from Kansas and California. Billy had the estate left to him by his grandparents total renovated and redecorated except for his grandfather's study and his grandmother's sewing room. He left he just the same. He had so many memories there as a young boy of hiding as he played hide and seek with him. His grandfather never thought to look there because he didn't allow playing in his study. When he would walk pass Billy would rush out and touch base safely.

Justin arrived home to see his tuxedo had arrived from the tailor's and the corsage for Rae was delivered from the florist. "Ring! Ring! West Maine Bank" Rae Salazar speaking?' Hello honey are you ready for tonight!" "Hi you! I am, I just hope I can live up to your expectations of me?" "You do and I'll see you at 6:30" Justin confirmed to her. "Sure, darling that's sounds great! She replied getting off the phone smiling looking again at her hand in disbelief. Justin had given her a diamond promise ring the night before. He really enjoyed being with her. They went skating and bowling all the things he wanted to do with Menae. He took her to many functions given by the hospital. She was proving to be the one for him he thought. She was beautiful and very independent and could turn up the heat for she loved her man!

Billy's parent had come in from Washington State and the estate was buzzing with movement and laughter and the wonderful smells of the evening's entrée. Tetra had helped the chef and his staff make plans for her son's celebration. She had also met Annie Clark when she came by to check on the flower delivery for Billy. Tetra looked forward to seeing and speaking with her at the family's time together later this evening. Tetra sat for a moment thinking about Jillian. She was her son's fiancée who was taking away tragically during September 11th but except for Annie's long blonde hair she had no resemblance to Jillian. She appears to be a nice young lady, she thought getting up to see what the boys were up to.

David and Tommy were running around the estate enjoying some of the many area's they had not explored before. David Michael had opted to stay with his grandparents for the day instead of going to Dana's it was Saturday. She had said she wasn't going out to the ranch today. Dana had a hair appointment after work, so David Michael asked if he could go home since his grand-parents were there. David his grandfather said he would pick him up from school today. He was now thirteen but Billy was having a lot of renovations done to the estate and he didn't want him getting in the way or getting hurt by falling debris. "Be careful when you run by the swimming pool David! Tetra shouted as the two boys ran out the back door and across the yard. It was winter and it was too cold and frigate for swimming. The pool looked wonderful. The protective covering had been rolled back so that guest could enjoy its beauty. The crystal blue waters sparkled with the pools lights that were embedded underneath the icy blue water. The pool man had cleared all the leaves and debris from it, so it could be enjoyed as one strolled around the grounds of this large estate. The pool house had also been redecorated and fresh linen, and towels were there for anyone needing to spend the night in it. Tetra was making sure her instructions for the candles were accurately carried out and the new staff seemed so far to be promising of what was needed to run this large estate. 'Grandma is it all right if

Tommy and I go to the tree house?" David asked because it was a bit further out on the estate and the evening sun was about to go down. The gardeners had kept the grounds in order and well maintained but Tetra would still feel better if and adult accompanied the boys this time of day. "Go and find something to do closer to the main house she said there's always tomorrow, "Grandma does that mean Tommy can spend the night!" "It's okay with me as long as his parent's say it's okay." "Thanks grandma he said running of to who knows where she thought. "David are you going to get dressed the hour for guest to arrive is quickly approaching" she told him. "Yes dear". He was sitting in the study looking at some of his father's papers he had left in the desk. "Tetra came in and sat on his lap. "David I never told you your father apologized to me for the treatment he gave me when we were dating". David looked at her. "Treatment? he questioned. "Well I never told you this, but your dad was against our marriage from the start." "I know, but I told him I was going to marry you because I loved you! "I know and I told him the same exact thing." "But when he started sending you on those business trips with your secretaries to get you away from me, he told me it was best for everyone and that we would thank him for it one day." David started to speak. "But before you say anything, I forgave him! do you hear me David! I forgave him! and you must do the same. "I loved Mr. Parker and he loved our child and me in his own way! He would say he was born in a time where everyone stayed with his own kind". But you David Parker went against the grain! And I love you for it! And he did ask for forgiveness before he left this world and I held him in my arms and I forgave him" she admitted crying and hugging David in her arms. "I love you Tetra Parker, I love you! David affirmed.

Justin was getting dressed when is mom Katherine called. "Hello! Hello Justin I hear there's going to be a big party out at the estate to celebrate William Parker winning his trial". "Now mother where in heavens name did you hear such nonsense" he implied? "From the society page of today's news! She stated. "And you were not going to tell me, were you? Justin didn't want Katherine to know because honestly, he didn't want her to pester him about coming. He knew David and Tetra would be there and she was not invited. "Well mom I didn't say anything because it was invitation only" he remarked. "Well what does that mean to you, you're family!" "You see, there you go pulling rank! Billy invited me mom, and I can't just tell you to come." "I could simply go as your date! Kat, I have a date! 'Look I'll call you tomorrow" by the way did you get that package I sent you in the mail?" "Yes. "Then good night we'll talk soon", love ya!

Dana had let her feelings fall into the hands of another married man. She felt this was different somehow because the wife was ill and she and her husband had not been intimate for years. She and Rusty would take long rides out on the ranch. They had started having picnic lunches and really enjoying one another's company. She knew he loved his wife he said it every time her name came up. But let's be real he was a man in need and twenty some years older than this pretty filly that was interested in him. I'm in a safe place Dana thought, I can't get hurt. Rusty would never hurt me intentionally. And Donna well to be honest she doesn't exist to me! Dana reasoned in her mind moving around her office. She had invited Rusty to be her date for the family celebration but he had to think about it. Rusty confessed the relationship was moving a little to fast for his pace. They had gone out riding horses again Friday after she came home from the salon. She brought a picnic basket from home and she and Rusty were having another wonderful time together before the celebration Saturday. As they rode back from the trail the housekeeper informed him Donna his wife had called twice. He hurriedly dismounted his horse and ran to the phone calling her. Dana looked on as he talked to her lovingly. Then he said "I have to go! and hurried into the house. Dana made sure the ranch hands put away both horses and went in to speak with Rusty. "Mr. Higgins is in the shower and asked not to disturbed" his housekeeper stated with a matter of fact attitude. Dana didn't understand but she was sure he'd call tomorrow and explain. She got in her car and left. She was just about to enter the freeway from the dusty road that led to the ranch when Rusty's truck came flying pass her. He waved almost running her off the dusty trail. "Something must be wrong with Donna she thought pulling her Porsche back on the road heading home for the evening.

Adele had walked home from school and saw the progress the owner had made on the house. Surely someone else will get it before she does. Her mother had them packing their boxes after she read the letter about them having to move. She had left two days prior to find a place for them to stay and still had not returned. Adele worried all night about a place for her and her brothers to stay. She knew it would be up to her to find them a place to live. Adele had expected to walk out of Billy's office with some money in her hand. But then she remembered how long it took for the county to send her mother's first check. So, she reasoned it was the same type of situation and settled her nerves another day.

When she went by the next morning, he had painted the whole house inside and out. And new carpeting had been installed. They didn't have carpeting where they lived only cement floors. The owner had fertilized and cut the back and front yard and watered it. The lawn was a beautiful lush green. "Wow you have done a lot in a few days! She told him passing by has she had done everyday. She thought by passing letting him know she was still interested was keeping anyone else from renting it. It looked so nice. "Are you fixing this house up for anyone yet?" 'Oh, some good family will move in" the old gentleman shared. He had four other younger men now working with him. He needed to get the work finished by tomorrow he told her.

Adele walked home speedily. She slowed down as she came to the mailbox. It had been a few days and she was expecting a letter to tell her what to do next to get some money for the beautiful house. She put the small key into the ragged mailbox carrier. The postal service tried to keep then fixed up but the tenants either moved or didn't change address so they forced the mailboxes open to get the mail or lost the keys. Taking out the mail she almost screamed when she saw a letter addressed to her. She ran into the house. The boys were not there yet. She thought she was alone and let out a scream of excitement. She hadn't even opened it yet! Then she heard a moan from the room. She ran in to see her mother sleeping in bed still intoxicated. The smell of her room to Adele was nauseating. She quietly tiptoed back into the living room. She knew a bulldozer wouldn't wake her in that state. She put the other mail on the table and sat down and opened her letter. It wasn't a letter at all! It was a check! A check for $10,000 dollars made out to Adele Hodges. WOW! She had never seen this much money she thought. 'Wait, okay let's think! Oh my! She was excited. The checks stub had the names of each one of her brothers. "Wow! We can get the house! She ran in the boy's room a grabbed one of their bibles and put her hand on it and said "thank you." She didn't know why she just felt like doing it. Her clothes were in the closet in the living room. She hurried and got her best outfit she had and put it on. It was Wednesday so she had a day off from the Burger Hut. The boys would play until about six before they came looking for something to eat. She had a lot to do and a short time. She hurried back toward the school it was about a forty-five-minute walk. But she ran it in about thirty minutes. Hello Mister, she said, he was putting the last paint can back into his truck. Yes, he said seeing her come toward him. "I have the money for this house! "You do! he said. "Yes, I'll bring it to you tomorrow after school". That's fine" he said. "Is it still $545.00 like you said before you fixed it up?" she asked. Yes, dear to move in will be $1090.00 dollars that includes the cleaning deposit he told her. "That's it! That's it he smiled. She took out her small tablet and wrote it down. And what's your name?" she asked. "Reverend Morris" he replied. 'Okay, I'll be here tomorrow! "I want that house" she said hurrying off to catch the bus to the bank. She went in to open and account in her name. She had her identification and with a few pertinent questions answered and a phone call to Billy's office from the bank she was on her way with a cashier check in the amount of $1090.00 made out to Reverend Morris. Her next stop was Sears for furniture and other household furnishings. She bought a microwave to match the nice new white stove and refrigerator the owner had put in. Then she needed some beds. The ones they had were run down and she didn't have a bed she slept on the couch and let the boys have that thing they called a bed. She looked so mature has she shopped for their new home. She didn't purchase the MOST expense beds she could find. But was told by the salesman they were very good. She picked out a living room set and a dinette set also. All total including the house, when she walked out of Sears, she had spent a little over $5000.00 dollars. Half of what she had. They promised her delivery of tomorrow.

She put each amount spent down in her small tablet she had in her purse and left the store. Then she got back on the bus and headed home. When she arrived, it was close to 5:30 and her mother was sitting up watching the small television set, Adele walked in." That's what I forgot! she said looking at the small fuzzy black and white television. "Where have you been?" her mother scorned. "I found us a place to live mama! It's nice and it's near our school". "Where did you get money to buy a house?" she asked puffing on her cigarette. "Did my check come early?" "I don't know here's your mail" handing it to her. She looked hurriedly, there was a letter in there for her from the county. But for her in was not good news. They shared with her she would have to go to a facility for help with her problem or her funds would be discontinued. She was upset and mad and used a few four lettered words. Okay a lot of four-letter words! She walked around looking at the boxes packed around the apartment. "Where is this house and how much does it cost Adele?" she questioned walking around with her cigarette hanging from her lips and her hands on her hip. "The same has we were paying here. Is it worth it?' she asked. 'It's nice mama! The man fixed it all up when I told him I wanted it". "What man?" slapping Adele across her face. "I don't know, he says his name is Reverend Morris." "Oh, her mother smiled "he's a minister of the gospel. "A minister?' Adele asked. "Yes, Adele that's what a Reverend is! Her mother stated again. "Okay, I thought that was his first name" I sure hope he can cash this check I made out to him, she thought to herself.

Dana sat that next morning waiting for Rusty to call. She didn't know what to make of his sudden exit as he left speeding away from his ranch. "Hello, may I speak with Rusty?' she asked calling his ranch. "Mr. Higgins is unavailable right now; you'll have to call back" his housekeeper told her. "Thank you, she said hanging up. She had gotten everything ready for the evening with the Parker family and Rusty still had not said if he would escort her tonight. She didn't care that he was older. She liked him a lot. He was kind and gentle and caring and most of all honest. All the things she needed in a man. She called and spoke a few minutes with her son and sat back down watching television. It was now about 5" o clock so she thought she'd try his number again. This time she only got a recording. She hung up and called the hospital facility where is wife was to see if something had happened to her. "Dana was a doctor so she didn't lie about that. Using it she was able to persuade the nurse into giving her some information. She found out Donna had been moved to another facility out of state. But that's all she would say. "Thank you" she said hanging up and reaching for her keys and heading out the door. She got into her car and headed down the highway to the ranch. She had driven this way so much it seemed to have gotten shorter. It was exactly 45 minutes from her home and she knew every bump in the road getting there. As she was about to turn down onto the dusty road, she saw the housekeeper's truck go past her speedily. Dana kept going toward the ranch. She saw the horses grazing in the fields and a few cowhands far in the distance. As she approached the farm's entrance, she noticed the very large gate was closed. That was unusual. All the months she had been coming here this gate was never closed she thought. She got out of her car and saw a huge padlock on the gates end. And looking upon the ranch from the distance there was no movement at all. "What's going on she thought? She took out her cell phone and called getting only voicemail and answering machine. She tried desperately to call to the ranch hands she could barely see in the distant. But her cries went faint and she got back into her car and drove slowly down the highway. She couldn't believe what she had just witnessed? what has happened? Had she been used again! Dana walked in to see a blinking light on her answering machine. She knew he had not let her down. She ran over to hear the message. Rusty's voice was clear. "I love her Dana, "We're moving again to a different climate maybe there she will get better. I have to try I love her". Those words pierced Dana's heart over and over as she played it listening to Rusty's voice. She had fooled herself into thinking just because she had not seen Donna that she didn't exist. She sat by her phone and cried her eyes out. Again she was alone! "SHE DOES EXIST! She cried out loud over and over again.

Adele and the boys moved around their small apartment getting the few clothes and other items they had of value to them in boxes. She hadn't shared any of the good fortune news with them only that she had found another house and they were excited. She also celebrated by ordering pizza and soda that was a treat for them. 'Adele where is our new house going to be?" Fletcher asked. "Very near the school" she replied. "Those houses over there are big! Riggins said. I won't mind telling people where I live then" Hansen added. Adele was smiling to. She had looked at that check over and over again she couldn't believe this had happened. After their pizza and soda arrived, they all sat down on the floor in front of the small television. Adele had already made a note to herself to buy a large clearer colored television for them to enjoy. They all took napkins and put two pieces of pizza on them. Adele hurried and sat down and joined them. She picked up her pizza and took a bite. "Wait! Fletcher said. we have to give thanks! That's what we do at the church Adele! Riggins said. "Okay, she put her pizza back down on the napkin. And bowed her head after looking at the others. "Thank you, lord, for this food you allowed us to eat. And thank you for our new house amen." The boys started laughing and eating and enjoying this rare occasion of pizza together. Their mom had left earlier she said to go find them somewhere to live until she gets her check'. Adele couldn't tell her what she had gotten. Her mother would hound her until she had every bit of it. This was for her brother's and their new home and hopefully a new start. She later wrote Billy and thanked him for her new home and new start. She had spent the money so wisely that she had enough to buy dishes and other items needed for the house. Their cabinets and new refrigerator were full of nourishing food for growing boys. And their large back yard was put to use. Not only by the boys but their mother spent more time at home too. She didn't question it after Adele convinced her this money was coming from a lawyer's office. But she never disclosed to her mother the amount. By force from the county she was made to go to a rehabilitation facility for her alcoholism. Only time will tell if it works. Adele had saved just enough for a down payment on a new car. She held on to what was left from the first check she had and was saving to buy some type of transportation for them. But every two weeks like clockwork she receives over $2,000.00 to assist her in caring for her brothers from the trust fund. Knowing that she would now be able to buy anything needed she could concentrate on her studies. Knowing how good news travels Ariel soon came by the new place. She sat down and questioned Adelle intensely about her funds. Adelle told her about an attorney named Jeffery. As soon as Ariel heard the address, she knew Justin had something to do with it! Of course, she couldn't push the issue Justin always wanted to help. Even more meaningful for Ariel than her younger sister trying to protect the secrecy of the money Justin had given her for she and the boys, were the smiles on each one of their faces as they showed her around in their new home and bedrooms. And now these Sunday's as Hansen, Riggins and Fletcher leave to catch that colorful bus brightly painted with children's smiling faces Adele also goes along as well.

CHAPTER TWENTY-EIGHT

Can't say goodbye

Dana sat crying alone in her home, when her phone rang. It was her son David. She let her answering machine pick up the message she didn't want to be disturbed. Dana was crying uncontrollably on the arm of her big chair in her living room. "Dana this is Davie, I'll call you back again! his voice said across the phone. Dana's heart was hurting and socializing was not at the top of her list. She just wanted to be alone with her thoughts and her broken again heart. After nearly an hour sobbing, she sat up and wiped her eyes. I can't keep doing this to myself, she thought. This beautiful face is causing me nothing but heartache. I'm an intelligent woman but the decisions I make are all totally wrong! The men I'm attracted to are always in love with someone else. The only sure thing in my life is my son. And that's where I'm going. She knew he had called because she should have been to the estate by now. Her makeup had smeared on her face. And her gorgeous Klein dress was wrinkled from the long ride from the ranch. She looked a mess she reasoned as her reflection looked back at her as she passed in front of her bedroom mirror. "Get it together Dana" she voiced quickly headed to her shower, and change into a beautiful red beaded gown by Purcell. She removed and applied on new makeup and headed out her door. She was going it alone to be with her son who by the way had called again before she left her home. She returned her son David's call after she got into her car so he wouldn't worry about her. She rode along in her Porsche 911 getting her mind together for the evening. She knew this could happen with Rusty. She knew he loved his wife. She just didn't expect it to be so soon if at all! When she arrived at the estate Dana was escorted out of her car and greeted by a valet who opened her car door and took her keys. She walked into a luxurious entrance at the estates front doors. Billy had renovated the 60,000 sq. feet estate that boasted an entire front entrance with a beveled smoke colored glass motif. Entering just behind the magnificent entrance was David her son. He was sitting in the foyer decorated in expensive Scandinavian design furnishings waiting for his mother to arrive. "Hello Dana, her son acknowledged as she came into the elegantly decorated family space of the home. "Well let me see you! she replied. "You're quite the gentleman" she added turning him around in a circle. Dana tugged slightly on his small black tie, then straightened it. "Nice" she smiled. He was sporting a tuxedo as were all the men there, she noticed as her eyes browse the large room. David Michael lifted his arm and Dana entwined it walking around greeting guest. Tetra and David, Billy's parents hugged and welcomed her in. She still had not seen Billy. Then looking quickly, she saw him over standing by a wheelchair. "Oh, Glen must have come to the celebration too! She thought still holding her son's hand moving through the crowd. "Hi! She greeted coming up to Billy sharing an embrace. "Glen, Cheryl Reed, this is Dr. Dana Williams." "Glen looked almost in shock, he knew her as a young girl Dorca but she had transformed he thought into a goddess! She was beautiful he shared with Billy tugging his coat sleeve in a teasing way. "Pleasure meeting you" she said shaking Cheryl's hand and then Glen Reed's" smiling at him with an embraced hug. "It has been a while" she continued. Billy had shared years ago about his accident that left him in a wheelchair. David was trying all he knew how to get moving again he wanted to show Dana something outside. Obliging, Dana waved and moved on through the crowded room of guest toward the back entrance. She saw Desmond and Mostalgia Owens and reacquainted herself with them meeting his brother Sidney, "Congratulations on your outcome" she said shaking Sidney's hand. "Thanks, I had some very good attorney's" he acknowledged. And it helps when you are innocent, Sidney added. "that's so right, by the way I'm Dana Williams and this is my son David Michael Parker." David wanted anxiously for her to go outside to see something, but he had learned to be still until his mother finished her conversation. "Sidney Owens, but you probably know that from all the publicity" he commented." "It's a pleasure meeting you" she said again and walked away with David pulling her arm. Many of the people there had met at a social event, the office party, or funeral sadly to say. But this was a time of celebration and socializing and laughter were all in order.

Dancing in the other adjoining room was Justin and Rae Salazar. Dana nodded a smile at the size of her rock she was wearing on her finger. Dana had met many of Billy's co-workers and fellow attorneys from the law firm where he worked on her occasional visit's concerning their son. Dana waved as she walked by many of the guest smiling as she didn't know all by name. Looking back, she noticed Rae was having a wonderful time meeting the Parker family and showing of her new flawless diamond ring Justin had given her the day before. Then she looked over in the sitting room to see Leron and Martha Owens Desmond's parents were now chatting with Billy and Annie who had joined them coming in from the other room. Knowing Billy, he was no doubt talking about the trials out come she imagined. She just smiled and waved as Billy noticed his son still pulling her through the crowded room. The butlers made their way through the gathered crowd of guests of each room filled with much laughter and smiling, drinking expensive champagne and caviar which was securely balanced on a sterling silver tray. 'Thank you, was heard as each removed a glass of champagne or a piece of caviar from his tray. "Come on Dana you have to see the pool! David Michael said pulling her out of the crowds an eventually to the back door. It looked magnificent she thought standing out in the garden like setting that surrounded it. Billy's architects and designers had put a lot into this renovation. It almost appeared to be a different estate altogether THAN SHE REMEMBERED, more modern. Dana thought. She contemplated as she looked around at all of the renovation changes Billy had IMPLEMENTED. Suddenly over the airways came a voice. "Where's David Michael?" It was Tommy he had arrived with his parents. And the intercom he was standing by in the foyer was picking up his question loud and clear. Charles, Tommy's dad looked at him and Lily tapped his hand. "Tommy behave"! His mother admonished him standing there all dressed up in his fashionable little tuxedo. Tetra and David Parker greeted them coming in. "Oh, he's fine, he and our grandson use the intercom all the time around here, David Parker replied. "I'm sure wherever David Michael is he's heard it and will be here soon. "Extending his hand David introduced themselves." I'm David Parker and this is my wife Tetra Parker, David Michael is our grandson" and William Parker is his father our son. "And you must be Tommy's parents?" "Yes, Charles McCormick and this is my wife Lily". "Pleasure meeting you! "Do come in and enjoy the celebration! Davie came running back into the house. "I heard my name over the intercom outside is Tommy here?' "David Michael mind your manners" Tetra expressed. "Oh, I'm sorry grandma" taking a breath from running. "Hi Mr. and Mrs. McCormick," "hello David, both replied smiling. "Can we go now please?" "sure" Tetra smiled shaking her head and they both headed off. "God only knows what those tuxedos are going to look like in and hour! Tetra laughed allowing Tommy's parents to join the others in the great rooms. Dana stood out in the night's air taking in the estate's beauty. The night sky was brisk from the winter's weather and the sky was filled with bright shiny stars. It looked even better than during the day she was told by Davie, who of coursed lived there now with his dad. She could hear the music playing softly on the inside and all the laughter and conversations being exchanged. Many guests were eating and drinking and dancing and having a good time. "Hi! A voice behind her said. "Are you alone tonight?' the voice was Billy's. She promised herself she would not cry or feel sorry for herself. David Michael had run off with Tommy and yes, she was alone but not in that sense. "Looks that way" she stated turning around trying to force a smile. Billy had come to know Dana his childhood friend better now. "Want to tell me about it?" he said hugging her around her arms shielding her from the night's cold breeze as they stood outside overlooking the sparkling water. Why did he ask that? She thought silently. He knows it makes me cry the more, her thought said silently. "No not really turning away to wipe the tears. He pulled her up close and put his arms around her and she laid her head on his chest. "Well anytime you need to talk Dana, let me know. I'm here!

THE END